ANATOMY OF .

ANATOMY OF A LIE
Decoding Casement

by

PAUL R. HYDE

Word_well_

To the memory of my parents

First published in 2019
Wordwell Ltd
Unit 9, 78 Furze Road, Sandyford Industrial Estate, Dublin 18
www.wordwellbooks.com

Front cover image—Roger Casement from a photograph with John Devoy (not shown). Courtesy National Library of Ireland.

ISBN (Paperback) 978-1-9164922-1-9
ISBN (eBook)) 978-1-9164922-3-3

British Library Cataloguing-in-Publication Data.
A catalogue record for this book is available from the British Library.

Typeset in Ireland by Wordwell Ltd
Copy-editor: Emer Condit
Index: Author and Wordwell Ltd
Cover design and artwork: Wordwell Ltd
Printed by SPRINT-print

After such knowledge, what forgiveness? Think now
History has many cunning passages, contrived corridors
And issues, deceives us with whispering ambitions,
Guides us by vanities.
Gerontion, T.S. Eliot. 1920

'Everything secret degenerates ... nothing is safe that does not
show how it can bear discussion and publicity'
(Lord Acton).

Contents

Foreword

To mark the coronation of King George V in 1911, Roger Casement was granted a knighthood. This public recognition was considered by his peers as a worthy acknowledgement for an exceptional consular official, although, in private, Casement had little time for Britain's imperial honours system. Aged 45, Sir Roger Casement's public service record was impeccable, and he was renowned for his investigations on behalf of the British Foreign Office into atrocities on the frontiers of empire. This defence of 'native people' had helped to reinvigorate Britain's global reputation after the humiliations of the Anglo-Boer war (1899–1902). His courageous involvement in the Congo reform campaign and his formal reporting of the violence resulting from the extraction of latex rubber from the rainforests of the north-west Amazon were ground-breaking investigations. Today both of these interventions are upheld as integral to the evolving history of human rights. Beyond his influence at an official and imperial level, Casement's work catalysed a radical movement identifying and challenging new forms of slavery. In that year of 1911, Casement's name was associated with moral authority, integrity and an empathetic concern for people oppressed by unequal power relations.

Those who knew Casement were aware of his strongly held views supporting Irish Home Rule and Ireland's cultural revival, but few considered how these beliefs and opinions would compromise his official work. References to Casement before his open political commitment to Ireland describe him in exceptionally positive terms. The novelist Arthur Conan Doyle immortalised Casement in his 1912 bestseller *The lost world*, which is just one example of how Casement's fame percolated through into popular culture.

By the summer of 1916, however, Casement was standing in the dock accused of high treason for consorting with the king's enemies. The letter he had written to the British Foreign Secretary, Sir Edward Grey, accepting his knighthood back in 1911 was used by his prosecutors as indicative of his 'sudden change in allegiance'. This transformation of Casement from humanitarian hero to disgraced renegade traitor created great confusion in those who had known him. Added to the mix of misunderstanding were press rumours that 'a diary' had been found that revealed Casement not as an official of integrity but as someone who, in the words of the memorandum placed before the cabinet in July 1916, had 'completed the full cycle of sexual degeneracy'.

For over a century now, an inordinate amount of time and ink has been invested in understanding Casement's path to the scaffold at the height of the First World War. The 'diary' mentioned in 1916 that helped to alienate public support for Casement and to railroad him to the gallows has played a large—some might say disproportionate—part in his interpretation and the representational wars that persist over who he was and what he stood for. Since 1916 an identifiable tradition of inquiry has maintained that the Black Diaries (as they are now called) are forgeries and a vicious legacy of the counter-insurgency strategies emanating from British intelligence agencies during the First World War.

Paul Hyde's *Anatomy of a lie* is more than another voice in an overcrowded field; it is a vital contribution to comprehending key dimensions of the diaries controversy. In the chapters of this book, Hyde builds logical arguments based on carefully researched answers to fundamental and lingering questions that have sustained the confusion for too long. The analysis that he provides answers contradictions about the archive, about the provenance of the diaries and about the management of this story that have previously evaded scrutiny. By critically interrogating the primary sources and the official arguments bolstering authenticity, Hyde exposes the patterns of duplicity, misinformation and selective framing which have produced the contemporary consensus. For instance, he makes the crucial distinction between the police typescripts, which were shown in the weeks before Casement's execution, and the bound diaries, which were not shown in 1916 and were only released into the Public Record Office by the British Home Office in 1959. Almost all biographers treat the typescripts as if they were true copies of diaries for whose existence at the time there is no independent witness testimony. Hyde demonstrates that this remarkable absence of evidence is far from being accidental.

Looking back over this controversy, it is possible to read the political expediencies and security requirements that have managed, revived and subdued the argument in different directions in both Britain and Ireland. These bitter twists and turns offer insight into the contingencies and tensions separating the politics of Anglo-Irish history from the history of Anglo-Irish politics. Because Casement's 'treason' extends from his apparent loyal and distinguished service to the British Empire, his legacy has demanded very careful handling and, as Hyde demonstrates, archival encryption. But Casement belongs, too, to Ireland's history, not just in terms of the long genealogy of resistance to English rule but also in his aspiration to define a specifically Irish form of international relations based on empathy and rights. This intersectional schism in his identity as both 'traitor' and 'patriot' has resulted in his Janus-faced meaning.

Those who come to this story with an appetite to know what happened should never underestimate the level of revulsion and hatred that Britain's governing class felt towards Casement once his 'treason' was identified in 1914. Although Casement was in many ways an advanced Liberal in terms of much of his political outlook, his radicalisation stemmed from the political failure to deliver Home Rule in Ireland. But once Home Rule became conditional on Ireland's participation in the First World War, Casement was incensed. This shedding of Irish blood was a step too far, and he decamped to Berlin in a deliberate and bold act of treason.

In the wake of his capture, trial and execution, two very different Casements emerged. In nationalist Ireland he was revered as a revolutionary martyr and held close to those who participated in the 1916 rebellion. In imperial Britain, however, where understanding of the Irish struggle was limited, Casement was reviled and, in the atmosphere of war, malicious rumours escalated into a smear campaign that undermined his support base. Ever since, the ongoing dispute has endured as an effective way of obfuscating Casement's journey into open resistance to the ruling establishment. At the same time, it has been used as a diversion to obscure his critique of colonial power by robbing him of the moral high ground and much credibility in his investigation of colonial violence in the Congo and the Amazon.

The period that defined Casement's place in history and framed the diaries controversy for later generations might be traced back to the 1950s. This was a consequence of various political and cultural dynamics. A resurgent interest in Casement among nationalist and republican circles in Northern Ireland was overtly demonstrated in the naming of the GAA stadium in West Belfast Casement Park and the setting up of an annual

Casement Commemoration event in Murlough Bay, where Casement wished to be buried. Both events happened within a few months of each other in 1953.

This triggered a strategic response from within the Unionist/Conservative Party tradition, most notably from the Ulster Unionist MP, barrister and popular historian H. Montgomery Hyde. In Britain, the disagreement over the authenticity of the diaries contributed to the public discussion on sexuality. Both the publication of the Wolfenden Report in 1957 and the process that led to a partial decriminalisation of homosexuality in the Sexual Offences Act a decade later become part of the broader context to the dispute. What the fusion of the controversy with a public discussion about sexuality successfully achieved was to weld the dispute over the authenticity of the Black Diaries to the question of Casement's sexuality.

Among many public intellectuals who stepped into the ring to offer their view on the matter was Galway-born Thomas 'Tommy' Woods (1921–61). Considered by his contemporaries as one of the most brilliant minds of his generation, Woods rose rapidly through Ireland's Department of External Affairs to become permanent representative to the Council of Europe. Remembered still for his nurturing of Irish relations with continental Europe, his real vocation was not diplomacy but literature and philosophy. He wrote regularly for the main publications of the day using various pseudonyms, including Thomas Hogan, and under that name he made some measured interventions in the 'Black Diaries' debate.

In an article in *The Irish Times* (27 April 1957), Woods/Hogan commented: 'The point at issue, it cannot too often be emphasised, is not whether Casement was a homosexual. It is whether he was the author of the diaries.' This is the critical distinction to be made and one that many people who think about the diaries either forget or ignore. The authenticity of the Black Diaries has little to do with the status of Casement's sexuality.

On 14 August 1959, shortly after the release of the Black Diaries into the Public Record Office by the British Home Secretary R.A.B. Butler, *The Irish Times* ran an opinion piece by Hogan—'The Casement case: new fields of controversy'. He pointed out that their release proved merely that they existed and not whether they could or should be trusted as authentic sources. He was critical, too, that 'a new polemical atmosphere' had been created by the manner of the release, providing 'just another opportunity for extending the controversy'. There were justified concerns that journalists could comment and pronounce on the question of authenticity before historians had examined the evidence. At the end of the piece, Hogan posited:

'Can the diaries actually be shown to be forgeries? That the originals themselves are now available for inspection has raised hopes that this might now be done. The fact is that if they are competent forgeries, then they certainly are highly competent ones. ... But if the documents were forged, the only way it can be shown is by internal evidence. This will entail lengthy and tedious checking and cross-checking by a scholar with a detailed knowledge of the period and of Casement. It will have to be carried out in a critical and objective fashion. The results cannot be pleasing to partisans on both sides—they may even be not satisfactory to either.'

Woods not only focused on the fundamentals of the problem but signposted the necessary research that should be undertaken before the public reached any informed decision. He died in 1961 in Strasbourg, just a few months shy of his 40th birthday. His analysis was insightful and posed questions that were both measured and judicious and remain relevant, but little heed was paid to his views. Instead, the dispute over the diaries stayed trapped inside a paradigm of press sensationalism and the heightening political tensions over resurgent insurgency in Northern Ireland.

After Casement's bones were returned to Ireland in 1965, all voices arguing that the Black Diaries were forged were largely silenced. For the next 30 years there was a steady flow of publications in Britain that framed Casement in terms of the Black Diaries. Casement's interpretation now became indivisible from the Black Diaries. But the cross-checking and internal analysis that Tommy Woods had considered necessary to a balanced assessment were not undertaken.

During this period the most significant and influential intervention came from the historian and journalist Brian Inglis. Although Inglis considered himself Irish, he was very much a figure of Britain's post-war media establishment. A self-defined West Briton, born in India, educated in the English public-school system and raised in Malahide, he had served as an RAF squadron leader during the Second World War. He then went on to research a Ph.D at Trinity on the history of press freedom in Ireland, which was supervised by one of the founders of *Irish Historical Studies*, T.W. Moody. Inglis forged some of his closest friendships with Ireland's mid-century historians and journalists writing for *The Irish Times*, where he wrote for several years the anonymous 'Quidnunc' column, but in the depressed climate of 1950s Ireland he returned to London to build his career in the British media.

In 1954 Inglis joined the editorial staff of *The Spectator*, the weekly journal articulating the views of the Tory Party establishment in Britain. Shortly after his arrival that publication started to run regular stories about the Black Diaries. From a successful stint as editor of this influential weekly journal, Inglis became a well-known TV presenter on the current affairs programme *What the Papers Say* and a popular history programme, *All Our Yesterdays*. When the publishing house Hodder and Stoughton launched his biography *Roger Casement* (1973), it was work that had been in the making for over twenty years. It was widely reviewed in both mainstream newspapers and academic journals and had widespread influence in shaping opinions. By that stage of his career Inglis was one of the most respected journalists bridging the Irish Sea, and his biography became the standard and popular work on Casement for the next three decades. As Hyde argues here, however, it was a biography that was purposefully flawed.

For a work that claimed to be academically rigorous there were no source references, and Hyde has done invaluable work in explaining why this is and what Inglis is essentially obfuscating by this omission. Furthermore, in his analysis Inglis chose to ignore the measured questions asked by Tommy Woods and refrained from carrying out the lengthy and tedious cross-checking of the internal evidence. Hyde shows how Inglis's biography established the parameters of deception upon which contemporary consensus is based.

By the mid-1990s it had become almost a heresy to continue to argue for the forgery of the diaries. In 1993 Ireland liberalised its own Sexual Offences Act and thereby initiated a process that led to the Marriage Equality Referendum of May 2015. Once again the Black Diaries became a way whereby Ireland mediated an acceptable public discussion on sexuality. In the UK, the release of the diaries in 1994, followed by the declassification of much documentation held back under the Public Records Act (1958), saw the story once again revive. The open release of the documents allowed for different kinds of interrogation. In the light of postcolonial studies and deconstructionist approaches to the production of history—coupled with an increasing awareness about the instrumentality of the archive—the Black Diaries started to look different under different analytical lights.

My own engagement with this story in the early 1990s arose from interest in learning more about Casement's investigation in the Upper Amazon. The realisation that most of the Black Diary material dealt with 1910 and 1911, the years when Casement carried out his investigation into the activities of a British-registered rubber company, the Peruvian Amazon Company, compelled me to look closely at the documents and establish their veracity in terms of Casement's interrogation of a very public atrocity. If the diaries are extracted from the bitter history wars underpinning English–Irish relations and placed in the context of the representational hostilities fought on the frontiers of the Amazon, where the Black Diaries must either stand or fall as verifiable sources, then they start to take on a very different meaning. I edited and published two volumes, *The Amazon Journal of Roger Casement* (1997) and *Sir Roger Casement's heart of darkness: the 1911 documents* (2003), to facilitate a deeper level of internal examination of the Black Diaries' narrative for 1910 and 1911. The fact that the entire 75-day period of Casement's investigation of the Putumayo as published in his Amazon Journal is covered by parallel entries in the Black Diaries allowed for some deep intertextual comparisons. The variances in these analogous narratives called for a re-examination of the relationship between the Black Diaries and Casement's comprehensive archive documenting crimes against humanity. Much of this comparison is yet to be done.

The period from 1993 to 2012 was one of intense publishing about Casement, which I tried to capture in an article—'Phases of a dishonourable phantasy'—published in *Field Day Review* 8 (2012). This mapped how the deceptive foundations laid by Inglis and other biographers had been accepted almost unanimously with little questioning or critical reasoning by a new generation of journalists and academics. In 1998

Martin Mansergh, an Oxford-trained historian and, at that time, special adviser to the taoiseach, entered the fray. Mansergh had emerged as a critical negotiator behind the Good Friday Agreement and felt that there were adequate grounds to open what he later described as 'a minor but longstanding affair of state'. But efforts to encourage another type of interrogation of the Black Diaries—evidenced by the colloquium held in the Royal Irish Academy in May 2000—were met by a new offensive to reinforce their authenticity.

In 2003 both the BBC and RTÉ decided to produce their own documentaries on Casement but collaborated in co-financing an examination of the diaries by a qualified document examiner. Under the guidance of a Steering Committee of Irish and UK academics, the accredited Audrey Giles was commissioned to inspect the conflicting diary material. Giles, it transpired, had served for twelve years as a document examiner for the British Home Office and the Metropolitan Police. This was the very agency that had allegedly discovered the Black Diaries and, under Basil Thomson's authority, had helped to mastermind Casement's character assassination. Whether the choice of Giles constituted a potential conflict of interest was not mentioned, but the choice was never adequately explained. After several weeks, Giles proclaimed the diaries to be genuine and the two documentaries were broadcast simultaneously. Professor W.J. McCormack, who chaired the Steering Committee, adopted a tone of unassailable 'authority'. As Hyde shows, however, this was another instance of distorting optics and excluded perfectly reasonable concerns about the internal contradictions and questions to do with motive and probability.

If Casement's story remained alive in Ireland, there was now remarkably little appetite in Britain to remember his traitorous turn. Perhaps the last significant intervention was by the columnist and popular historian Ben MacIntyre, who wrote an article in *The Times* published on 31 July 2015 under the heading 'The traitor who deserves a royal pardon'. MacIntyre made the argument that the British state should make 'a formal apology', claiming that the government-inspired homophobia that hounded the brilliant mathematician and cryptanalyst Alan Turing to take his own life was the same homophobia that led to Casement's execution. He suggested, too, that Casement died not for Ireland but 'for being a gay man'. Certainly, the smear campaign activated by the rumours of the diaries destabilised Casement's support in high places, but to confuse this with the institutional homophobia of 1950s Britain that led to the deplorable imprisonment of hundreds of men for contravening the Sexual Offences Act and drove Turing to bite on an apple laced with cyanide was confusion indeed. As one of the few British interventions about Casement in the Decade of Centenaries, MacIntyre's opinion demonstrates how the Black Diaries had successfully eviscerated Casement's historical relevance.

The commemoration of 1916 in 2016 allowed for a further sanitising of the intersections and layers of Casement's colliding identities and an even more determined effort to deepen the sexual dimension of his interpretation. Official Ireland was keen, understandably, to keep the 1916 centenary as non-confrontational as possible. A promiscuous Casement investigating human rights violations in pursuit of the dual causes of gay liberation and national liberation was the Casement that the Irish state wished to support. This was Casement as New Man: the perfect supplement to a commemorative intersection that aspired to be both progressive and redemptive.

A procession of historians and senior figures in the judiciary marched forth to endorse the Black Diaries in the public domain, oblivious to or ignoring the arguments contesting their authenticity. State funding was channelled towards arts projects celebrating Ireland's sexual liberator. There was a plethora of exhibitions, plays and public lectures, from Sydney (Australia) to Abuja (Nigeria) and São Paulo (Brazil). Casement became the standard-bearer of the global dimension of the Irish revolution. Fintan O'Toole, towards the end of the year, made the point that 'If Casement symbolically replaced Patrick Pearse as the most magnetic figure of the Rising, it is because his doubleness is deeply attractive to a culture that has become more comfortable with, and more interested in, mixed feelings' (*The Irish Times*, 29 October 2016). In the next sentence O'Toole invoked a line out of Brian Friel's classic play *Translations*—'confusion is not an ignoble condition'—underscoring the attraction of an ambiguous Casement.

Paul Hyde's agenda has been to strip away the confusion by going directly to the primary sources and mapping where and how meaning and analysis start going awry. His study dissects the murky provenance of the Black Diaries and the skilful blending of fact and innuendo by a procession of Casement biographers in support of their perspectives. Hyde's reasoning eliminates the misinformation that has accrued over decades and provides answers to those fundamental questions identified by Tommy Woods back in the 1950s. By unpicking these stratified layers of secondary interpretation, he refocuses analysis on those months between 1914 and August 1916 when Casement's life and legacy hung in the balance and a desperate remedy was required to destroy the credibility of a committed and enduring enemy of the British Empire.

Angus Mitchell

Acknowledgements

I am grateful to staff at the following institutions: Windsor Castle Archives, National Library of Scotland, National Library of Ireland, UK National Archives, National Archives, Dublin, New York Public Library, Public Records Office of Northern Ireland, Mitchell Library, Glasgow, Essex Records Office, Belfast City Corporation and Belfast City Libraries.

The following persons have encouraged my research and have offered valuable comment and criticism: Dr Angus Mitchell, Ciaran Hyde, Dr Martin Mansergh, Lord Alton of Liverpool, Gerry Danaher SC, Brian Leahy, Martina Devlin, Julian Burnside QC, Jack Lane, Prof. Declan Kiberd, Prof. Richard Kearney, Prof. Adam Geary and Prof. Giampaolo Dalle Vedove. Thanks are also due to Marcel Matley, James Horan, Kate Strzelczyk and Susie Bioletti. I owe Angus Mitchell a particular debt of gratitude for patiently allowing me to exploit his remarkable in-depth knowledge of the Casement story and for encouraging me to prepare this book. I also thank my son Ciaran for his help with the project and for his invaluable critical comments on rendering my arguments clearer and more accessible. Special thanks are due to my publisher, Nick Maxwell, who firmly believed that *Anatomy of a lie* deserved a reading public.

Abbreviations

FO	Foreign Office	PRO	Public Records Office
HO	Home Office	PRONI	Public Records Office of
IRB	Irish Republican		Northern Ireland
	Brotherhood	RH	Rhodes House
LSE	London School of	RIA	Royal Irish Academy
	Economics	RIC	Royal Irish
MEPO	Metropolitan Police		Constabulary
NLI	National Library of	TNA	The National Archives
	Ireland		(UK)
NYPL	New York Public Library		

Introduction

'For, with me in their hands … the English government will try how [*sic*] most to *humiliate* and *degrade* me … they will charge me with something else—something baser than "high treason"—God knows what—& what chance of a trial will I have on any charge they choose to get up against me?'

—Roger Casement, 26 March 1916 (NLI 17026)

The construction of the historical narrative about Casement is not yet complete 100 years after his execution. In his afterlife he still provokes painful and profound questions about the nature of loyalty, integrity and the state, questions about authority, justice and power. In his introduction to *One bold deed of open treason*, Angus Mitchell (2016, 17) writes, 'Even if Ireland still finds it hard to accept Casement …', without indicating why Ireland finds it hard. Perhaps this is because there are so many Casements to choose from, because his historical identity is so fissured. Heroes, like martyrs, are usually of one piece. The multiple kaleidoscopic identities of Casement have still not coalesced into the coherent understandable unity required for closure. He was a man of terrifying integrity or of none, a megalomaniac or a man who 'eliminated self', a defiant enemy of imperial power or simply a traitor, emotionally unstable or rational and lucid, a homosexual or a man besmirched by his enemies. Most people today have chosen their Casement, but it is always unwise to choose without complete knowledge of the 'product'.

Research for this book was carried out from 2014 to 2018 and the focus has been on determining the authenticity or otherwise of the diaries attributed to Casement. This has necessitated an in-depth scrutiny of the Giles Report of 2002, because this is the only examination of the diaries which received widespread publicity and which furnished conclusions of authenticity. The research has also necessitated a close scrutiny of the anomalies in and contradictions between the two diaries for 1910. In the light of the conflicting official and unofficial records, the question of the provenance of these diaries, allegedly discovered in 1916, is also examined at length.

In an ideal world, the question of the authenticity of these controversial diaries would be settled with certainty by scientific tests such as those used in the 1983 case of the Hitler Diaries, but the policy of the UK National Archives is that no such 'hard science' tests will be carried out on the Casement volumes. This has left comparative handwriting analysis, which is the weakest method for determining authenticity of documents since it cannot produce more than a subjective expert opinion. The Hitler Diaries, although forged to order, managed to deceive no fewer than three handwriting experts. Handwriting analysis is not an exact science; indeed, it is not a science at all.

Two rhetorical strategies have been used to impress upon readers that the diaries are authentic. These are the 'wealth of detail' and the scale of the alleged forgeries. Although neither of these are arguments, they are nonetheless persuasive because they are calculated to inhibit a credible response. Where and how would a forger have found the vast quantity of mundane detail that the diaries contain? Why would a forger risk writing so many thousands of words when a few forged letters would have been equally effective? That these two points are expressed as interrogatives indicates that they have no probative aspect and that no response is anticipated. Tacitly they insinuate that the form and content of the diaries are *de facto* a sufficient proof of authenticity. These strategies, however, find striking parallels in the case of the forgeries of the Hitler Diaries. It was precisely the vast number of Hitler diaries and their utterly banal content that convinced eminent historians to authenticate them; they simply could not imagine that anyone could forge such a quantity of material. They also felt that the wealth of banal detail could not have been invented—and, indeed, it was not; it was copied from another published source. The audacious scale of the operation had the psychological effect of excluding *a priori* the possibility of fraud. The form and content alone of the Hitler Diaries were taken to be a sufficient proof of authenticity. This conviction was then confirmed by three noted handwriting experts. Only 'hard science' testing established that the diaries had been forged in the previous two years, with some of them taking no more than a few hours to produce. On this basis, in both cases, scale and detail are an integral part of the plan since they act as powerful incentives to convince. Nevertheless, they prove nothing about authenticity.

While scientific testing was successful in the Hitler case, consultation with scientists in the UK, the USA, Poland, Ireland and Australia has confirmed the limitations of 'hard science' testing in that conclusive results cannot *in every case* be obtained from spectroscopy, DNA, pollen, ink and paper analysis. There are many variables and no serious scientist will claim a decisive result from probabilities. In short, there is no guarantee that any data obtained from such testing will be sufficient to substantiate a definitive conclusion.

This leaves only one investigative approach to the authorship of the diaries attributed to Casement. That approach is logical analysis of the documents and of the circumstances in which they were and are known, and an analysis of the reasons why they are widely held to be authentic. This approach, which essentially seeks to *decontaminate* the basic sources of information, has never been attempted.

The principal weakness of the authenticity position is the absence of anything that resembles an argument. There is simply no evidence that Casement was the author of the diaries. The authenticity position rests entirely on a resemblance in handwriting and on the word of hostile government officials. Resemblance is not identity. Handwriting resemblance is not an argument but it can successfully deceive when disguised as an argument. The principal weakness of the position against authenticity is that the arguments lack focus and therefore penetration. This is the result of confusion and futile speculation. It is also due to the secrecy in which the diaries were kept until 1959 and the secrecy of important files in government possession. Official refusal to allow the diaries to be rigorously and impartially tested nourished suspicion and further speculation. In addition, many crucial documents are missing, believed destroyed by the British authorities.

The positions both for and against authenticity have failed to provide logical investigation in the sense of constant, sceptical and clinical scrutiny of sources. Both have been weakened by bias and by a reliance on non-probative circumstances and conjecture rather than verifiable facts. Neither position appears to have perceived that there is no verifiable record of the bound-volume diaries being shown to anyone in 1916. Absence of such record indicates that there is no proof that the diaries existed in 1916. In addition to this, there is the unresolved question of the provenance of the diaries.

The Casement controversy is burdened with contradictions, anomalies, suspicions and confusions, and by a lack of verifiable facts concerning the diaries. Responsibility for this situation lies with the British authorities, who for many decades behaved in a manner as if calculated to produce suspicion. As recently as the early 1990s applications to view the diaries were still being refused. Today the diaries are kept in a safe-room at Kew as if they were state treasures or state secrets, but no one has ever claimed that they were state treasures.

The controversy is also burdened with an extraordinary quantity of innuendo and misinformation that has its origin in an evident predisposition to defend the British authorities at all costs by upholding authenticity in the absence of testable evidence. The principal authors are Inglis, Sawyer, Reid and Ó Síocháin, whose deployment of rhetorical strategies and selective framing enables them to distract the reader from ever arriving at the central questions. Some examples of this innuendo and misinformation are examined briefly in Chapter 10. An impartial reader would ask why these authors felt it necessary to mix facts with innuendo but would pose that question only if able to make the distinction between fact and innuendo. The answer can be found by noting what the innuendo and misinformation relate to and what their effect is. In all cases the innuendo and misinformation relate to the diaries and to the behaviour described therein, and in all cases the effect is to persuade the unwary reader of the diaries' authenticity.

That successive Irish governments since 1921 declined to raise the question with the British authorities has also nourished suspicions of collusion between Dublin and London. Although these suspicions were strongly denied in 1956, no explanation for official Irish disinterest was offered. Absence of a reasonable explanation for that disinterest weakens the official denial and increases the suspicion. The Ahern initiative in 1999 was quickly undermined and became a *private initiative* that produced the privately funded Giles Report.

A history that is composed of facts mixed with falsehood has no more value than pulp fiction. That the widely accepted Casement 'history' is a pulp fiction finds an indirect confirmation in the film screenplay written by noted author John Banville. In this very modern endeavour Casement is portrayed as homosexual, but his diaries fail to convince and therefore need to be forged. This formula seeks to satisfy all those who know little or nothing about Casement, which is a vast number of people. That the film was never made is a considerable contribution to impartial study of the controversy. Another noted novelist who fails to render the complex dynamics of the Casement story into fictional form is Mario Vargas Llosa, whose novel *The dream of the Celt* hovers uncertainly between historical biography and imaginative fiction offering a portrait of a tragic fanatic, thus avoiding the very issues which have generated the century-long controversy. In a generous act of confused sophistry he asserts that fiction can reveal truths that cannot be revealed by verifiable facts, and with this Vargas Llosa reveals how he has been unable to defend himself from the propaganda that has nourished his novel. Everyone chooses his or her own pulp-fictional Casement.

The century-long controversy over the diaries attributed to Casement is a triumph of opinionated confusion, deception and misinformation. Even before the centenary year of 2016, however, a widespread consensus had been achieved, which was that the notorious diaries were indeed the work of Casement. This consensus rested mostly on two events: the result of the 2002 Giles Report and the 2008 publication of Séamas Ó Síocháin's lengthy biography. These two productions seemed to authoritatively close down all doubts.

To many it appeared that the only dissenting public voice was that of historian Angus Mitchell, who continued to argue that the diaries had been fabricated. Early in 2015, however, Mitchell's isolated voice was joined by that of the present author, a newcomer to the question. Mitchell noted that his approach was different; he was more analytical and penetrating and he took nothing for granted.

This author began to probe where no researcher had gone before, at least not publicly. Rather than conjecture about how an alleged forgery might have been carried out, he concentrated on hunting down the evidence for the alleged authenticity of the diaries. His first discovery was simple and startling: there was no evidence for the authenticity of the diaries. In place of evidence there was insinuation and rhetoric, opinion and conjecture. His second discovery was that there was no evidence that the diaries existed during Casement's lifetime. No one was shown the bound volumes before 3 August. Typescript pages prepared by the Metropolitan Police were circulated as alleged copies of original diaries and these pages were seen by a large number of persons from May 1916 until the execution. They included King George V, the US ambassador, journalists, politicians, clergymen and those involved in the propaganda war effort, but there was not a single independent witness who recorded seeing the bound volumes. The major studies since 1956 also failed to cite any showing of the volumes during Casement's lifetime. Moreover, government documents dating from 1959 confirmed that the Home Office possessed no evidence of the diaries' having been seen by independent witnesses in 1916. The conclusion was that their existence at that time had been merely *presumed* for 100 years. In 2017 officials at the UK National Archives admitted that they did not know of any evidence that demonstrates the existence of the diaries in 1916.

That discovery has yet to be refuted. Later research focused on a secret memorandum of 1914, which had been ignored or suppressed by all previous Casement authors. This document contains the earliest insinuation of scandal; analysis of the document's contradictory and implausible nature demonstrated that it was invented by Minister Findlay in Oslo. Nonetheless, the same allegation appeared in the police typescripts shown in the 1916 smear campaign. Therefore the single insinuation of scandal made first in 1914 and again more explicitly in 1916 is false in the first instance but allegedly true in the second. The obvious absurdity of this explains why the 1914 document was ignored by those authors whose prime concern was to establish the diaries as authentic.

Either of these arguments alters the parameters of the long controversy over authenticity, and together they stand as a formidable challenge to the alleged authenticity of the diaries. In order to meet that challenge, the material existence of the diaries in 1916 must be established beyond all doubt, and this has not been done in 100 years. Without that proof, there are no grounds for any claim of authenticity and the diaries must be considered to be of unknown authorship.

This author believes that the diaries now held in TNA were forged in their entirety after Casement's death and he proposes the following, based on known facts, as being the most probable scenario. He accepts that CID chief Basil Thomson possessed a genuine 1903 diary and the cash ledger, as he stated consistently. The diaries in TNA for 1910 or 1911 were not found and Thomson never mentioned these.

The text of the genuine 1903 diary was copied into a part-used 1903 diary with the addition of incriminating passages. Pages for the first six weeks of the 1903 diary in TNA have been ripped out, leaving fragments of handwriting on the torn remains.

The text in the Dollard 1910 diary was extrapolated from the Amazon Journal diary and other sources with the addition of incriminating passages. A typed copy of the Amazon Journal was in government possession.

The text in the 1911 Lett's diary was mostly invented, with the innocuous material being assembled from original documents that recorded Casement's travels and locations.

The text in the cash ledger in police possession was copied into an unused ledger with the addition of incriminating passages. The ledger as originally printed is not year-specific so that any comparable new ledger was suitable.

Thus the forging of the 1903 diary was mostly an exercise of faithfully copying existing handwritten text from the original 1903 diary found by Thomson, simulating the original calligraphy and adding the incriminating material in the same simulated calligraphy. The forging of the 1910 diary required simulation of Casement's handwriting from existing exemplars, using a master narrative (prepared by Intelligence operatives) that was edited down from the Amazon Journal. The forging of the 1911 diary was similar to that of the 1910 save that there was no *single* original account as a source of daily events and the innocuous narrative had to be assembled from disparate sources that might have included fragmentary diary entries and other notes. This lack of a single extensive innocuous account was compensated for by the vastly increased quantity (compared to the 1910 diary) of fabricated incriminating material.

Claims that a forgery operation on this scale would require many years to carry out are no more than uninformed speculation. Only an experienced forger can know the timespan of this operation. The fact that the innocuous text in the bound volumes was sourced from existing writings considerably reduced the time needed. In this respect the case of the forgery of the Hitler Diaries is worthy of attention. There were 62 diaries and these had been forged in approximately two years. Konrad Kujau stated that some of these diaries took him no more than two weeks to fabricate. Much of the text was copied from published (printed) material, which means that Kujau had only to focus on simulating Hitler's handwriting. His simulation deceived three handwriting specialists, including world-famous expert Ordway Hilton, who failed to detect that the control material was as false as the diary writings. Comparative handwriting analysis lacks experimental verification procedures and therefore cannot guarantee the conclusive results expected from scientific investigation; it can never be more than informed opinion. On this basis it is evident that a capable forger can produce a close resemblance to existing handwriting without difficulty and relatively quickly. There is no reason to think that the forgery of the Black Diaries took any longer than the forgery of the Hitler Diaries.

Paradoxically, it is the innocuous text that is of greater importance because it is intended to represent Casement's authentic experience, which it appears to do; the personality that 'speaks' in the innocuous material does seem to be the known Casement. The deception, however, should not surprise: that innocuous personality is indeed parasitic upon Casement's genuine personality, since the innocuous material was derived directly from his authentic writings. The illusion of authenticity is established in the innocuous material, which illusion transfers itself automatically to the incriminating material because of intimate association and because of identical handwriting on the same page on the same day. The transition is virtually seamless and it seems that there is but one voice speaking. The illusion is as complete as the illusions of standard fictional techniques in which entirely imaginary people speak, and we listen because the voice resembles a voice we believe we have heard. But in the diaries there are two voices: the first is a stolen voice and the second is a voice parasitical upon the first. It is an illusionary act of double ventriloquism.

The forger of the Black Diaries worked from two sources. The police typescripts were the primary source of the narrative texts—of the actual words to be written into the diaries. The secondary source was genuine Casement writings, which contained a great majority of those same words in the typescripts but in Casement's original calligraphy. The total forgery of each bound volume means that the handwriting is consistent throughout as the work of a single hand, which bears a close resemblance to original Casement handwriting in the secondary sources.

It is possible that the four volumes are the work of more than one forger. The narratives in the police typescripts were generated by some two or three persons working for British Intelligence, which during the war employed some of the cleverest men in the UK. The 1903 diary required the invention of a relatively small amount of new material to be inserted. Similarly, the 1910 Dollard diary contains only about 4% of compromising text but the innocuous framing narrative needed to be extrapolated and reworked from the typescript of the longer Amazon Journal. The 1911 Lett's diary contains a much greater quantity of sexually explicit narrative, which dominates the innocuous material; there are 97 compromising entries in a total of 154 entries (63%). Many of these compromising entries are so explicit that they contrast with the generally more allusive and muted compromising entries in the 1910 diary. These two diaries do not entirely share the same erotic personality and almost certainly the 1911 narrative was prepared by two 'authors'. The 1910 narrative appears to be the work of a single erotic personality who appears again in the 1911 diary along with a second, much more daring 'author'. The disproportionate amount of compromising material was due to a scarcity of original writings recording Casement's 1911 investigation.

The police typescripts (or parts of them) were shown from late May onwards, and it is recorded that the typing of the 1911 typescript was completed on 24 June, just two days before the trial started. It cannot be determined when the typing process began but it is recorded that four 1911 typescripts were made. It is possible that the creation of the narratives proceeded in tandem with the typing process.

No explanation has ever been proposed for this extraordinary typing operation, which fact leaves a serious interrogative: why was it felt necessary to undertake the typing? The use to which the typescripts were put is beyond dispute, but possession and display of the bound volumes would have made it easier, faster and more economical to achieve a result that would have *eliminated all possible doubt at that time and since*. There is no record, however, either by HM government or by independent witnesses, that the volumes were shown before Casement's execution, whereas there is testimony from independent witnesses of the showing of the typescripts. The absence of a simple and credible answer to this interrogative after 100 years reinforces the only logical and common-sense answer that can be proposed: the volumes could not be shown because they did not exist. Their non-existence made it necessary to prepare the typescripts as a temporary substitute so that the smear campaign could proceed.

A number of quite valid questions have been asked over the decades about the extraordinary secrecy in 1916 and the official no-comment policy that lasted until 1959. What circumstance can explain the British government's behaviour in that period? The answer lies in the fact that silence and secrecy are defensive strategies. What had to be defended was the integrity of those involved in the smear campaign, and those involved included very prominent people in the state—cabinet ministers, high-ranking police and Intelligence officers, senior civil servants. Many of these were still alive during that period and they, too, had been honoured by the Crown. They were members of a post-WWI élite. A smear campaign is considered to be unworthy of high state officials, but their involvement was as undeniable as it was considered justifiable against a renegade traitor in wartime. This is a delicate balance, however, because it places 'men of honour' in a precarious position. Anything that disturbs the balance will potentially taint their honour, and the élite can only fall from grace. At all costs nothing was to be done which might reveal the smear left on their reputations. These men of honour had judged Casement long before his arrest and had determined that he was to be killed. The publicised show trial was the spectacle that would disguise the state's vengeful hatred of its own knight who had turned against the empire and whose accusatory writings in *The Continental Times* had revealed official secrets and attacked Grey, Bryce, Churchill and Balfour, the most powerful statesmen in Britain. The judgement of the men of honour was motivated by revenge, and the execution was no more than a legalised revenge killing. In order to take their revenge on Casement, the honourable men had first to compromise themselves and thus compromise the state's *moral* authority to judge Casement. That compromised moral authority was concealed by silence and secrecy, which was a refusal to confess the shame of the state's men of honour. Shame is consciously felt but unconsciously exhibited. It was exactly Casement's moral standing which compelled the men of honour to make his name unspeakable so that they could take revenge.

After the restricted release of the diaries in August 1959, the first sceptical reaction was published by Roger McHugh in 1960. In a surprise conciliatory gesture, the British government finally conceded the return of Casement's remains to Ireland for a state funeral in 1965, but this was followed in 1966 by Herbert Mackey's book that openly claimed forgery (Mackey 1966). It seemed to the British authorities that, despite the gesture, access to the volumes had failed to convince and that forgery claims would continue unless rebutted. Thus began what amounted to a print campaign to defend the state from the sin it dare not confess because by then it was too late. The first response was the publication of the Inglis study in 1973, followed in 1976 by Reid's biography in the US, both claiming authenticity. In 1984 Sawyer's first book appeared, again claiming authenticity. That made three books in eleven years about a man executed over 60 years earlier and whose name had long vanished from public consciousness and from the history books. It was the era of the Cold War, of new technology, of nuclear danger, of the Falklands War and the imminent implosion of the Soviet Union. Despite the fall of the Berlin Wall, the end of the Soviet era and the redrawing of borders in Europe, Casement would not go away. The Inglis study was republished in 1993 and a second book from Sawyer appeared in 1997. This amounts to five publications in 24 years about a man of whom most people born after WWII had never heard. Within a few years another three books appeared, all accepting authenticity, and Inglis's book was reissued in 2002 to coincide with the Giles Report. Finally, after many years in preparation, Ó Síocháin's weighty volume was published in 2008, yet again claiming authenticity. It is a remarkable and significant record—nine publications in 35 years about this strange, 'enigmatic' traitor/patriot/ srevolutionary, relic of a bygone imperial age, whose name scarcely appears in any histories of the period but whose ghost somehow will not lie down. The number and frequency of these publications suggest a widespread ongoing interest in Casement matters, which, if true, is perplexing, since he has long been eliminated from the story of human rights and very few in either the UK or Ireland know much about him or are interested in him. One might ask why the authenticity claim has required such persistent support, especially since that claim has been obediently endorsed by the mass media. Perhaps, however, these authors interpreted Lord Acton's observation as a warning: 'Everything secret degenerates ... nothing is safe that does not show how it can bear discussion and publicity'. The voice of dissent has been marginalised and more or less silenced.

The extraordinary amount of material aimed at rebutting the very few so-called 'forgery theorists' and diary sceptics seems unnecessary, especially when they have no political voice, no media support and have not published a single study focusing on the grounds for forgery since 1966. At the same time, the years of research and thousands of pages supporting authenticity have yet to provide conclusive proof of authenticity that would satisfy an impartial court. An impartial person seeking to inform him/herself about the controversy would find on the bookshelves mostly books dedicated to supporting authenticity; this example of saturation marketing is not accidental.

The Irish establishment has obediently acquiesced to the consensus view emanating from the UK, with, for example, two prominent figures, a former attorney general and a president of the Royal Irish Academy, speaking publicly in 2016 about the diaries and revealing that personal research is not required, since a ready-made consensus judgement is available which can be proclaimed with the arrogant certainty that derives from woeful ignorance. One of these prominent figures blithely invited listeners to imagine any kind of Casement they wished, while the other called for the public lynching of those who refused the dogma of authenticity. Sadly, this is symptomatic of the level of debate, which has been afflicted with duplicity, contempt and cowardice.

There is dissent, but it is constrained more or less to a resigned silence reminiscent of totalitarian cultures. The complex controversy requires in-depth analysis of documents and facts and a ruthless emotional detachment in order to establish what can be stated with a sufficient degree of certainty. This is both difficult and time-consuming. The combination of confusion, secrecy and misinformation is intended to make the task daunting and beyond the capacity of most people. The authoritative voices in both Ireland and the UK declaiming authenticity for many decades constitute a powerful disincentive. Radically altered attitudes to the complexity of human sexuality have conditioned and confused perception of the issues which generated the controversy, with the result that it now appears irrational and reactionary to question authenticity. Nonetheless, the issue remains one of childlike simplicity: are the diaries held in TNA the authentic writings of Casement or are they of unknown authorship?

Probably the most frequently asked question in the controversy over the Black Diaries is why the authorities would take so much trouble to vilify a man already in their power. Minor variations of the question ask why the extensive forgery was undertaken when it had no connection with the charge of treason. These are perfectly valid questions. The answers are also perfectly valid and penetratingly true.

The answers were provided by two very eminent persons representing Church and State on 2 August 1916, one day before Casement's execution. That morning, after a 90-minute cabinet meeting to deliberate for the last time on the fate of the condemned man, Home Secretary Herbert Samuel wrote that a reprieve would 'let loose a tornado of condemnation ... would profoundly and permanently shake public confidence in ... the government', and admitted that 'had Casement not been a man of atrocious moral character' (Reid 1976, 446) the decision to execute him would have been much more difficult. On the same day, the archbishop of Canterbury, Randall Davidson, met Lord Chancellor Buckmaster and advised that 'a reprieve would be wiser than an execution', but then added that 'the well being and safety of the Empire' required his execution. Davidson completed his justification by describing Casement as 'morally unhinged'.

These answers respond perfectly to the questions above; moreover, they penetrate to the core of establishment anxiety. The questions seek to understand (A) why it was felt necessary to vilify Casement before and after his conviction, and after his death on the scaffold, and (B) why an extensive forgery was felt necessary when irrelevant to the legal charge.

Neither Davidson nor Samuel had seen the bound diary or diaries but both were certain that the condemned man was a traitor and an unspeakable degenerate. Samuel had seen the police typescripts, as had many others, and Davidson had been reassured by Reverend John Harris, who also had seen the typescripts on his behalf. Davidson was concerned with the empire and Samuel with government stability; these concerns were both immediate and future-oriented. It seems scarcely credible that one man awaiting execution could have caused such anxieties to the most powerful empire in history, to a military superpower whose warships controlled the seas and whose monarch counted his subjects in hundreds of millions. Nonetheless, the answers of these eminent men—*expressed separately*—reveal their views that a reprieve threatened both government and empire. It is unthinkable that these two influential men were alone in their opinions.

Casement was the empire's very own VIP traitor. There had been a mutual but facultative symbiosis between Casement and the state until 1912. The empire lacked but desired Casement's genuine compassion, and so by honouring Casement it shared by proxy his humanitarian aura. Thus the empire became like Casement—noble, virtuous, altruistic. Following the symbiotic phase, however, Casement progressively betrayed the unspoken code of honour, the *omertà* that safeguards every power-sensitive organisation. In his published writings and speeches he denounced the ruling Oxford oligarchy as a criminal conspiracy.

To synthesise: the legal charge alone was sufficient to put Casement in the dock and to convict him but was not *morally* sufficient to put him on the scaffold. That insufficiency was compensated for by the campaign of vilification. His new identity as degenerate traitor was very recent, however, while his career as moral hero of the Empire was of longer standing and could not be discounted so easily. It was essential that Casement become more than a traitor and that he become also 'a man of atrocious moral character', something he had vaguely foreseen on 26 March 1916 when he wrote: '... the English government will try how most to humiliate and degrade me ... they will charge me with ... something baser than "high treason"—God knows what ...'. The defamation was the vital key in overcoming a vacillating cabinet and the many appeals for clemency; it ensured Casement's execution. Therefore to ask why the vilification and forgery were necessary is to ask why his execution was necessary. Samuel and Davidson provide the correct answers.

In 2000 London's Royal Courts of Justice saw a perhaps unique example of false history being put on trial. Historian David Irving ignominiously lost his libel case against US academic Deborah Lipstadt when the judge decreed that he had falsified the historical record concerning the Holocaust. Far from being a matter of revision of historical evaluation in the light of new research or of reinterpretation of events, this was a case of pure and simple lying. The emotive weight of the Holocaust, the scale of suffering involved and the verified testimony of surviving witnesses in every country made the Holocaust a special case that could not be rationally denied—a denial, moreover, that would implicitly sanction genocidal murder. Irving may well be no more than an eccentric *provocateur* who over-reached himself in his appetite for attention.

The principal authors on Casement have also falsified the historical record but much more cleverly than by Irving's crude negationism. Close reading of their works reveals a systematic operation of duplicity and selective framing, an abundant but revealing use of rhetorical devices rather than arguments based on verified facts and, most tellingly, a persistent reliance on innuendo. These tactics alone would disqualify them from being considered impartial historians in the same measure as Irving lost his claim to being a serious historian. History is a political discipline and history is written by politically conditioned people. The works produced by the Casement authors are politically conditioned to protect and continue the deception of 1916. In short, these authors have undertaken state propaganda, which they have disguised as scholarly, unofficial and impartial research. They have been dishonest rather than incompetent, knowing that cohesive narrative is a potent weapon in neutralising problematic questions. Theirs is not a naïve falsification, however, and their use of innuendo, selective framing and rhetoric indicates that their works emerge from a *necessary* state of cognitive dissonance which allows them to write what they know is false. Like Irving, they have lied, although not to gain attention but rather to protect their faith in state integrity, which they confound with higher values and which values they find within themselves. They have lied and deceived to protect the state's official truth.

The question of honest belief was raised by the judge in the Irving trial as a possible explanation for Irving's falsifications. The same question might be raised on behalf of the Casement authors. If a person honestly believes that what he/she has said or written is the truth then he/she has not knowingly lied. In Irving's case this was dismissed because it was demonstrated that he had manipulated his own written facts in later publications and had changed his version in an anti-Semitic direction. He had reinvented his own facts. The Casement authors are not guilty of reinvention but of presenting as true that which is not supported by proven evidence or by documents and which is demonstrably false. They do this by exploiting the readers' understandable lack of knowledge and research in order to provide an 'in-depth' but heavily manipulated version of events, and they do this with such skill and persuasiveness that the discrepancies are not evident to an unwary reader who has no reason to be suspicious. A single example from Inglis might illustrate this technique of deception.

When he was in Germany in 1914–16 Casement kept a diary, which contains no compromising entries such as those in the Black Diaries. This diary was never in the possession of the British authorities. In order to explain the absence of compromising material, Inglis added the following in an appendix to the paperback edition of 1974:

> 'Of the other two surviving diaries, one was written while he was in Germany, under constant police surveillance, he would have been unwise to include any compromising material'.

The distorted logic of Inglis's statement betrays his presumed impartiality. The innuendo is that the compromising acts were performed despite constant police scrutiny but that Casement cunningly did not record these acts in his diary and thereby protected himself from prosecution. Thus police scrutiny functions as an incentive rather than a deterrent to criminal activity. Inglis absurdly implies that the police will only act to prevent crimes if *post facto* they find the crimes recorded in a diary. With this verbal legerdemain Inglis reveals that Casement is guilty *whether or not he records his behaviour in a diary*, and even the absence of evidence becomes evidence. And with this single example of duplicity Inglis abandons all pretence of being an impartial historical biographer. His work must therefore be dismissed as worthless because it is dishonest.

Similar although sometimes less subtle forms of deception infect the works of other Casement authors. The notion of honest belief raised above cannot be considered for the Casement authors unless one wishes to accuse them of rank stupidity and ignorance, which is far from the case.

In 1959 Alexander Clutterbuck, British ambassador to Ireland, advised his government that the arguments of the scholars over authenticity would continue but would cancel each other out. This statement admitted that there was no proof of authenticity beyond reasonable doubt because the British authorities lacked essential evidence to support such proof. Therefore authenticity could only be *presumed* by those disposed to make that presumption on trust. Authenticity thus became a matter for persuasion and hence for the deception and calculated misinformation which found first expression in the Inglis biography. After the 43-year-long official silence, the authorities began to speak through selected ventriloquists.

REASONABLE GROUNDS

Are there reasonable grounds for the suspicion that the Black Diaries might not be authentic? Reasonable grounds would arise from unsatisfactory answers to reasonable questions posed by a reasonable and impartial enquirer.

- *How were the diaries found?* Not known—various conflicting accounts.
- *Who found the diaries?* Not known—various accounts.
- *When were the diaries found?* Not known—various contradictory accounts.
- *Who first made the insinuation of hidden scandal?* British Minister Findlay in Oslo in 1914.
- *How was that allegation made?* It was an allusion made in a top-secret memo written by a legation official who never met or saw Casement; the memo was sent to Foreign Secretary Grey and passed to British Intelligence.
- *What was the reaction of Casement's friends, colleagues and associates to the 1916 allegation in the typescripts?* Astonishment and disbelief; those who had known Casement personally and professionally had no suspicions.
- *Why were the diaries kept secret by the British authorities until 1959?* Not known.
- *Why were the bound-volume diaries accessible only to persons vetted in advance by HM Home Office after their release in 1959?* Not known.
- *Have any exhaustive forensic tests been carried out on the diaries?* None of the examinations carried out meet forensic standards (i.e. court standards).
- *What were the results of the 1958 investigation?* An opinion of 93 words that failed to identify authorship and did not satisfy the Home Office.
- *What were the results of the 1970s investigation?* No formal results were

published of this non-professional and unofficial intervention.

- *What were the results of the 1993 investigation?* Unclear and cautious but favouring authenticity.
- *What were the results of the 2002 investigation?* Claimed authenticity of the diaries.
- *Where can the results of these investigations be seen?* For the 1958 investigation see HO 144/23481; for the 1970s and 1993 investigations, not known. The text of the 2002 investigation can only be found in the Royal Irish Academy book on Casement (Daly 2005).
- *Have the British authorities now released all Casement documents to public access?* No; a number of files are still classified for reasons of national security.
- *How did the British authorities exploit the diaries in 1916?* They did not exploit the bound-volume diaries at all in 1916. Police typescripts were shown to influential persons, who were told that these were true copies of diaries in their possession.
- *Were the bound-volume diaries now in TNA shown to anyone in 1916?* There is no verifiable record of the bound-volume diaries being shown to anyone in 1916, as confirmed by HO 144/23455 of 6 March 1959. There is no record of independent witnesses being shown the bound-volume diaries during Casement's lifetime. In 2017 officials at TNA admitted that they do not know of any evidence demonstrating the existence of the volumes in 1916.
- *Why did the police prepare typescripts instead of making photographs of the diaries for showing?* No answer to this question has ever been proposed.
- *Where are the original photos and police typescripts that were shown to influential persons?* The photographs are believed to have been destroyed; the typescripts are held by the NLI and by TNA.
- *Who were the sources of the scandal allegation in 1916?* The sources were all British Crown officials and all hostile to Casement: Findlay, Thomson, the two Halls, Smith and Blackwell. None of them had met or seen Casement before 1916.
- *Did the authorities produce any eyewitnesses to support the allegation?* After the trial one person signed a contradictory police statement.
- *What was Casement's reaction to the allegation?* He never saw the police

typescripts that were shown. When informed of it by one of his legal team, he indignantly denied the allegation.

If one accepts that these questions are reasonable, one must then decide whether the answers are satisfactory or unsatisfactory. An unsatisfactory answer is one which fails to provide the information sought in the question or which leads to further uncertainty. If, on balance, the answers are held to be unsatisfactory, it follows that there are reasonable grounds for suspicion concerning the diaries.

WHO'S WHO

Ernley Blackwell*—legal adviser to the cabinet; one of those responsible for showing the police typescripts.

Adler Christensen—a young Norwegian hired by Casement in New York as his servant on his secret trip to Oslo and Berlin. On the Norwegian ship, Casement travelled first-class, disguised as New York businessman James Landy. Christensen travelled second-class under his own name. The main biographers portray Christensen as treacherous and as plotting to betray Casement. He did not betray him during his year of service and Casement remained grateful to him.

Mansfeldt de Cardonnel Findlay*—minister to the British legation in Oslo and originator of the scandal insinuation; he was obsessed with Casement's capture or assassination and issued a written bribe of £5,000.

Stephen Gaselee*—Foreign Office librarian, one of those responsible for showing the police typescripts.

George Gavan Duffy—the solicitor who assembled Casement's defence team and consequently was forced to resign his legal partnership in London.

King George V—of the royal house of Saxe-Coburg and Gotha and first cousin of Kaiser Wilhelm of Germany. The monarch was shown the police typescripts. He noted in his personal diary on 3 August that Casement's execution was well deserved.

Arthur Maundy Gregory—one of Thomson's informants. According to

Thomson, it was Gregory who suggested to him the use of incriminating diaries to destroy Casement's reputation. None of the biographies mention this shady character, who was behind the 'honours for sale' scandal.

Edward Grey*—Foreign Secretary whose admiration for Casement led to his knighthood in 1911.

Major Frank Hall—MI5 intelligence officer and one of Casement's interrogators; an Ulster Unionist and secretary of the UVF in 1914.

Captain Reginald Hall*—head of Naval Intelligence in WWI; one of Casement's interrogators and a man of strong convictions.

John Harris*—Baptist missionary and one-time associate and admirer of Casement.

Brian Inglis—journalist, popular historian and author of *Roger Casement* (1973), the most influential biography.

René MacColl—leading journalist and author of *Roger Casement: a new judgement* (1956).

William J. Maloney—neurologist and author of *The forged Casement diaries* (1936).

E.D. Morel—journalist and founder of the Congo Reform Association and close associate of Casement.

Alfred Noyes—professor of literature and poet; author of *The accusing ghost, or Justice for Casement* (1957). Noyes was convinced by the police typescripts in 1916 but a 1937 poem by Yeats caused him to rethink the matter.

Gustav Olsen—reception clerk at the Grand Hotel, Oslo; he collaborated in Findlay's plotting against Casement.

Séamas Ó Síocháin—Irish academic and author of *Roger Casement: imperialist, rebel, revolutionary* (2008).

B.L. Reid—US academic and author of *The lives of Roger Casement* (1976).

Roger Sawyer—author of *Roger Casement: the flawed hero* (1984) and *Roger Casement's diaries: the black and the white* (1997).

Peter Singleton-Gates—a young Fleet Street reporter and confidant of Thomson, who gave him police typescripts in 1922 under an oath of secrecy. Banned from publishing these in 1925, he finally published them in 1959 in Paris to avoid prosecution in Britain.

F.E. Smith*—attorney general, member of the cabinet and Casement's prosecutor; an ardent Unionist and devout imperialist with a personal antagonism towards Casement. One of the cleverest men of the period, Smith rose from modest origins to become attorney general and lord chancellor. He appointed himself as Casement's prosecutor and personally blocked Casement's appeal to the House of Lords; he threatened the government with his resignation to prevent a reprieve, thus ensuring Casement's execution. Another man of 'strong convictions', in his imperial delirium he was considered extreme by fellow reactionaries: '... it is for us, who, in our history have proved ourselves a martial ... people ... to maintain in our own hands the adequate means for our own protection and ... to march with heads erect and bright eyes along the road of our imperial destiny' (7 November 1923).

A.M. Sullivan—Casement's defence lawyer, he took on the case for a large fee and for career advancement.

Basil Thomson*—head of Metropolitan Police CID and the alleged discoverer of the diaries. Previously a colonial administrator and prison governor, he had no police experience. He fell from favour in 1921 in unclear circumstances and left the Metropolitan Police, taking with him considerable quantities of official papers, photographs and records. His contradictory accounts of the diaries' provenance have undermined claims for their authenticity.

Those marked with an asterisk were knighted after WWI.

REFRESHER READING

The Black Diaries

The Black Diaries consist of five bound volumes: an Army notebook, a Lett's pocket diary for 1903, a Dollard office diary for 1910, a Lett's office diary for 1911 and a cash ledger relating to expenditure in 1911. The last four contain homosexual writings, the most explicit being the 1911 diary. They are held in the UK National Archives and are formally attributed to Roger Casement. The provenance of these volumes has been controversial since 1916, when the Metropolitan Police allegedly found them in a trunk belonging to Casement.

Today it is undisputed that a planned smear campaign was conducted by British officials from the time of Casement's arrest until several weeks after his execution. This campaign was intended to destroy his reputation and thereby offset the many appeals for reprieve and to prevent him from achieving martyr status in Ireland and the US. The campaign, however, was based *not on the diaries* but on police typescripts that were shown from May 1916 onwards. There is no record of any of the diaries being shown to anyone *at that time*. It is undisputed that the police typescripts and a few photographs of extracts from them were shown. It was alleged that the typescripts were copies of the diary contents.

Two of the bound-volume diaries, the 1910 and 1911, were shown to Michael Collins on 6 February 1922 in the House of Lords by prior arrangement with Lord Birkenhead, Casement's prosecutor. The 1903 diary could not be located at Scotland Yard at that time. Collins left no record of his reaction to seeing the diaries.

Also in 1922, a British journalist, Peter Singleton-Gates, was given a set of the police typescripts by Basil Thomson, former head of CID and one of Casement's interrogators after his arrest. The journalist's plan to publish these in 1925 was blocked by the Home Office and by Birkenhead. From 1916 to 1959, official policy was to refuse all comment about the diaries.

Casement's execution did not extinguish the controversy about either his life or the scandal. Two biographies appeared in 1930 and in 1936, and in the latter year William Maloney, a medical doctor, published *The forged Casement diaries*, a detailed study of the smear campaign which revealed the extent of the plot by agents of British Intelligence. In 1956 leading journalist René MacColl published a biography that claimed that the diaries were genuine. This was followed in 1957 by *The accusing ghost, or Justice for Casement* by Alfred Noyes, his account of having been deceived in 1916 when he was shown the police typescripts. Noyes had become a convert to the forgery argument. In 1959, after the publication by Singleton-Gates in Paris of *The Black Diaries*, based on two of the typescripts in his possession, the government transferred the five volumes to the Public Records Office for restricted access by accredited persons on application to the Home Secretary. Restricted access remained the rule until 1994.

That the controversy was rekindled after 1959 is due to the simple fact that the existence of the diaries had been confirmed at last. Their contents made it clear that the previous forgery theory was without foundation. This earlier theory had proposed that in 1911 Casement had sent the Foreign Office an obscene diary by a Peruvian criminal, and that this material had been used against him in the smear campaign.

In the decades that followed, a number of works appeared that supported the authenticity of the diaries. The first was by Brian Inglis in 1973, quickly followed by B.L. Reid's US edition of *The lives of Roger Casement*. Roger Sawyer published *Roger Casement: the flawed hero* in 1984 and *Roger Casement's diaries: the black and the white* in 1997. In the meantime, Inglis's book had been reprinted in 1974 and republished in 1993.

What these books share is a failure to distinguish between the police typescripts that were shown and the bound-volume diaries now in the archives but for which there is no record of any showing *at that time*. They also share a heavy reliance on innuendo and unsupported assertions posing as facts. Above all, none of them offer any treatment of the origins of the allegation of 'unnatural vice', which dates from October 1914, fully eighteen months before the alleged discovery of the diaries. Also missing is any treatment of the evidence that Casement's trunk was located shortly after he went to Germany in 1914 and not in 1916. Many of those who believe in authenticity are on record as believing that the diary or diaries were found some fifteen months before the official date of April 1916.

Support for authenticity continued with Adrian Weale's *Patriot traitors: Roger Casement, John Amery and the real meaning of treason* (2001), Dudgeon's 2002 volume, McCormack's *Roger Casement in death* of the same year and yet another edition of the Inglis volume. As if this was not enough to consolidate authenticity, Irish academic Ó Síocháin's detailed biography finally appeared in 2008. A total of nine works plus two reprint editions were in the authenticity field.

But 2002 was a special year in the Casement controversy. In February the privately commissioned Giles Report announced that the diaries were genuine, and the press welcomed this apparently scientific conclusion. Handwriting expert Dr Audrey Giles had examined all the volumes at the request of Professor W. McCormack; her fee was paid by the BBC and RTÉ, with a small contribution by the Irish government. Both broadcast organisations produced lengthy TV documentaries covering Casement's career and the diaries scandal. Millions were now informed that 'the truth' had at last been revealed. What was also revealed, however, was that Dr Giles was a former employee of the Metropolitan Police, the body that had produced the typescripts in 1916. In his enthusiasm for authenticity, McCormack 'forgot' to appoint a non-British expert as a minimal gesture towards impartiality. Two distinguished US handwriting experts strongly criticised her report for its lack of detail and clarity, and for its failure to demonstrate how such definitive conclusions had been reached. One expert described the report as 'forensic junk science'. The 'Steering Committee' supposedly behind McCormack remained silent, and the instruction remit to Giles was clearly biased in favour of authenticity. Giles herself committed a major error by claiming that Collins had authenticated the diaries in 1922.

Despite these serious shortcomings and notwithstanding the 1982 scandal of the forged Hitler diaries which were authenticated by three handwriting experts, the Giles Report achieved its aim of appearing to give scientific certainty to authenticity by means of well-prepared press reporting which stressed the magic word 'forensic' to create an aura of scientific rigour. Two new works plus the new edition of the Inglis volume were issued in 2002, but with so many books already upholding authenticity it appeared to close observers that the adage 'less is more' had been reversed.

Perhaps the most persuasive appeal for authenticity is found in the 1973 Inglis book, an untested assertion that has been repeated by other authors: 'No person or persons, in their right mind, would have gone to so much trouble and expense to damn a traitor, when a single diary would have sufficed. To ask the forger to fake the other two diaries and the cash register (and if one was forged, all of them were) would have been simply to ask for detection, because a single mistake in any of them would have destroyed the whole ugly enterprise.' If it is indeed the case that a single mistake is capable of proving forgery, then there is an abundance of such mistakes—many hundreds. The Inglis innuendo, however, is that no such mistake has been found, and his many tens of thousands of readers over 30 years have not examined the volumes or the typescripts in search of errors. Inglis himself, in his many years of research, must have noted some of these mistakes but he mentions none. He certainly noted the errors in the 1914 memorandum that contains the original allegation of 'unnatural relations', since he quotes selectively from this contradictory document. He fails to inform his readers that, by word count, only 7% of the content can be verified as factual. A close examination of the *two diaries* for 1910 reveals hundreds of inexplicable anomalies and contradictions. Likewise, scrutiny of a single page of the 1911 volume and typescript exposes over 100 mistakes in the entries for a few days only. In those same typescript and volume entries an entire event-filled day, 20 December, is abruptly cancelled on the 21st as if it never happened and a mysterious vacuum takes its place. The anomaly of cancelled days leaving inexplicable time vacuums also appears in the 1910 Dollard volume and typescript.

The assertion that a single diary would have sufficed has a superficial plausibility until one realises that a single diary is less convincing than three diaries and the ledger. A single diary might be forged but it seems highly improbable that four volumes would be forged. In the Hitler diaries scandal, it was the number of diaries—some 62—that convinced many of their authenticity. With the Black Diaries, the greater quantity of incriminating material increases their claim to authenticity by making scepticism more difficult.

The above-cited authors have reinforced the authenticity position for over half a century, but they have done so by avoiding five crucial weaknesses in that position.

- The anomaly of several conflicting versions of how and when the diaries came into police possession has never been satisfactorily resolved.
- None of the authors have addressed the fact that Basil Thomson of the CID in his later writings claimed consistently that he had found *only one diary*, that for 1903. His own published versions give differing times for the discovery.
- The memorandum of 29 October 1914 containing the original innuendo of 'unnatural relations' is not mentioned in any of the works save that of Inglis, who gives no source reference and cites only the 57 words of the insinuation, thus ignoring the anomalies and contradictions in the remainder which expose the document as manifestly invented by Minister Findlay. So obviously false was this memo and later attempts to corroborate its claims that it was laid aside by the intelligence services until July 1916. Only the poison of the innuendo was of interest in 1915.
- The authenticity experts are divided about when the diaries were

discovered, with many believing that the trunk was found at least fifteen months before Casement's arrest. Therefore, if scandalous diaries were discovered at that time, the intelligence services kept them secret from everyone and thus protected Casement from exposure and ruin. There is no reference in the KV intelligence files to the finding of any incriminating diaries in 1914–15.

- It is when we examine the smear campaign in the summer of 1916 that we find records of the police typescripts being shown to influential people, including the monarch, clergymen, journalists, members of parliament and ambassadors, but *no record whatsoever of any of the bound volumes being shown to anyone*. Indeed, the files of the 1959 Home Office Working Party reveal that no such record exists (PRO HO 144/23481), a fact ignored by all authors. It follows that the material existence of the bound-volume diaries during Casement's lifetime has never been proven. In the thousands of pages published by the main authors not a single verifiable instance of the diaries being shown is offered. Instead, there is a persistent but deceptively simple conflation of the typescripts and the diaries, as if these were identical.

Contrary to the claims in these books and in the press and the TV documentaries, impartial scrutiny of the controversy reveals that there are very solid grounds for believing that the typescripts were the originals invented in 1916 and that the Black Diaries now in the National Archives were fabricated after Casement's execution.

The public life
Roger Casement was probably the most famous Irishman of the Edwardian period. He first came to public attention in 1903–4 following his investigations into the atrocities perpetrated on the natives of the Congo by the Belgian administration of King Leopold. By then he was 39 years old and had spent eighteen years in Africa; he had been HM consul for eight years. In December 1903 Casement returned to England and met the humanitarian campaigner E.D. Morel. Together they founded the Congo Reform Association in March 1904 as a means of increasing public awareness and mounting pressure for radical change. It was a significant step in Casement's concern for the human rights of oppressed peoples

everywhere. His Congo report to the Foreign Office appeared to cause some embarrassment, and perhaps incredulity; the whistleblower had blown his whistle too loudly and the published version was toned down, much to Casement's disappointment. The Belgian government set up a commission of enquiry into the evidence in his report; Casement was 'on trial' rather than King Leopold.

By the end of 1904 Casement had temporarily resigned from the consular service, had joined the Gaelic League and faced a long period of unemployment, which he spent mostly in Ireland. He was awarded the CMG for his humanitarian services but, scorning all honours, he avoided the London ceremony and the postal packet containing the medal remained unopened throughout his life. In November the Belgian commission finally vindicated his report and Casement triumphed as 'Congo Casement'. Throughout 1905 he was writing anonymous articles on Irish history and the cultural revival.

Unable to find suitable employment, Casement rejoined the consular service in 1906 and was posted in October to Santos in Brazil. By this time the consul had joined the Sinn Féin party of Arthur Griffith and had embraced Irish independence as a central purpose in his life. His disaffection from imperial colonialism had begun in the Congo and was still evolving. In June 1907 he left Brazil for England and at once crossed to Ireland, where he spent the summer with Gaelic League friends visiting the *Gaeltacht* areas. By March the following year Casement was back in Brazil, in Pará, the busy Amazon port for the export of natural rubber extracted from the vast forests of Colombia and Peru. After a two-month convalescence in Barbados and the publication of his Consular Report, Casement's doctor advised him to leave. By December he was back in Ireland.

In 1909 the 45-year-old Casement sailed to Rio de Janeiro to take up his promotion as consul general for Brazil. Neither the climate nor the lifestyle of Rio suited him, however, and he preferred the diplomatic city of Petropolis, where he made friends with the British and German ministers. In March 1910 Casement took extended leave and departed Rio, never to return.

Reports of abuses and atrocities in the rubber industry in Peru reached London in 1909, and it appeared that a London-registered company with prominent English investors was involved. This 'British-owned Congo' had to be investigated, and Grey called for Casement. In July 1910 Casement set out yet again for Brazil, this time in the company of an investigative team of five Englishmen employed by the Peruvian Amazon Company. His official task was to investigate the conditions of British subjects, natives of Barbados, working for the rubber company, but during his 75 days in the Putumayo region he went beyond his remit and exposed in detail a system of brutality and horror even worse than that in the Congo. This time he was dealing with genocide. He kept an extensive diary, handwritten on foolscap pages, as a graphic record of his experience. The diary, now in National Library of Ireland, became known as the Amazon Journal. The various notebooks that he wrote up have never been located. When his Putumayo reports were submitted, the Foreign Office and the world were shocked and Casement was once again the hero of the hour. In July 1911, on Grey's recommendation, Casement was knighted by George V.

From 1912 onwards the Home Rule issue drew Casement into the increasing tensions of Irish political affairs. Alarmed at the prospect of Home Rule, Ulster Unionists signed the Solemn League and Covenant in September 1912 and began recruiting the Ulster Volunteer Force to oppose by force of arms the introduction of the Government of Ireland Bill, which passed the Commons in January 1913. The oncoming crisis over Home Rule caused by Unionist and Conservative opposition contributed to Casement's decision to resign his consular post definitively in August of that year. In November the Irish National Volunteers were founded in Dublin and Casement was soon co-opted onto its provisional committee. The touring campaign that he began early in 1914 brought in many thousands of recruits all over Ireland. In March British officers at the Curragh indicated that they would refuse orders to act against Carson's Ulster Volunteers and the Westminster government backed down. A month later the Ulster rebels landed a massive cargo of arms illegally imported from Germany. Casement watched with keen interest and in May began planning a similar, smaller-scale operation for the Irish National Volunteers, whose numbers had grown to over 140,000. An unarmed organisation of such dimensions alarmed Redmond, leader of the Irish Parliamentary Party at Westminster, who demanded and obtained a controlling role; the Irish Volunteers split, the majority following Redmond, and Casement lost control. This event persuaded him to go to the US to discuss a new strategy with the leaders of

Clan na Gael. He sailed from Glasgow and reached New York on 18 July 1914.

Casement's activities had been monitored closely by the RIC in Ireland for some time, and during his 89 days in America he was under surveillance by British agents reporting to London as he visited Baltimore, Chicago and Philadelphia, speaking at public meetings and fund-raising among Irish-Americans. Among his many contacts were John Devoy and Joseph McGarrity of Clan na Gael and lawyers John Quinn and Bourke Cockran. The new strategy was Germany and the oncoming war in Europe. Contact with German Minister von Bernstorff was made in New York and Casement's plan to seek German support was approved. Financed by Devoy and with top-level introductions from von Bernstorff, Casement prepared for a secret trip to Imperial Germany via Norway.

On arrival in New York Casement had met by chance a young Norwegian, Adler Christensen, and now he employed him as his manservant for his mission to Germany. This would turn out to be a mistake. Although he had little education, Christensen spoke Norwegian and sufficient German, languages unknown to Casement, but the disparity in age, manners, education and life experience would puzzle many in the following months. In October Casement travelled first-class as an American citizen with the passport of a Clan na Gael member, James E. Landy of New York, faking an American accent and with his beard shaved off. Christensen travelled second-class as guide and assistant to New York businessman Landy. This ruse, Casement hoped, would conceal his identity and any Irish link should the SS *Oscar II* be intercepted *en route*. In fact, the vessel was stopped by a British warship, searched and taken into Stornaway harbour for two days. Casement's ploy succeeded, however, and his ship arrived in Christiania (now Oslo) at midnight on 28 October.

The following 39 hours in Oslo Casement spent mostly in his hotel room. His later account shows that his presence was already known to officials at the British legation headed by Findlay. The events in Oslo are still subject to confusion and conflicting interpretation but two documented facts are undisputed. First, unknown to Casement, a secret memorandum was dispatched to Grey in London by Findlay on the night of 29 October. This four-page document contained an allegation of 'unnatural relations' between Christensen and Casement. The seed that was to grow into the

1916 diaries scandal had been planted. Second, Findlay attempted to bribe Christensen to betray Casement and eventually signed a written promise to pay him £5,000 for information.

On 30 October, Casement and Christensen proceeded by train towards Berlin. Casement's mission to Germany had three aims: to obtain a statement of goodwill towards Ireland from the German government, to recruit an Irish Brigade from Irish POWs, and to obtain arms and officers for rebellion in Ireland. The first succeeded but the second failed miserably, which had an impact on the limited success of the third aim. The failure of the Irish Brigade despite repeated efforts depressed Casement and his health suffered. Meanwhile, communications with Ireland and the US were being intercepted by British Intelligence in Room 40 at the Admiralty.

Casement's seventeen months in Germany were spent in frequent despair and ill health and growing disillusionment with Germany's interest in Ireland, as revealed in the diary he occasionally kept. By early 1916 Casement knew that his position was hopeless and he longed to leave Germany and return to Ireland. In April he persuaded the authorities to provide a shipload of arms and munitions for the forthcoming rebellion and to transport him separately by submarine to the west coast.

Within hours of landing at Banna Strand on Good Friday, Casement was arrested by the RIC and taken to Dublin and then onwards to London, where he was met by Scotland Yard officers on 23 April. Three interrogation sessions were conducted by police chief Basil Thomson, Captain Hall of Naval Intelligence and Major Frank Hall of MI5. After the third session, Casement was placed in military custody in the Tower of London.

Two figures enter the story at this point: the flamboyant Attorney General F.E. Smith and legal adviser to the Home Office Ernley Blackwell, both nourishing a visceral hatred for Casement which was shared by the general public. As the guns fell silent in Dublin and the army took hundreds of Volunteers into captivity and began the courts martial and summary executions of the leaders, Scotland Yard typists were busy preparing lengthy typescripts intended to create a new and very different identity for the renegade knight and one-time humanitarian hero. The lethal scandal that had been dormant for eighteen months since the allegation in the 1914 Oslo memorandum was about to explode. On 15 May, with the Dublin executions over, Casement was placed in Brixton Prison to await a civil trial for high treason. In May, to Casement's public identity as rebel and traitor a new and more heinous dimension was added: he was now a sexual deviant and degenerate. The police typescripts were being shown and rumours of an abominable obscene diary spread rapidly. Casement was doomed.

The trial opened on 26 June at the Old Bailey with six counts of treason against Casement. The attorney general, F.E. Smith, had already appointed himself as state prosecutor. The treason charges derived from a law of 1351 written in Norman French, the legal language in England over five centuries earlier. The unpunctuated text, incomprehensible to the jury, was given the widest interpretation to include acts committed outside the jurisdiction. On the third day Casement's defence lawyer, Sullivan, collapsed in court and withdrew entirely. On the last day Sullivan's defence strategy, continued by his counsel, fell apart when the jury returned the inevitable verdict of guilty. Casement then delivered his speech from the dock, which was clearly addressed to posterity and to a world far beyond an English law court. The judges donned the black caps and pronounced the death sentence. The show trial was over.

The appeals for reprieve started before Casement's appeal to the Royal Court of Appeal was dismissed on 18 July. Simultaneously, the police typescripts were being shown to journalists, political figures, clergymen and the monarch himself—indeed, to anyone who might sign an appeal for clemency. The typescripts crossed the Atlantic, where they were used to manipulate any sympathy in influential political circles. On 25 July Smith refused to allow an appeal to the House of Lords, which act left only the royal prerogative of mercy. That in turn required prior cabinet assent, but the cabinet, although vacillating, was advised by Blackwell, who advocated that the law should take its course. Smith, a cabinet member, made his point clearer; he threatened to resign if the hangman was not summoned.

Casement was doomed, but the clemency appeals came in from notables in England, Ireland, the USA, South America and Africa. In late July, as the typescript campaign went on, Thomson attempted to provide corroboration for the ongoing defamation of the condemned man. Photographs of handwriting were sent to America and statements were gathered in Oslo by the legation. A former hotel worker was brought from Oslo to London to sign a police statement testifying to a contradictory version of Findlay's later inept attempts to corroborate his original allegation of October 1914. A police inspector returned from Philadelphia with an unsigned police statement allegedly made by Christensen.

As Casement prepared for the end, appeals were made directly to George V, to Asquith and to the Foreign Office. The signatories included prominent clergymen, academics, scientists, authors and editors; in New York, lawyer John Quinn raised 25 legal signatories in a day or so, all of them pro-British. Senator Cabot Lodge pushed a resolution through the US Senate calling for clemency. Casement's friends in Ireland furnished a significant appeal and others arrived from the Vatican, the president of Colombia and the Negro Fellowship League. But all was in vain against the determination of Blackwell and Smith. On 2 August, after a last cabinet meeting, Home Secretary Samuel admitted that the decision to execute would have been even more difficult 'had Casement not been a man of atrocious moral character'.

On the morning of 3 August 1916, a small crowd gathered outside Pentonville Prison to rejoice at the execution of Roger Casement.

Part 1—Symptoms of confusion

The story of the Black Diaries is as confused today as it was 100 years ago. All attempts to impose coherence on the official version and to defend the claimed authenticity of the diaries have failed to eliminate the anomalies, contradictions, errors of fact, discrepancies and unsupported assumptions that are integral to the story. Those who defend the official narrative have failed to address these multiple confusions, preferring mostly to ignore or suppress them. This has proved a useful strategy since it does not draw attention to the confusions. Yet they remain as symptoms that are indications of a health problem, of a possible illness. The symptoms had long been discernible in several biographies of Casement's life. They appeared again in 2002 during the BBC documentary broadcast to announce the results of the Giles Report and in press reporting of that event. In the centenary year of 2016 the symptoms became widely manifest. An impartial outsider would conclude that the Casement story was seriously confused.

In order to identify the nature of the illness that has afflicted the Casement story it is necessary to examine the symptoms carefully and impartially to discover what they might have in common. Only then might it be possible to determine the underlying cause of the malaise. The symptoms include errors of fact, discrepancies, anomalies, innuendo, omissions, contradictions and unsupported assumptions. Moreover, the symptoms are often difficult to distinguish from one another, which frustrates a prompt diagnosis. Perhaps more than a state of confusion, the Casement story is in a state of delirium.

1

Recipe for a delirium

Innuendo, confusion and corroboration

In 1916 the authorities made various attempts to corroborate the authenticity of the police typescripts. It has yet to be explained why, since the authorities claimed to be in possession of Casement's authentic self-incriminating diaries, such corroboration was thought necessary, unless these attempts were intended to deflect any demands to see the bound-volume diaries that might be made by those unconvinced by the typescripts. Nor is it clear for whom the corroboration was intended, but it is very clear that showing the bound volumes at that time would have made the clumsy and often botched corroboration quite unnecessary.

The first attempts at corroboration included the so-called affidavits commissioned from Oslo by Thomson, the photographing of extracts from the 1911 typescript and an alleged eyewitness statement inspired by Minister Findlay at the British Legation in Oslo. A personal initiative was undertaken by Major Frank Hall of Military Intelligence; this was a much more professional endeavour and therefore it is dealt with separately in Chapter 9, 'Manufactured evidence'.

In 1959 the Paris publication by Peter Singleton-Gates of two of the police typescripts reignited the Casement controversy. Already in 1958 a Home Office Working Party had been set up to advise the government on future policy concerning the Black Diaries. In the following decades interventions of a corroborative nature were made by various experts, including Roger Sawyer and Professor Christopher Andrew, official historian of the British Secret Services.

The result of these interventions—many of which were clumsy and patently unconvincing—was to add confusion to confusion, error to error, speculation to inaccuracy; the Casement story became a delirious cocktail of pompous *pronunciamenti* and misinformation, intentional and unintentional. Subtle ingredients included innuendo and insinuation. Less subtle ingredients included both stark ignorance of verified facts and disregard of facts. What had once been a secret recipe controlled by British intelligence evolved over the decades into a free-for-all. Those sipping this cocktail would soon find themselves able to believe anything whatsoever. Having swallowed the mixture of perplexities, confusions and misinformation, they would understand nothing at all.

Useless testimony

In the later months of 1910 Casement was in the Putumayo area investigating human rights abuses worse than those encountered in the Congo. For around three months he was in the company of five Englishmen who were employed by the Peruvian Amazon Company, registered in London. Their names were Barnes, Bell, Fox, Bertie and Gielgud, and they were experts in various aspects of the company's business. Casement was on cordial terms with them and saw them frequently, often playing bridge with them in the evenings.

In July 1916 Casement had already been condemned to death and efforts to seek a reprieve were under way in Britain, Ireland and the US. CID Chief Basil Thomson was seeking corroboration to strengthen the moral condemnation of Casement that had resulted from the showing of the police typescripts. Strangely, he sought this corroboration in Oslo, where Casement had spent a mere 39 hours in late October 1914 while *en route* to Germany. In a very short time Thomson obtained what have been described as eight affidavits from various Norwegians, but he was somewhat disappointed with these because they were little more than gossip; he wrote to Blackwell on 26 July 1916: 'Not much in them' (HO 144 1637 311643 140).

It remains to be explained why Thomson sought testimony from foreigners who did not know Casement and who lived in a city where he had spent a mere 39 hours. It would have been more logical to seek testimony from the group of professional Englishmen who certainly knew Casement and who had spent much time in his company. There is no record in the public domain to show that these Englishmen were consulted by Thomson, who might therefore be guilty of negligence in this respect. That Thomson was negligent is improbable, however, given his anxiety to obtain corroboration against Casement. That his anxiety was urgent is demonstrated by his soliciting testimony from foreigners *who did not even know Casement*. The impartial enquirer asks why Thomson sought testimony from unknown Norwegians when he could more easily have obtained the testimony of several English gentlemen who had known Casement very well over several months.

That there is no record in the public domain does not mean that Thomson was negligent in not consulting the five Englishmen. If he did consult them, there are three possibilities:

- Thomson obtained testimony damning to Casement but he suppressed it;
- Thomson received a 'no comment' from all five and he suppressed it;
- Thomson received unacceptable testimony and he suppressed it.

The first of these is not credible and can be dismissed. If Thomson was indeed convinced that Casement was guilty of the behaviour depicted in the Black Diaries, he would certainly have sought corroboration from Englishmen whose word would have counted a great deal more in England than the imprecise gossip and hearsay of unknown hotel staff, a self-declared 'gentleman' and a tax inspector in Oslo, none of whom knew Casement. If he did not consult the Englishmen, it suggests that he knew that any consultation would be futile. If he did consult them, he suppressed the second or third result of the consultation.

False evidence

Professor Christopher Andrew, a renowned authority on the world of intelligence and official historian for MI5, is yet another Casement expert and has made his contribution in favour of the authenticity of the Black Diaries. Unfortunately his contribution does not withstand scrutiny. In an essay entitled 'Casement and British Intelligence', published in *Roger Casement in Irish and world history* (Daly 2005), he writes: 'One of the reports from Findlay . . . included the statement that Casement and Christensen had "unnatural relations" . . . they began when he was a seaman aged only fifteen or sixteen and Casement was British consul in Brazil. According to Christensen, Casement followed him into a lavatory in a Montevideo hotel where they had sex. Christensen jumped ship and began an affair with Casement lasting for about a month.'

This appears to attribute to Findlay comments supposedly made to him by Christensen in 1914, but Findlay did not make any such report concerning events in Montevideo. The alleged interview with Christensen in Philadelphia was purportedly conducted on 23 May 1916 by Chief Inspector Ward of Scotland Yard CID, who claimed in his long report that he had travelled from London for that purpose (TNA KV 2/9-3, 15–30). Close scrutiny, however, reveals this corroborative exercise to be astonishingly inept and foolish.

There are two typed documents. The first, of ten pages and dated 5 June 1916, is headed 'COPY' and bears Scotland Yard's address. This is a summary report (TNA KV 2/9-3, 15–30) by Chief Inspector Ward of his alleged meeting with Christensen in Philadelphia on 23 May in the office of the Acting British Consul. The second typed document, of six pages, is headed 'Philadelphia' and dated 23 May. This account is purportedly in Christensen's first-person voice but is unsigned. Both documents were typed on a police typewriter in Scotland Yard at the same time. Therefore the alleged first-person typed statement is not an original account by Christensen but is the work of Inspector Ward. It is Ward's version of a narrative allegedly originating from Christensen some two weeks earlier. There is nothing to guarantee its authenticity or to demonstrate that the typed words in the statement were ever spoken or written by Christensen, but there is strong evidence to demonstrate that the statement attributed to Christensen is entirely invented—that it is an example of ventriloquism. Ward describes the meeting as an interrogation, which implies questions and answers, but the alleged statement contains no questions and no answers. Both documents are hopelessly beset by errors and contradictions that expose this enterprise as just as inept and false as the Findlay memo.

The timing cited in both Ward's report and the following alleged statement does not hold up under scrutiny. The Montevideo event allegedly occurred 'about 10 or 11 years ago', which would be in either 1905 or 1906. Casement was not in Brazil (or in South America) until mid-October 1906, when he began work as consul in Santos. It is not credible that he immediately absented himself and spent a month in Montevideo, some 1,200 miles away, nor is there any evidence that he did so.

A second error of timing appears on page 2 of the statement attributed to Christensen. 'In November 1914, by arrangement with him, he having obtained an American passport from a Mr Landz . . . we sailed for Norway on the S.S. *Oscar II* 2nd.' The ship carrying Casement to Norway departed New York on 15 October 1914. That vessel was the SS *Oscar II*. In November 1914 both Casement and Christensen were in Berlin. Casement carried the passport of a Mr James *Landy*. The Christensen who travelled with Casement to Norway on that same ship certainly knew the date when he boarded the vessel and also knew the correct spelling of Casement's alias, but the Christensen represented in Inspector Ward's alleged 'statement' did not know.

The spelling of several words further betrays the falsity of this endeavour. The names Findlay, Devoy, Meyer, Nordenflycht, Landy and

Christiania are all misspelt in both Ward's ten-page report and the alleged statement (TNA KV 2/9-3, 15–30). Christensen knew Findlay and Devoy personally and knew the correct spelling of their names. He equally well knew the correct spelling of Christiania, the capital city of his own country, but since the pages were typed in Scotland Yard on 5 June Christensen was not present to make corrections. More precisely, Christensen never saw these pages, let alone signed them.

There is no mention of sex in the police typescripts, although the innuendo was attractive enough for Andrew to state as a fact that Christensen *had confirmed* that the alleged relationship was sexual. This is a clear echo of Findlay's reports to the Foreign Office in 1914–15, and indeed this 'Philadelphia exercise' was intended to recover something of Findlay's false memo, which planted the seeds of scandal.

Both documents prepared by Inspector Ward claim that Casement was in Montevideo to meet the German minister Baron von Nordenflycht. No evidence is offered. Casement did know the German official but not in 1906; they only met in August 1909 in the diplomatic community of Petropolis, and Casement became a frequent visitor to the Nordenflycht home. Roger Sawyer verifies the meeting in 1909: 'A friendship which began at this period was with the German consul-general, Baron von Nordenflycht' (Sawyer 1984, 75).

The language and the grammatical structures used in the alleged and unsigned statement are those of an Englishman and not those of Christensen, a non-native speaker of US English with very limited schooling. We are invited to believe that Christensen himself spoke Ward's stilted formal English. There are no traces of Christensen's US English in the text, which is not a verbatim version of anything written or spoken by him. The text is Inspector Ward's version of an entirely imaginary first-person account attributed to Christensen, many elements of which derive directly from Findlay's invented memo of October 1914 and his subsequent inept attempts to corroborate.

Therefore the 23 May date of the alleged statement is false, since it was typed in London at the same time as Ward's summary report. No original handwritten notes made by Ward in Philadelphia accompany the typescript; if Ward was ever in Philadelphia, he relied on a remarkable memory. The spelling errors listed above are common to both the report and the alleged statement. As if to add authentication, Ward wastes over 100 words in relating how he arrived at the purported meeting. Although Christensen allegedly refused to disclose his address in Philadelphia, somehow the acting consul managed to arrange the meeting at very short notice. Most noticeably, there is in Ward's ten-page report no description of Christensen's appearance, although brief descriptions of others are given. Also of note is that Ward, a senior policeman, states on page 3 that Christensen and Landy (Casement) sailed 'from Norway' 'about November 1914' and, further, that the real Landz was indeed a real estate agent in Nassau Street, NY. On page 9 of his report he contradicts the imprecise November date and cites the correct date of departure from NY (15 October). One further minor detail confirms that the first-person statement allegedly by Christensen was not copy-typed by Ward from any original written by Christensen: the archaic spelling 'shews' (for 'shows') is used in both documents, on page 9 of the report and on page 5 of the alleged statement.

That this document is not referred to by any of the principal biographers indicates that they categorised it with the Findlay memo as self-evidently false and better suppressed. It is unthinkable that Professor Andrew, an expert on intelligence, genuinely believes in the veracity of this alleged statement, which is without probative value. Perhaps he felt that pretending to believe it was a risk worth taking. We must therefore thank him for revealing it and, by so doing, adding strong evidence for the weakness of his own position.

The camera never lies

The 1911 police typescript is held in the National Archives (PRO HO 144/1637/311643/139 Ref. 20261). In the margin beside the entry for 18 September the word 'Photo' is handwritten in crayon. It is reasonable to conclude that the marginal note is an instruction to photograph this entry or perhaps the entire page. It is a verified fact that photographs were made and shown. Other pages of the 1911 typescript also show marginal markings in crayon. The question that arises is obvious: why photograph the typescript rather than the original handwritten page?

There must be some factor that prevented the simple photography of the appropriate pages of the 1911 handwritten diary. That British Intelligence preferred to go to the trouble of first preparing typescript pages and then photographing those typed pages is remarkable and revealing. Most people who consider themselves to be possessed of a functioning intelligence would deduce that the handwritten diary pages could not be photographed because there were no original handwritten diary pages. They would deduce this in the absence of any plausible reason being found for not photographing the handwritten diary pages said to be in the possession of British Intelligence. This is the only credible explanation that satisfies common sense. If those handwritten pages did not exist, it follows that the 1911 bound-volume diary did not exist at the time when the photographs of the typed pages were taken. If the bound volume did not exist at that time, it did not exist before that time. Therefore it came into existence after that time. It is recorded that the 1911 typescript was completed on 24 June 1916 and from this it can be deduced that the 1911 bound-volume diary came into existence after that date. Since Casement was in prison at that time and about to undergo trial, it can be deduced that he did not have the opportunity of writing the 1911 diary after 24 June 1916. Therefore someone else wrote the 1911 bound-volume diary after 24 June.

Proof that the photographs taken were photographs of the typescript/s comes from HM government itself: 'The Ambassador was given photographs of two passages from the typescript' (History of the Casement Diaries. March, 1959, Working Party. PRO HO 144/23481). These were given by Thomson at the ambassador's request. Although Thomson allegedly held the bound volumes, he preferred to show the US ambassador photographs of the typescript/s. There is no record anywhere of photographs of the bound-volume diaries being made and shown. Something prevented the taking of such photographs. Until the existence of the bound volumes at that time is proven, the matter of their authenticity is meaningless.

The existence of the bound-volume diaries 'at the time of the Casement trial' was also questioned by Lord Russell in 1955 (PRO HO 144/23455). Lord Russell's letter of 6 August to Home Secretary G. Lloyd-George received a 'no comment' response on 11 August. The existence of the diaries at any time could not be spoken of then.

Olsen's story

This is the only alleged eyewitness account of a homosexual act involving Casement. The alleged incident took place in the Grand Hotel in Oslo (Findlay letter 13 March 1915, PRO FO 95,776), where the chief reception clerk, Gustav Olsen, claimed to have witnessed Casement and Christensen in a compromising homosexual act. This claim was not made by Olsen himself but by Minister Findlay *on his behalf*, some four months after the alleged event and without naming Olsen. Some two hours after Casement's arrival in the hotel on the night of 28–29 October 1914, the German naval attaché asked for him at the reception desk. By Findlay's account, Olsen went to Casement's room, knocked and entered at once *without waiting for an answer*. It is unclear why Olsen did not wait for a response since he believed that Casement was in the room. This is highly improbable behaviour from senior hotel staff in a high-class, capital-city hotel. Secondly, Olsen did not report the alleged crime to the police. Thirdly, the 'offenders' were not asked to leave by hotel management—*ergo* Olsen kept silent and so became an accomplice. Fourthly, it is improbable that the *chief* reception clerk would have gone *in person*, leaving his desk, rather than sending another staff member or more simply making a telephone call to Casement's room. Olsen could have easily directed the German official to the room, especially since he was allegedly resident in the same hotel.

There is no independent corroboration whatsoever of this alleged event. Some 21 months later, in July 1916, Olsen travelled to London to see Inspector Sandercock and he identified Casement from a photo as 'Landy'—Casement's assumed name. Olsen and several other Norwegians made statements and it is clear that these were solicited by the British authorities, although they could play no part in Casement's prosecution. The motive for seeking these alleged affidavits therefore remains unclear. (An affidavit is a voluntary statement of alleged facts made under self-administered oath; the signature of the author is witnessed by an authorised person, *who does not verify the statement content*. The veracity of an affidavit can only be established by a court, and false affidavits are commonplace.) Scrutiny of these so-called affidavits reveals that none are in fact affidavits; several lack the jurat, several are reported hearsay and gossip, four come from one source, and those allegedly sworn are not sworn by the deponent. Even CID chief Basil Thomson admitted his disappointment that there was 'not much in them'.

It is improbable that *eight* Norwegians would spontaneously concern themselves, 21 months after the alleged event/s, to furnish these statements, and from the files at the National Archives (HO 144 1637 311643 140) it is clear *that they were invited to do so*. It is improbable that Olsen travelled to London at his own expense. It is unclear why eight statements were made when Olsen's alone would have sufficed.

Casement's vessel, the SS *Oscar II*, docked in Oslo at midnight on 28 October 1914. MacColl reports in his 1956 book that Casement left the vessel at 1.30am on the 29th and reached his hotel at around 2am. Olsen's statement claims that the compromising event allegedly witnessed by him took place around two hours after Casement's arrival in the hotel. This means that both Olsen and the German naval attaché were awake and on duty at around 4am that morning, and that the naval attaché, having risen from his slumber at 4am, could not wait a few hours until morning and that Olsen, the chief receptionist, acceded to his urgent wish that Casement be disturbed at 4am in the morning. It is verified that Casement left Oslo by train for Germany at around 5.30pm on 30 October. Allowing approximately 24 hours for Casement's two visits to the German legation, for packing and the trip to the railway station, for sleep and for meals, and deducting those hours from his total time spent in Oslo since arriving in the hotel (which amounts to 39 hours), we are left with fifteen hours. It was therefore during these fifteen hours that the Norwegian 'witnesses' noted non-specified compromising behaviour. At the time, however, they preferred to say and do nothing; rather like the many dozens of persons known to Casement over the previous twenty years, these Norwegians also conspired to be silent when faced with 'unnatural' behaviour. Only some *21 months* later, when they were persuaded to 'speak out', did they agree to furnish statements to officials of a foreign government.

The full Olsen story has *two conflicting versions*, one invented by Findlay in March 1915 and the second by the Metropolitan Police in July 1916.

Smith's story

A seventh version of the provenance of the Black Diaries was published in Attorney General F. E. Smith's 1926 book *Famous trials* and differs from all other versions. On page 252 Casement's prosecutor writes: 'Three coats were found, one of which contained Casement's diary'. This remarkable find happened on 21 April on Banna Strand, where Casement had landed from the German submarine along with Monteith and Bailey in the early hours.

Smith gives no evidence for this find, which seems to consist of one diary only. That it was allegedly found in a coat left on the shore signifies that Casement had brought the incriminating diary from Germany, which means that he took it with him to the USA in July 1914. In turn, this indicates that Casement kept the diary (or diaries) safe for almost two years on his travels in the US and then on his trip to Norway and into Germany, where he remained for eighteen months, but carelessly abandoned it as soon as he arrived in Ireland.

We must overlook, as Smith did, that this diary survived the landing from the submarine, which took some two hours and involved the overturning of the dinghy and the immersion of the men in the sea.

Presumably the coat and diary were found by the RIC officer who later arrested Casement and took him to Tralee police station. There is no record of how the sodden diary subsequently found its way to Basil Thomson in Scotland Yard.

Since Smith's book appeared a full decade after the trial and execution, we must assume that the author had not read Thomson's differing accounts of provenance published in 1921, 1922 and 1925. We must also assume that Smith was unaware in 1926 of the five bound volumes now held in TNA and was also unaware of the typescripts of three diaries and a ledger shown in 1916. It is unthinkable that he was also unaware of the two bound-volume diaries shown to Michael Collins in February 1922, an event which Smith himself had arranged. If so, then Collins was shown documents which Smith had never seen but vouched for as authentic. If Smith had never seen the two diaries shown to Collins, it could be that he had never seen the third diary or the ledger. And if Smith as Lord Birkenhead, one of the most powerful men in Britain, had not seen any of the bound volumes a decade after their alleged discovery, then it seems improbable that any lesser mortal had seen them. Yet in 1925 that lesser mortal Singleton-Gates had seen them.

Certainly Smith had seen the police typescripts and had passed these to Artemus Jones in 1916, but it is not credible that Smith believed that Casement had typed the A3 pages. It is also possible that by 'Casement's diary' Smith intended the singular to refer to a diary written by one Casement but in five volumes. In this case all five were found in the coat pocket. This was, therefore, an enormous pocket: the largest volume measures at least 22cm x 30cm and together the five books weigh perhaps as much as 3kg.

None of Casement's biographers mention a diary or diaries being found in a coat anywhere at any time. We can assume that Smith's account is invented. B.L. Reid, however, claims that the Black Diaries were on show to anyone who wished to see them: 'Apparently anybody of influence could have a look' (p. 418). Birkenhead, the state prosecutor, was certainly a person of influence, but it seems that either he did not ask to see them or, if he did, he was refused. Since he invented and published the absurd account in 1926, it can be deduced that he never saw the bound-volume diaries.

Diary contortions

In the introduction to his 1997 book *Roger Casement's diaries: the black and the white*, Roger Sawyer claims that the 1910 Dollard's diary was written by Casement when in Peru; it was his original diary, complete with compromising entries. At a later date—possibly after his return to

Europe—Casement wrote the much longer Amazon Journal (or Putumayo Diary), using the Dollard as source material or an *aide-mémoire*. According to Sawyer, the longer text was intended as preliminary material for a book. This explains why the longer text contains no compromising references; it is a 'cleaned-up' version of the shorter Dollard.

> 'Evidently it was written in the hope that it would eventually form the basis of a published work and ... it had the initial value of being a useful *aide-mémoire* for the official report ... ; [...] as he writes a fuller, official, version eventually intended to form the basis of a published work.'

Sawyer proceeds to contradict this thesis, however, when he seeks to authenticate the Dollard diary. His attempt at authentication is doubly inept but is performed with sufficient flair to deceive the unwary reader. He draws our attention to the Dollard entry dated 8 October: 'The man's name "Waiteka"—the fearless skeleton of *my diary* who denounced the "cepo" [emphasis added]'. In the Amazon Journal held in NLI Dublin we find the same date entry: 'I was smiling with pleasure that this fearless skeleton had found tongue ...'.

Sawyer emphasises that the Dollard reference to 'my diary' is a clear reference to the same date entry in the Amazon Journal, which, according to his main thesis, *has not yet been written*. It entirely escapes Sawyer that 'the fearless skeleton' in the Dollard could just as logically have been lifted from the already written Amazon Journal. It is the reference to 'my diary' that betrays the Dollard entry as an embedded authenticating device. Scrutiny demonstrates that it fails. The Dollard entry derives apparent authenticity from the authentic Amazon Journal by identifying the source of the words 'the fearless skeleton' in the Amazon Journal. The parasitical mechanism creates an illusory correspondence between statements in both documents so that the authenticity of the statement in one document passes imperceptibly into the statement in another document. But the repetition of the same words in the second document does not demonstrate that the same person wrote those words in the second document. Copying a Shakespeare quotation into one's diary does not demonstrate that Shakespeare wrote the diary.

Sawyer's affirmation would, however, prove that the Amazon Journal was indeed written *before* the Dollard, although Sawyer seems unaware that this contradicts his thesis that the Dollard was written first. His assertion leads to the following absurdity: Sawyer asserts that Casement wrote 'fearless skeleton' first in the Amazon Journal and then wrote into a second diary (the Dollard) an entry recording that he had already written the same words in the first diary. Sawyer does not explain why Casement would not only *consciously* repeat the same words in the Dollard but also refer to the first diary he had already written *as if he did not know what he had written in the first diary* **until** *he wrote it in a second diary*. These contortions drag Sawyer's notion of *l'aide-mémoire* into absurdity. And, indeed, Sawyer does not hesitate to propose a second *aide-mémoire*, with the result that both diaries are *aides-mémoire* and both are written first.

> So the last shall be first, and the first last: for many be called, but few chosen (Matt. 20:16).

Quandary

Tensions over the Black Diaries reached a critical point in 1958 and the British government was in a dilemma. More corroboration was urgently needed. A Working Party was instructed to investigate, evaluate and advise on a future policy that would relieve the Home Office. The Working Party soon realised that there was no proof of authenticity for the diaries, which had been in limbo for decades. The opinion of a handwriting expert was sought, and on 4 November 1958 Dr Wilson Harrison produced his opinion.

Roger Sawyer describes this opinion as a forensic test that declared authenticity (Daly 2005, 97). Unfortunately, Sawyer does not give any reference or source for this claim; he provides no citations from the results of this 'test', nor does he say whether he has seen any official papers prepared by Dr Harrison.

Very little attention has been paid to the Harrison report and for good reason. The *opinion* of Dr Harrison consists of three short paragraphs amounting to a mere 93 words in total. It is obvious that no tests were done and Dr Harrison does not claim to have performed any tests. Therefore this intervention was not a test of any kind, far less a forensic test. The word 'test' does not appear and neither does the word 'authentic'. It was no more than a brief handwriting comparison by a government expert.

The Working Party dealing with the government's dilemma must have been disappointed with the flimsiness of these 93 words, which lack conviction. This might explain why Dr Harrison's report was not publicised at the time or later, and why it still appears not to be in the public domain;

it is buried in a National Archives file of over 200 pages (HO 144/23481). Other Casement authors refer to Dr Harrison's intervention but none offer any details or quote from his report.

Dr Harrison was a Home Office forensic scientist and the author of *Suspect documents: their scientific examination* (1958). In this very brief report he carefully avoided any claim that the diaries were the authentic writings of Casement. He made no attempt to verify the authenticity of the control material provided for comparison, describing these files as 'attributed to Roger Casement'. Perhaps an attempt to authenticate the control material would have been 'indelicate' but both law and science require it. In brief, his opinion was that the diaries were written by one person only and that the person who wrote the diaries also wrote the control documents. He affirmed that the government attributed both writings to Casement.

That Harrison's report was of little comfort to the Working Party is clear from documents dated March 1959, when a formal committee of enquiry was proposed for the purpose of authenticating the diaries definitively. The proposal was soon aborted because the committee 'might refuse to conclude categorically that the diaries are not forgeries' (6 March)(PRO HO 144/23481). With regard to the Harrison report, it was feared that 'another expert might be found whose opinion would not accord with his' (9 March). The apprehension did not end there: '... if the remit were confined to the question of forgery, the committee would be entitled not only to examine the diaries, presumably with the assistance of a handwriting expert, but *to explore how they came into the possession of the police* and to see whether there was any evidence that they were being groomed for a particular purpose [emphasis added]' (9 March). The risk that the committee 'might refuse to say categorically whether the diaries are or are not forgeries' killed the proposal. In the end it was decided that the best way to cover up the cover-up was to give the diaries restricted release in the hope that, in Ambassador Clutterbuck's words, 'the verdicts of the scholars will at least cancel each other out'. To date no impartial committee has ever examined the Black Diaries.

Choose your Casement
In the centenary year of 2016 the experts had a field-day at the many Casement events. The misinformation of decades was now being blithely propagated by those who had tasted the delirious cocktail. Michael McDowell, noted barrister, politician and former attorney general, gave a

lecture on Casement to an invited audience of legal professionals in Green Street Courthouse, Dublin, on 4 May 2016. The lecture covered many topics—legal, biographical and historical—which might well have been familiar to such a learned audience. Casement was given the now-standard kaleidoscopic identity treatment: the enigmatic hero-martyr with a hidden and once-unspeakable secret. McDowell closed with a generous 'free-for-all': 'In the end, each of us is left at liberty to imagine and even to judge his real character *as we choose* [emphasis added]'. In other words, 'make it up as ye go along'.

In Part 9 of his lecture McDowell goes astray when he reaches Oslo and the Findlay Affair, and thereafter, not surprisingly, he loses his bearings with the Black Diaries. Indeed, most who tackle these interlocked aspects flounder quickly into confusion and error; the result is always more misinformation than analytical clarity. Perhaps McDowell does not understand how poisoned the Casement story has been since 1914 and how he misguidedly continues to perpetrate the misinformation intentionally created by earlier Casement 'experts'. It is clear, however, that he has done no original research and, without such critical exploration, he inevitably garbles the versions generated by others and now believed by many. The result is a confused but politically correct version that is not guided by a scrupulous passion for truth.

McDowell relies upon Ó Síocháin's discussion of the Black Diaries, which was relegated to the appendix of his 2008 volume. While this is more descriptive than analytical, it certainly presents a persuasive case for authenticity, but only for those who have not studied the question in depth. Ó Síocháin relies heavily on the Giles Report as being a definitive conclusion that offers scientific certainty. Here he makes the same mistake as Giles herself: both seek to confirm a specific thesis—authenticity. Hence the only evidence considered is that which appears to support this conclusion. This self-confirming approach excludes evidence that might negate the favoured thesis. Scientific investigation seeks to disprove a dominant thesis, not to confirm it.

McDowell cannot be blamed for failing to note Ó Síocháin's errors of approach, logic and fact, since he makes enough errors of his own. The errors of approach and logic are all-embracing and invisibly condition Ó Síocháin's treatment. Errors of fact are more visible. For example, on page 493 Ó Síocháin writes: 'Further evidence concerning this episode arrived in London in July 1916 as part of the prosecution's preparations for the trial'. Since the trial ended on 29 June, the alleged evidence arrived too late and could not in any case have been used by the prosecution since it concerned allegations of 'unnatural relations', which were not part of the charge *of treason* against Casement. The evidence to which Ó Síocháin refers is what he calls 'affidavits, eight in all . . .', concerning 'unnatural relations'. None of these statements are affidavits, however, and the principal one, that of Olsen, does not even contain the jurat which is fundamental to an affidavit. Even Basil Thomson, who solicited these statements *after the trial*, recognised their uselessness when he commented: 'Not much in them'.

Every paragraph in this last section of McDowell's lecture is woefully misinformed and corrupted by errors of fact, by intentionally imprecise language and by unsupported conjectures. Although he is a barrister, he fails to grasp the purpose of Smith's tactics. He misreports Mary Reilly as being shown 'diaries', and typescripts as being given to Morgan rather than to Jones. Clearly McDowell has never seen the so-called affidavits of 1916 and it is reasonable to suspect that he has not read the discredited Giles Report.

McDowell's error is the same as that made by Ó Síocháin and many others: he fails to distinguish between the typescripts and the bound volumes held in the UK National Archives and the role these have played in the long controversy. This failure means that he is unable to understand the relationship between them. It is a verified fact that the typescripts existed during Casement's lifetime; it has not been verified that the bound volumes existed in that period. McDowell speaks of a preponderance of evidence in favour of authenticity without realising that the evidence he has selected is false evidence. The material existence of the bound volumes before Casement's execution is a *presumption* based exclusively on the material existence of the typescripts, which he presumes are copies—but there is no proof that they were copies.

With magnificent contempt for verified facts, McDowell closes his lecture by throwing away any claim to informed scholarship and inviting us '. . . to imagine and even to judge his real character as we choose'.

Expert blunders

On 2 June 2016 another Casement event was held in the Irish embassy in London. Law professor Seán McConville and noted human rights lawyer Shami Chakrabarti were the guest speakers. The event, entitled 'The Life and Humanitarian Legacy of Roger Casement', was recorded for BBC TV and broadcast to many millions in the UK. Both speakers and the Irish ambassador, who hosted the event, are believers in the authenticity of the Black Diaries and therefore this topic, although mentioned, was taken for granted. After some 39 minutes, however, Professor McConville, who believes that the diaries are genuine, made the following statement:

> 'I think they [the diaries] were in British possession for quite a long while . . . they had these trunks from the moment that Casement started issuing pro-German pamphlets . . .'.

That moment was therefore in late 1914, some eighteen months before Casement's arrest, but two state documents from Scotland Yard record possession of the trunks on 25 April 1916, the third day of Casement's interrogation. Therefore Professor McConville believes that the interrogation transcript and the police list of effects found in the trunks are false. It also means that he believes that two of CID chief Basil Thomson's published accounts of discovery are false. It follows that McConville admits that his primary sources of information concerning provenance are contaminated with falsehood. Despite conceding this falsehood concerning provenance, he believes that the diaries are authentic. During the event he offered no explanation for not believing his sources and seemed oblivious of the contradiction, which amounts to saying 'I know the man is a liar *and so* I believe him'. McConville is a professor of law but it is evident that his belief in authenticity is not based on logical reasoning, on facts or on common sense.

I repeat: Professor McConville concedes that his sources are contaminated but this admission does not allow him to doubt the integrity of those dishonest sources when they inform him that the diaries are authentic.

It is clear to any impartial person that the authenticity edifice rests upon unstable foundations. Those foundations are unstable because they require the illogical reasoning behind McConville's belief in authenticity. Something other than logic and common sense has induced McConville's belief, perhaps something emerging from the grey zone of cognitive dissonance. Perhaps it was this unhappy condition that also induced him to mislead the audience of millions by stating that '. . . the diaries were circulated in London . . . Blackwell . . . was circulating these diaries at a time when Casement's fate had not finally been decided . . .'. This is manifestly false. Only typescript pages were shown, but this was a vitally necessary deception.

Given that the event was held in the Irish embassy in the presence of the ambassador to St James, one assumes that the Irish state accepts the unproven authenticity of the Black Diaries simply because it has now become politically correct and therefore necessary in Ireland to do so. The television transmission reached millions, who passed from being uninformed people to being *misinformed* people who believe that they are informed. It might be politically incorrect to describe this as propaganda but it is nevertheless difficult to distinguish it from propaganda. Thus, as Orwell warned, lies pass into history.

On-line truth

In March 2002 the BBC broadcast a major documentary on Casement to support the result of the Giles Report—*The secret of the Black Diaries*, produced by Paul Tilzey. No secret about the diaries was revealed and the film pointedly endorsed the consensus view of authenticity.

Tilzey's page on Casement on the BBC History website contains misinformation. He describes the Giles Report as a 'fully independent forensic examination' and as an 'impartial scientific analysis'. He ignores the critical peer-review comments by US document experts Marcel Matley and James Horan. Matley described the Giles Report as 'forensic junk science', while Horan stated that it failed to demonstrate how its conclusions were reached and could not be presented in a US court. Other critics commented that a convincingly impartial analysis required a non-British expert with no connections to agencies of the British state. Dr Giles is a former employee of the Metropolitan Police and as a leading expert is consulted by many state agencies.

Tilzey also states that 'the diary pages were distributed by the British authorities . . .'. This appears to mean pages from the diary; if so, it is false. The pages that were shown—not 'distributed'—were police typescript pages that the authorities alleged were copies of diary pages, which they did not display. Tilzey's bland comment could easily mislead the unwary reader into believing that the bound diaries were shown.

Like Dr Giles, Tilzey regurgitates the unsubstantiated claim that Michael Collins authenticated the diaries: 'Collins who inspected them in 1921 and was satisfied that they were genuine . . .'. This is wholly false. Collins saw two diaries on 6 February 1922 and he left *no written comment*. Collins never knew Casement and there is no verified evidence that he had ever seen Casement's handwriting, but Collins's silence on the matter allows Tilzey (and others) to indulge in mind-reading. Moreover, it is unclear why Collins's non-expert opinion would carry any more weight than anyone else's. There are only two indications of Collins's reaction to seeing the diaries. Upon his return to Dublin he opened a file that he called 'Alleged Casement Diaries'. In 1952 Father Patrick Doyle of Naas, Co. Dublin, deposited Witness Statement 807 in the Bureau of Military History, in which he recounted his memory of a confidential conversation with Collins on Easter Sunday 1922, two months after seeing the diaries in London. The Doyle statement reads: 'Collins told me that he was very familiar with Casement's handwriting and that if the book was not authentic it was a devilishly clever forgery'. This hearsay comment recalled after 30 years does not indicate that Collins was 'satisfied that they were genuine'. On the contrary, it indicates that Collins was unsure and even confused by seeing the two diaries. Once again, the absence of verifiable evidence allows innuendo and deceit to pose as historical fact.

2

The two 1910 diaries

In the National Library of Ireland there is a long, handwritten document which is the undisputed work of Casement and which is a detailed account of his day-to-day investigation into the Putumayo atrocities in the latter months of 1910. This document is referred to here as the Amazon Journal.[1]

In the UK National Archives there is a handwritten bound diary attributed to Casement, most of which is a partial account of the same period and which contains around 22 references that appear to allude to homosexuality. This document is referred to here as the Dollard diary.[2]

The precise relationship between these two documents has never been fully explained or, indeed, examined, and even where it is proposed that both are the work of Casement it remains to be determined which was written first. This is necessary, because those who hold that both are Casement's work claim that the Dollard was written first and that the Amazon Journal is a later version. The Amazon Journal consists of 128 handwritten, double-sided foolscap pages containing around 143,000 words detailing Casement's travel and investigations over 75 days from September to December 1910. This document is 10.22 times longer than the entries for the same period in the Dollard diary and it contains no compromising writings whatsoever. Its existence has caused some difficulties for those who believe that the much shorter Dollard diary was written by Casement in 1910, not least because the *principal reason* for thinking that Casement wrote the shorter diary is a resemblance in the handwriting. Whereas there is verifiable evidence that the Amazon Journal was written by Casement in 1910, there is no evidence to show that it was written later than 1910. To ease those difficulties, it has been suggested that both diaries are genuine and that the longer document is a later version of the shorter that has been purged of its compromising content. Therefore it is the inclusion in the Dollard of the contentious references that provides the only rationale for its existence. This, however, does not explain why anyone would write *c.* 14,000 words in 75 days merely in order to conserve 516 words of near-gibberish. Nor does it explain why the same person would later write 143,000 words in order to conceal those 516 words.[3] Nonetheless, there is an explanation.

Others have suggested that it is counter-intuitive to propose that a much longer document is a later version of a much shorter document; the usual motive for producing a second version of any document is that the first is too long, too dispersive and unfocused, and that a tighter, more concise version will achieve maximum effect with less effort. If this is accepted, then the Dollard diary is the pared-down version of the unwieldy Amazon Journal and not vice versa. This finds confirmation in common sense. Therefore the Dollard diary would be either an extract or a condensed version of the Amazon Journal containing only the essentials of the longer document, but there are serious difficulties also with this idea. Apart from the controversial content, however minimal, there is only a limited correspondence between the innocuous information in the Dollard and in the Amazon Journal. The Dollard contains information that is not recorded in the Amazon Journal as well as information that disagrees with that in the longer document. The locations and dates more or less correspond, as do many of the persons mentioned. Certainly there is some resemblance or overlapping in the information content. Nevertheless, there are many anomalies, discrepancies and contradictions between the documents, which act to frustrate understanding of the relationship between them. One of the most perplexing anomalies is the disparity of emphasis or importance between events as recorded in the two documents. Given that diary-writing is a personal activity in which one records significant experience and reflections upon events, it becomes problematic when an event given great importance in one diary is recorded in the other diary but is accorded no importance whatsoever. It is true that events tend to diminish in importance as time passes and, this being the case, it suggests that the two documents were written some time apart rather than in tandem day by day by the same person. The document that consistently attributes less importance to events is the Dollard.

Of course, a reasonable enquirer would ask why Casement would wish to write the Dollard diary as a variant of the first, and not only with the addition of incriminating material but also with information which does not coincide with that contained in the longer document. Similarly, the impartial enquirer might equally well ask why the author would repeat in the Amazon Journal any of the same innocuous information contained in the Dollard. To speculate, however, on Casement's possible motivation for writing a second diary, with or without the sexual references, is simply to add to the many conjectures that afflict the story and would not serve to decode the multi-layered enigma.

The idea that both documents were written by Casement in tandem, more or less simultaneously, during his investigation must be considered. This, too, raises the question of the motive for keeping two diaries for the same period, and the only motive proposed for keeping the Dollard is that he wished to record erotic experience. This might enjoy some credibility if the Dollard was indeed an erotic diary, but 96% of this 'erotic diary' is utterly non-erotic. The 3.62% erotic content in the 75-day period consists of non-events, mere observation and innuendo to a total of only 516 words. None of the 23 entries containing erotic references record Casement's participation in sexual activity. It is reasonable to expect erotic activity to predominate in any document motivated by the desire to record erotic experience; this vast disproportion has yet to be explained. If no explanation is found, then Casement did not write the Dollard in order to record erotic experience. Another motive must be found for writing the Dollard.

The argument that the Amazon Journal is a 'cleaned-up version' of the shorter Dollard is untenable and bereft of logical coherence—not only because the Amazon Journal is quite evidently not a version of anything else but more importantly because in 1910 or 1911 or 1912 Casement had no need to produce a 'cleaned-up version', since the Dollard was *allegedly* still in his possession during those years and remained so until late 1914 at the earliest. Therefore he had no incentive to produce a 'cleaned-up version' of the Dollard at any time before his capture in 1916. The motive would arise only if Casement had foreseen several years before 1916 the key role that any such diary would come to play in his destiny. Moreover, the Amazon Journal was *not intended to be read by others* and therefore would have served no purpose as a 'cleaned-up' version. Until February 1913 (more than two years after its completion) the Amazon Journal was not seen by others; this is evident from Casement's own description of it to Charles Roberts MP, chairman of the Parliamentary Select Committee, who asked to see it.[4]

The existence and survival of the Amazon Journal as an authentic record written in 1910 of Casement's experience has constrained three of his widely read biographers to produce contradictory accounts of its provenance. That three 'experts' contradict each other on a point of such importance is unfortunate for the experts but less so for the readers they wish to convince, because those readers might conclude either that none of the experts is an expert or that none of the experts is telling the truth.

> 'The other [diary] was a copy of his Putumayo diary, which he made
> for the use of the Select Committee investigating the affair. As he told
> the chairman, he was sending the copy because "naturally there is in it
> [the original diary] something I should not wish anyone else to see" '
> (Inglis 1974, Appendix III, p. 439).

The 'other' diary was the Amazon Journal, not a copy of that original document. The Amazon Journal was written in 1910, two years before the Parliamentary Select Committee was appointed, an event unforeseen by Casement at the time of writing the Amazon Journal. Inglis states that Casement *copied* the original Amazon Journal in 1912 and sent the copy upon request to Charles Roberts MP. This is false. There is no reference to a copy in Casement's letter to Roberts. There is no verifiable record that the document submitted to Roberts was a later copy of any other document, nor is there any evidence that a manuscript *copy* of the original Amazon Journal ever existed. Casement's own description of the document that he was sending to Roberts demonstrates very clearly that it was the 1910 original with all its defects: '... have not read it for two and a half years ... sincere and was written with (obviously) never a thought of being shown to others but for myself alone as a sort of aide memoire and mental justification and safety valve' (Casement–Roberts Correspondence, Letter to Charles Roberts MP, 27 January 1913. R.H. Brit. Emp. S22). In this matter of the alleged copy, Inglis is simply misleading his readers.

Roger Sawyer also provides a problematic account of the Amazon Journal. He derives his 'explanation' from a casual remark made by Casement on 24 August in his notes recording a conversation with Victor Israel, a businessman based in Iquitos.

> 'Should he [Israel] ever read this conversation—supposing I were to
> some day publish a book on my travels in the Amazon—he will
> doubtless deny every statement I here attribute to him ...'

From this passing supposition, Sawyer (1997, 2) attributes to Casement the following intention concerning the Amazon Journal:

> 'Evidently it was written in the hope that it would eventually form the
> basis of a published work and ... it had the initial value of being a

useful *aide-mémoire* for the official report …; […] as he writes a fuller, official, version eventually intended to form the basis of a published work.'

Sawyer's account is confused and confusing, and the wary reader will be alerted by the suggestive term 'Evidently'. On the one hand, Sawyer seems to claim that the Amazon Journal was written after Casement's return from the Amazon as preparatory material for the publication of a book. He suggests that the Dollard diary was his *aide-mémoire* for this later exercise, which in turn became a second *aide-mémoire* for his official report. The 'fuller, official, version' is the Amazon Journal, which Sawyer implies was written *after* the private Dollard diary and therefore was not written during Casement's 75-day investigation. On the other hand, Sawyer seems to confirm that the Amazon Journal was written *before* Casement submitted his final official report on 17 March 1911, which would mean that Casement was writing both the diary of 143,000 words and two preliminary reports delivered on 7 and 31 January plus the final report of 25,000 words all at the same time but after his return from the Amazon.

Thus Sawyer differs from Inglis in that he claims that there was no original Amazon Journal written in 1910. It follows that Sawyer claims that the document sent by Casement to Roberts in January 1913 was indeed the *unique original* and not a copy, but was entirely composed in early 1911. In this he contradicts Inglis. Sawyer offers no evidence to make this claim more credible, and this absence of evidence can only be explained by Sawyer's need to undermine the authenticity of the Amazon Journal in order to sustain the alleged authenticity of the Dollard. Sawyer's claim implies that Casement *faked* the entire Amazon Journal in 1911 and later intentionally and successfully deceived the Select Committee about its authenticity as a 'real time' record. Sawyer does not explain that the manuscript in the National Library of Ireland is largely written in pencil, is in parts nearly illegible and contains many irrelevant data—all facts that Casement admitted to Roberts when he wrote:

'It is often almost unintelligible altho' I can read it all. . . . If you want to go through it I advise you strongly to have it typed first by an expert. It will take an expert to read it and decipher it. . . . The value of the thing, if it has any value, is that it is sincere and was written with (obviously) never a thought of being shown to others but for myself alone as a sort of aide memoire and mental justification and safety valve. . . . There is much, as you will see in my diary, would expose me to ridicule were it read by unkind eyes . . . The diary is a pretty complete record *and were I free to publish* it would be such a picture of things out there, written down red hot as would convince anyone' [emphasis added] (letter to Charles Roberts MP, 27 January 1913. R.H. Brit. Emp. S22 Casement–Roberts Correspondence).

Editors are not known for their kind eyes but this is Casement's description of his own manuscript, which Sawyer claims was written 'to form the basis of a published work' and thus for the approval of editors. In the two years between his return from the Amazon and the dispatch of the Amazon Journal to Roberts, there is no evidence that Casement was seeking publication; indeed, he stated that he had not even read his diary in those two years. Ironically, if Casement ever contemplated 'literary' fame, he achieved it for the works he did *not* write rather than for those he did.

If Casement wrote at the average handwriting speed of 31 words per minute, the Dollard's 75-day section of *c.* 14,000 words would have required about 7.52 hours over those days, which means a mere 6.01 minutes of writing per day. Therefore Casement's many references in the Amazon Journal to spending many hours writing that diary at night would be part of his alleged plan *in 1911* to deceive Charles Roberts MP and the Parliamentary Select Committee—about which he knew nothing in 1911— two years later in 1913. Sawyer offers no credible motive for this alleged deception because no such deception occurred.

No one would suggest that these two distinguished authors did not 'do their homework' and carry out meticulous research. Therefore the only conclusion that an impartial enquirer can reach is that both decided to mislead their readers. Their joint recourse to this tactic demonstrates that both were intent upon concealing the truth about the Dollard diary.

'My own conclusion on the many suggested "contradictions" is that, in virtually all cases, the arguments made for them are tendentious and that they fail to stand up to critical analysis' (Ó Síocháin 2008, Appendix, p. 486).

Ó Síocháin disagrees with both Inglis and Sawyer in that he accepts the fact that Casement sent Roberts the original manuscript written in 1910 rather than a copy. Therefore he rejects both of their arguments concerning the provenance and circumstances of the Amazon Journal. He does not explain why he disagrees with Inglis and Sawyer. Despite this major difference of judgement, Ó Síocháin agrees that the Dollard diary is authentic. Unfortunately, much of his conviction rests on the Giles Report, which he accepts without question, calling it 'an important milestone in the debate ...', while the rest of his conviction is based on rather flaccid reasoning, acceptance of official explanations and dismissive comments such as 'Most of the "discrepancies" dissolve under analysis'. He concedes that discrepancies and contradictions exist but engages with only one of these—how Casement's eyesight problem is treated in both diaries. For his response to this question he relies completely on the Giles Report, which flatly denies the evidence that Casement's handwriting was affected by eye illness. None of the other anomalies are confronted, perhaps because Ó Síocháin claims that they 'are signs of authenticity' rather than of falsity. Thus the discrepancies that disappear when analysed magically reappear as 'signs of authenticity'—or vice versa, which means that these 'signs of authenticity' vanish when analysed. Either way, the discrepancies are too fragile to be analysed and Ó Síocháin wisely does not take the risk.

Falling back on the 'wealth of detail' argument, Ó Síocháin undermines his entire position by the use of persuasive but vacuous rhetoric: 'It is impossible to imagine how a forger could ...'—so that the fact that we *don't* know something becomes proof that we *do* know something. The fact that we don't know how it was done means that it wasn't done. This is proof *ex nihilo*, belief derived from ignorance, and as such it stands outside rational process and belongs to the domain of propaganda.

Ó Síocháin rather naively asserts that to challenge authenticity is 'to suggest that certain branches of the British establishment were themselves taken in by the forgery'. He seems to regard this as an impossibility but he does not explain why. The impartial enquirer searches in vain for the critical analysis of the contradictions that Ó Síocháin claims have failed to stand up to this analysis.

Facts about the 1910 Dollard diary

The Dollard diary does have the appearance of a genuine diary, and because the handwriting resembles Casement's one might identify it as Casement's work. The discrepancies between it and the Amazon Journal would probably not be detected since it is only the compromising content that has caused it to be scrutinised. A pedant might ask why Casement wrote two diaries at the same time and might be told that the Dollard was Casement's *aide-mémoire* for the much longer Amazon Journal, but the quantity and quality of information in the Dollard do not support this thesis.

The Dollard entries for the 75 days contain surprisingly little text of a sexual nature—a mere 516 words in 23 entries, amounting to only 3.62%. Even these 23 entries are not dedicated exclusively to sexual matters. Moreover, these 23 contentious entries record non-events in which there is no sexual activity. They are merely allusive, insinuating sexual interest or desire or observation. Consisting merely of innuendo and allusion, the Dollard diary is non-pornographic by any standards. There is very little that is explicit and there are no graphic descriptions of sexual encounters such as might be expected in an erotic diary. By comparison with the 1911 diary, the 1910 Dollard is muted, tame and minimal. Certainly no one would accuse the author of recording his sexual exploits in these 23 entries, but it might be said that he found a surrogate satisfaction in recording his desires rather than in fulfilling them.

Since the Dollard contains so little compromising text, it is unreasonable to believe that recording erotic experience was the principal motive for writing the diary. Had the author wished to keep a private erotic diary, he would have excluded 96% of the Dollard content because it is non-erotic. The quality of the compromising content is unconvincing because it lacks emotional intensity and passion. The author seems to be more a voyeur than a protagonist. The 516 words are, however, embedded in many thousands of words of diary writings which *appear* to record a day-to-day reality experienced by the author, and from this context of apparently verifiable reality the compromising text borrows its own reality. *The compromising text does not allow of any kind of verification.* In total contrast with the innocuous material, which contains potentially verifiable data, the compromising text contains none at all. This is the crucial distinction.

The disproportionate percentage of innocuous writing in relation to the controversial content is of maximum significance for the following reason. It is the *quantity* of the innocuous writing that acts to convince the reader that this is an authentic diary written by Casement. The compromising content can be vague and minimal because the reader is primed to identify such material by its vagueness and innuendo, so that the two words 'big one' or 'fine types' always resonate as if erotically charged. This compromising innuendo is set in juxtaposition with text that appears to be authentic Casement writing, complete with apparently verifiable mundane facts which act to convince the reader that the entire text, *both innocuous and compromising*, is genuine. The reader automatically transfers his truth conviction from the innocuous text to the compromising material, no matter how vague that material is. Each time the reader finds the terms 'big one, fine type, offered, wanted awfully', he or she automatically responds to the encoded terms as programmed. The reader deciphers the code without being aware of the decoding process. Therefore the compromising text contains only allusions to *possible* sexual encounters; most entries are allusions such as 'went to square but none'. In these there is no reference to any sexual act or even to sexual desire—nor does there need to be, since the reader is by now conditioned by the code and co-operates by attributing the desired meaning to the phrase.

If 'none' means that nothing happened, why does the author want to record a non-event? The principal requisite of an erotic diary is that there should be erotic experiences to record in the diary. It is more probable that these non-events would be forgotten as being of no significance whatsoever. In this diary non-activity is recorded as if it were activity and that which did not happen becomes proof of sexual *intention*—a significant mental event. Lacking explicit detail of real sexual encounters, these non-events are nonetheless part of the encoding technique; graphic details are not needed.

Another significant feature of the Dollard diary is the lack of sentences of future aspect. The Amazon Journal has many such sentences, which resonate strongly with authenticity because they express the flux of time as lived, whereas if the writer does not render temporal dynamics in the text under composition it indicates that the writer is physically outside the original time flux, and this means that composition is taking place *after the closure* of that original time-frame. To simulate the awareness of the original time flux in sentences of future aspect requires imaginative gifts and trained narrative skill, which are rare. This strongly suggests that the Amazon Journal was written day by day in 1910 while the Dollard was written some time after the events recorded; the retrospective aspect which dominates the Dollard is in marked contrast to the intimate continuum of the narrative voice in the Amazon Journal. It would appear that the author of the Dollard was unable to create the temporal dynamics that render the Amazon Journal so convincing as a narrative written in 'real time' day by day.

The average length of an entry in the Dollard is 190 words (based on 27 random entries over 75 days). Casement was a prolific writer and almost certainly wrote at some speed. Average handwriting speed is 31 words per minute, so each average Dollard entry of 190 words would have taken only 6.12 minutes. The average length of the entries in the Amazon Journal is 1,654 words (based on 27 random entries in 75 days). In the Amazon Journal Casement frequently records spending many hours writing often late into the night, and he stresses the need to set down in writing the events as they happen in order to record them accurately and fully. Therefore when Casement refers to time spent on writing he is referring to the Amazon Journal and not to the Dollard, which, in fact, he never mentions. Equally, there is no mention in the Dollard of many hours being spent on writing anything, although it is not disputed that extensive writing was a daily activity for Casement.

The idea that Casement intended the Amazon Journal for publication is untenable, given his own description of the manuscript to Charles Roberts MP. The time to offer anything for book publication was immediately after his knighthood in 1911, when his reputation was at its highest, but there is no evidence that he did so. Indeed, there is evidence that publication was not an option.[5]

It was said that the now-infamous Giles Report of 2002[6] was intended to put an end to the controversy, but it failed to convince anyone who was not already convinced and therefore it failed to resolve the issue. Opinions, however expert, about handwriting resemblance are subject to cognitive bias and will never resolve the question of authenticity. Expert opinions remain opinions; all of the so-called forensic opinions so far are British establishment opinions, and none would be accepted by an impartial court of law because they all fail to meet forensic court standards. The 'evidence' that Casement was the author of the diaries held in the UK National Archives rests on the perceived resemblance between the handwriting in those diaries and his unquestioned writings. Resemblance is not identity, *but resemblance is sufficient to facilitate belief in identity.*

The arguments that have induced many to believe in authenticity are principally the one proposed by Inglis[7] and a second—the wealth of specific detail. The Inglis argument fails to resist scrutiny because it is facile and lazy rhetoric. The wealth-of-detail argument *assumes* that the detail is correct but does not demonstrate its accuracy. It is based on the easy presumption that a great quantity of detail is evidence of veracity of every detail, an inference belonging exclusively to psychology and propaganda rather than to logic. The author of the 1910 police typescript had more than enough sources for the wealth of detail, perhaps too many, but used them hurriedly and unsystematically.

Notes

[1] References to the Amazon Journal are to the handwritten manuscript held in the National Library of Ireland: MS 13,087 (25).

[2] References to the Dollard diary are to the version published in *Roger Casement's diaries: the black and the white*, edited by Roger Sawyer (1997).

[3] The overall length of the Dollard is approximately 24,000 words. There are about 55 compromising entries, amounting to 916 words.

[4] Charles Roberts MP requested the diary and Casement sent it on 27 January 1913, describing it as 'sincere and was written with (obviously) never a thought of being shown to others but for myself alone as a sort of aide memoire and mental justification and safety valve'.

[5] 'The diary is a pretty complete record and were I free to publish it would be such a picture of things out there, written down red hot as would convince anyone' (letter to Charles Roberts MP, 27 January 1913. R.H. Brit. Emp. S22 Casement–Roberts Correspondence). That it was never intended for publication is also confirmed by René MacColl (1958, 163).

[6] Privately masterminded by W.J. McCormack, the Giles Report was strongly criticised by US experts for failing to demonstrate how its conclusions were reached. Dr Giles is a former Metropolitan Police document expert.

[7] Brian Inglis, author, historian and TV broadcaster. His influential and readable book appears balanced, but with regard to the authenticity question its contradictory logic cleverly conceals its hidden bias from unwary readers.

3

Casement tried and tested

'Forensic science is not immutable ... and the biggest mistake that anyone can make ... is to believe that forensic science is somehow beyond reproach: it is not! The biggest miscarriages of justice in the United Kingdom, many of them emanate from cases in which forensic science has been shown to be wrong' (Michael Mansfield QC, barrister and legal scholar).

The history of investigating the Black Diaries, attributed to Roger Casement, is by now as confusing as the history of the diaries themselves. The results of the 1958 examination were not made public and were effectively suppressed by being quietly buried in a 200-page Home Office file; the 1972 investigation was amateurish and the 1993 investigation was inconclusive, and certainly none of these interventions met international forensic standards.

In 2002, however, the Giles Laboratory was commissioned by Professor W.J. McCormack to examine the controversial diaries. Sadly, this investigation failed to surpass the earlier tests.

Nonetheless, on 12 March 2002 Professor McCormack, addressing a Casement conference, declared his indifference to the outcome of the investigation before announcing the result. The diaries were authentic—at long last. The British and Irish press obediently reported that the question was definitively closed. In his book *Roger Casement in death* (published a few months later and therefore in preparation before the Giles investigation), McCormack's indifference was largely compromised by his dismissal of those unconvinced by the Giles Report as 'Casement vindicators'. His book is strongly in favour of authenticity, which signifies that when he commissioned Giles he was not impartial regarding the outcome of her investigation.

In the years since this intervention work on Casement has progressed, and different questions might now be asked of the McCormack–Giles enterprise.

Forensic

The term 'forensic' does not mean scientific and is not a synonym for scientific. The term 'forensic' means related to law (Latin *forensis*), and a forensic report or evidence is a specialist report or evidence presented in a court of law to help determine the outcome of a legal dispute. Such reports are not binding on the court. Forensic reports and evidence must meet specific standards and they are prepared and presented by professional experts who must explain and *demonstrate* to the court how their conclusions have been reached. Many but not all such forensic experts are scientists or technicians qualified in the exact sciences. All must have specific training and experience of forensic reporting to courts. Their reports and evidence have the status of an impartial expert *opinion* and their conclusions are expressed in terms of *probability*. Therefore a forensic report can only play a conclusive role if a court of law decides that it plays such a role. Outside a court an expert opinion has no legal (forensic) status and its role and significance are decided by private persons for their own purposes. For an expert opinion to become a forensic report it must be prepared to precise court standards, otherwise it will not be accepted by the court.

The forensic expert owes a *duty of truth to the court* and not to the party who commissions and pays for the expert opinion. It follows that if a report is not presented in a court it does not have the *juridical* status of a forensic report and there is no duty of truth. This remains the case even where the expert opinion is prepared in accordance with forensic standards.

The Giles Report

The initial commission given to document examiner Dr Audrey Giles by Professor McCormack was that she authenticate the questioned documents: 'The Steering Group have set the initial proposition to be that the documents at Kew known collectively as Roger Casement's Black Diaries are genuinely written in his hand throughout'. This instruction is fundamentally biased and compromises both the examiner and the subsequent examination. For this reason alone the report would not have been accepted by any court of law. Moreover, the 'Steering Group' remains inexplicably anonymous.

Dr Giles should have pointed out the limitations of handwriting examination and that it might be impossible to reach a definitive conclusion. Having accepted the commission, she proceeded to authenticate the documents. It is axiomatic, however, that *scientific investigation seeks falsification*, not verification. The dominant paradigm is tested by looking for weaknesses, contradictions and anomalies. Therefore the Giles investigation cannot claim scientific validity because it started from compromised premises. Moreover, the report does not fulfil the requirements of a *forensic* report to be *demonstrated in a court of law* because it lacks scientific detail, definitions and clear parameters. Quite simply, the conclusion is not demonstrated. Furthermore, in an astonishing statement Dr Giles confirmed that certain tests were not carried out because she had already foreseen the results of those tests *without performing them*. She stated in the RTÉ TV production of Alan Gilsenan's documentary *The ghost of Roger Casement* (March 2002):

'We could go ahead and carry out analysis of the inks, there are some problems there. There has to be a recognition that if indeed the Diaries are substantial forgeries, then they would have been produced at about the same time as the documents are dated or not long afterwards. So they are going to be produced using materials of the age, so I doubt whether in the end any close analysis of the ink is going to tell us a great deal about them.'

This statement alone is sufficient to convince the sceptics that the Giles/McCormack enterprise was planned as a media event rather than an impartial scientific investigation. It perfectly demonstrates the error of seeking verification rather than falsification of a thesis; the examiner selects only those techniques and methods that will produce the desired result. In this case the methods used were those of comparative handwriting analysis, which, by Dr Giles's own admission, are subjective:

'Handwriting examinations are necessarily to some extent subjective. It relies on my judgement to determine whether features are the same or different' (RTÉ TV documentary, March 2002).

If anything, the Giles Report raised more doubts than had existed before. Marcel Matley, a US document examiner, in his devastating sixteen-page critique stated: 'Even if every document examined were the authentic writing of Casement, this report does nothing to establish the fact'. Apart from scientific inadequacy, media publicity including two TV documentaries suggested that the entire enterprise was a political/publicity stunt masquerading as scientific investigation, an impression compounded by press misreporting that ink, pollen and DNA tests had given definitive conclusions when no such tests had been carried out.

The report was peer-reviewed by US document examiner James Horan, who stated: 'As editor of the *Journal of Forensic Sciences* and the *Journal of the American Society of Questioned Document Examiners*, I would NOT recommend publication of the Giles Report because the report does not show HOW its conclusion was reached. To the question, "Is the writing Roger Casement's?", on the basis of the Giles Report as it stands, my answer would have to be I cannot tell' (see Appendix, below).

Indeed, the Giles Report was not published and therefore was not deposited in major libraries as promised. Its fate was much the same as that of the earlier investigations, save that the media campaign proved successful not only in perpetuating the official thesis of authenticity but also in regenerating that untested thesis as definitively tested and proven. To doubt the 'conclusive tests' became heresy. Thus scientific investigation had become political propaganda.

In the section entitled 'Background' on page 206 of the version published by the Royal Irish Academy (Daly 2005) we read the following: 'As part of this campaign portions of a Diary or Diaries were covertly circulated or disclosed. … [M]ost of the influential figures to whom it was shown in the original transcript copy or photograph form accepted it as Casement's. The latest instance of material being so used seems to be in 1921 when Michael Collins was shown two diaries. He accepted the writing as that of Casement, which he knew.'

This is an ominous start to what purports to be a scientific report. The multiple instances of confusion and misinformation here came from McCormack, the guiding spirit of the enterprise. 'Original transcript copy': a copy is not an original, and the term 'transcript' *presumes* an original. 'Diary or Diaries': but was there one or more? Casement did not make the typescripts and these were not diaries at all but simply typed pages. 'The latest instance' was in 1925, when journalist Singleton-Gates was shown bound-volume diaries; Collins was not shown diaries in 1921. He saw two bound diaries in February 1922. There is no verifiable evidence anywhere that Collins knew Casement's handwriting and Collins left no evidence that he 'accepted the writing as that of Casement'. Further, Collins never met or corresponded with Casement. The inclusion of this misinformation indicates the bias in favour of authenticity that compromises the Giles investigation. As she holds a doctorate in philosophy, Dr Giles should have known better than to use the *argumentum ad verecundiam*—appeal to a prestigious name—and particularly when the 'authority' was both unqualified and silent.

Cognitive bias

Leading US experts, including Andrew Sulner (fellow of the American Academy of Forensic Sciences, lawyer and former state prosecutor) and Professor Dan Simon, have explored cognitive bias and flawed forensics.

Mr Sulner has pointed out that too many handwriting experts still believe that training and experience shield them from the biasing influences proven to affect the accuracy of visual observations and decision-making of ordinary mortals.

In a paper titled 'Cognitive and motivational causes of investigative error', presented to the American Academy, Professor Simon demonstrated various dangers in forensic investigations, such as *selective framing* (inquiry is framed in terms designed to influence the outcome), *selective exposure* (the information provided is chosen to influence the outcome) and *selective stopping* (inquiry ends when the hypothesis appears to be confirmed but all possibilities have not yet been considered). The Giles Report is afflicted by all three of these defects.

It is now increasingly recognised among the US forensic science community that experts are reluctant to acknowledge the possibility of mental contamination of evidence in the form of cognitively biased evaluations. As highlighted in the National Academies of Science report *Strengthening forensic science in the US* (2009), research in behavioural science and information obtained from reviews of errors in high-profile cases have clearly established the adverse impact that contextual and motivational biases have on human judgement and on the accuracy of forensic evaluations of evidence.

Scrutiny

Deep scrutiny exposes the following lethal defects in the Giles Report.

Firstly, while document examiners do use the term 'consistent with' despite its lack of precision, 'consistent with' says no more than 'might be' owing to a degree of observed similarity. An imprecise degree of similarity is *insufficient for positive identification* and therefore is inconclusive. A series of 'consistent with' results is more *persuasive* than one or two such results because the apparently repeated similarity *suggests* a lower probability of error in each observation. It does not, however, guarantee error elimination—the key word is 'suggests'. It is here that cognitive bias plays a determining role by unconsciously programming the search for repeated similarity. The subjective perceptive mechanism becomes less impartial as it is progressively conditioned by a cognitive bias *created by previous observations*; we see what we have previously been conditioned to see. The process is called *recognition*.

Dr Giles reaches 'conclusive' evidence by repeating the expression 'if taken together' in the preambles to her conclusions; this expression, following the imprecise 'consistent with', overlooks the distinct features of single contentious entries. A number of 'consistent with' assertions grouped under 'if taken together' produce what she calls 'conclusive evidence'. But 'consistent with' is not a constituent of conclusive evidence because it is an intermediate term on the scale of value determination; any number of *identical* inconclusive terms cannot produce a conclusive result.

This is a misapplication of the 'Law of Large Numbers', which requires *variant input values* in order to produce a result higher than *some* of the input values: 2+3+4+5 divided by 4 = 3.5, which is higher than two of the input values, but 3+3+3+3 divided by 4 = 3, which is identical to all input values. Therefore a series of 'consistent with' input values *cannot produce a result higher than any single input value*. Identical inconclusive values cannot produce conclusive results. The final Giles conclusion ought to be 'consistent with', which is inconclusive. This outcome would be 'consistent with' the 1993 result of 'correspond closely'.

Secondly, the term 'consistent pattern' appears on six different occasions in the report. What is meant by 'consistent pattern' goes unexplained, but it clearly refers to the 'contentious entries'. Regarding the possibility of forged entries, Dr Giles states that she 'would expect to find evidence of this in the form of: a consistent pattern of contentious entries'. Without an explanation, one must guess at possible meanings. Does she mean that the contentious entries should show features that distinguish them as a group from innocuous writings? Does she expect the questioned writings to be labelled for easy identification? If they were easy to identify by virtue of shared distinctive features, then the hypothetical forger would have utterly failed. Dr Giles does not even explain *why* she would expect to find any pattern. Surely a repeated detectable pattern acts like a label and is exactly what the forger would avoid?

At another point she discusses the difficulty of simulating another person's handwriting owing to the need to suppress the writer's own handwriting during simulation. 'Whereas this may be done over a small portion of handwriting, this becomes extremely difficult over more than a few lines of handwriting.' Is she referring to a beginner or to an experienced forger? No one disputes that the writings, if forged, were done by an expert, and an expert is someone who is capable of doing what most of us cannot manage. Even this misses the point, however. The Giles examination presumes that these are genuine Casement diaries that might have been doctored by forgery of the contentious entries; this presumes that the innocuous writings are genuine. There are no grounds for that presumption, which excludes *a priori* the possibility that none of the diary content was written by Casement. Her many comments about the brevity of the contentious entries are therefore factually true but irrelevant and misleading. Indeed, by noting the brevity she unwittingly dismantles her own argument about the difficulty of lengthy simulation.

When Dr Giles discusses the 1911 Lett's diary, which contains contentious writings 'on virtually every page', her argument does not improve. A 'curious' comment follows: 'It is easier *to identify areas* where the entries are non-contentious rather than where they are contentious'. No explanation is given for this easier distinction. This is strange, because the two types of entries are, by her own account, free of any 'significant differences' and therefore should be indistinguishable. The only difference would then be semantic—one with sexual references, the other without. To someone without English, these writings would be identical *if there are no significant differences*. Dr Giles is English, so we must assume that she detects the difference without noting semantic content, but on what basis she does not explain. This distinction, however, would constitute a significant difference requiring reasoned explanation. Even stranger is her later comment: 'The contentious entries are a large and integral part of the entries of this Diary and *cannot be separated in any way* from the innocuous entries'. This contradicts her earlier separation of contentious and non-contentious entries.

In her quest to provide another form of 'proof', Dr Giles explains that special instruments were used to detect alterations, deletions and erasures. On two separate occasions she states that limited testing for erasures was done on *blank pages* and no evidence was found. The tests were limited because 'unfortunately, without some manipulation, the Diary pages cannot be subjected to ESDA (Electrostatic Detection Apparatus) examination'. On a separate occasion the erasure test is again performed on *blank pages*; again these pages 'are not suitable for' the ESDA technique. No evidence was found.

Therefore limited erasure tests were applied only to pages *without writing* and *by chance* those blank pages were unsuited to ESDA testing. *No erasure tests were done on any written pages to detect suspected interpolation of contentious writing.*

Further evidence of bias can be found in the 'verification' of the pages lent to Dr Giles as comparison material by the National Library of Ireland (NLI). These pages are an extract from the so-called Amazon Diary written in Casement's handwriting and their authenticity has never been contested. It is therefore unclear why Dr Giles subjected them to a process of verification as to authenticity. These pages were compared to those provided to Dr Giles by the London School of Economics (LSE) and, after examination, the NLI pages were found to be authentic. Dr Giles did not, however, subject the LSE pages to any verification process; it follows that the documents used for the authentication of the NLI pages had not been authenticated by Dr Giles. From this it follows that the NLI pages were not, in fact, authenticated at all, since the LSE comparative material had not been authenticated by Dr Giles. The conclusion is that neither set of documents, whether from the NLI or from the LSE, was authenticated by Dr Giles.

Perhaps the most awkward facet of Dr Giles's approach is when she noted differences in the questioned writings but made them 'disappear' by not counting them as significant because such differences must be explained. Unable to find reasonable explanations for significant differences, they became insignificant. She did not, however, find comparable significant differences in the *unquestioned* writings because she did not look for them. Their 'absence' in the unquestioned control material constitutes sufficient reason to consider the differences found in the diaries as significant and as potential evidence of forgery. This point was also made by US document examiner Marcel Matley in June 2015: 'In reality Giles unwittingly proved at least some "contentious entries" were by a different hand'.

The Giles Report, described by one document examiner as 'forensic junk science' and by another as failing to meet court standards, raises questions about the author's competence. If these questions are false, the only remaining explanation is that the report's failures are due to what in cognitive science is known as confirmation bias—an unconscious predisposition to seek confirmation of a proposition and to disregard data that refute. The English philosopher Francis Bacon described it in his *Novum Organum* in 1620: 'The human understanding when it has once adopted an opinion ... draws all things else to support and agree with it. And though there be a greater number and weight of instances to be found on the other side, yet these it either neglects or despises, or else by some distinction sets aside or rejects.' Confirmation bias explains why Dr Giles failed to demonstrate her conclusions.

Earlier investigations

The investigation conducted in 1958 was carried out by Dr Wilson Harrison, a recognised scientific document expert. Very little is known about his examination, save that Dr Harrison was director of a Home Office forensics laboratory and that he undertook not to give press interviews. The results remained unpublished and buried in a 200-page file at the UK National Archives (HO 144/23481). That file clearly reveals (a) Home Office dissatisfaction with the brief opinion, which failed to securely identify authorship, and (b) fears of a second, contradictory report. Certainly its 93-word opinion does not meet forensic standards and was not intended to do so. Nor can we know what instructions were given, and there was no authentication of the control material.

Even less is known about the investigation carried out in 1972. The two persons involved were not qualified document examiners. No formal results were published and there is only an imprecise anecdotal account in the public domain. We do not even know which documents were examined or what methods and instruments were used. Those involved were Peter Singleton-Gates and Dr Letitia Fairfield. The former is well known in the Casement controversy, since he was co-author of the 1959 book that claimed to publish the diaries for the first time. By his own account, he obtained the typescripts for his book from 'a figure of some authority' in 1922. Many now think that this figure was Casement's former CID interrogator Basil Thomson, but this has not been verified and Singleton-Gates refused to identify his source, while conceding that his source was dead. Very little is known about Peter Singleton-Gates. In his 1960 article on the diaries, Roger McHugh states: 'Mr Gates ... admitted that he had been "guilty in the past of literary fraud" ... In 1921, representing himself as "Lieutenant Colonel Singleton", Mr Gates faked a news story about the finding of Lord Kitchener's body. A few years later he was severely censured by a judge for trying to obtain money by confessing to this.'

Dr Fairfield was a well-known public figure, a medical doctor and lawyer with Irish connections who had a long-term interest in the Casement affair. At the time of their investigation Singleton-Gates was 81 years old and Dr Fairfield was 87, and neither had formal training in document examination. With so little known and with no verifiable results, it is reasonable to categorise this investigation along with those done by the Home Office in 1958 as being of no practical use to an impartial enquirer.

The 1993 investigation

This was carried out by Home Office expert Dr David Baxendale and was featured in a BBC Radio documentary. The result of this rather brief intervention was decidedly cautious, if not ambiguous. Dr Baxendale stated that 'the bulk of the handwriting in there is the work of Roger Casement'. With reference to alleged interpolations he stated that 'the handwriting of all the entries which were of that nature correspond closely with Mr Casement's handwriting'. This caution might be explained by his awareness of the Hitler Diaries fiasco of some years earlier, in which some 62 *diaries* were forged in only two years by Konrad Kujau and were subsequently authenticated by handwriting experts and eminent historians before the fraud was discovered by Dr Julius Grant, a forensic paper expert, and by the West German Bundesarchiv.

In plain terms, 'the bulk of' means that the greater part of the handwriting is Casement's, and 'correspond closely' means almost identical or very similar. In either casse the ambiguity remains. It is reasonable to expect that a skilled forger would produce almost identical writing, otherwise there would be little point in the exercise. It is also reasonable to deduce from 'the bulk of' that the remainder is not identified as Casement's writing and therefore might be the writing of someone else. In neither case has forgery been excluded. Dr Baxendale confirmed that before proceeding with the investigation, he signed a Home Office 'secrecy declaration' (Mitchell, 2001).

Conclusion

The Giles Report was certainly the most important investigation of the Black Diaries and it attracted widespread attention in the media, but its claim to be scientific and definitive is untenable. McCormack succeeded in manipulating both Dr Giles and the media. Instead of lucid exposition, what precedes the conclusion is a verbal smokescreen composed of ambiguity, repetitions, irrelevant data, deceptions, omissions, *ex cathedra* pronouncements and disinformation.

The entire Giles investigation was predicated on the assumption that the diaries are genuine Casement diaries that might have been 'doctored' by the addition of interpolated incriminating writings. That the diaries are original works written by Casement and later compromised is merely a presumption, but that presumption allows Dr Giles to restrict her search for significant differences to a comparison between the innocuous writing and the contentious entries in each diary. To be more precise, this presumption permits her to avoid specific comparison of the diary writing with the unquestioned control material, the 66 letters provided by the London School of Economics, and no examples of such comparisons are given. In the absence of any evidence that the bound volumes existed during Casement's lifetime, such an assumption prejudices the investigation by substituting a biased question (which parts of the diaries were written by Casement?) for the real question (did Casement write any part of the bound volumes?).

Appendix
James J. Horan, John Jay College of Criminal Justice, New York: 'How did the Giles Report investigate Casement's handwriting?', *British Association for Irish Studies Newsletter* **31** (July 2002).

For a report to be accepted in courts in the United States it must present not only the findings but also the data which backs up those findings. Under the Federal rules of evidence, a report must include the results of the tests and all the notes and charts required to demonstrate the findings based on all the documents examined. Dr Giles' report as it stands would not be accepted in the courts in America because the report is lacking in backup material. Where are the photographs of the evidence examined, the charts, and supporting detail necessary for anybody to review the report?

When you examine known writing, especially in a case like this, it is very crucial that you determine the validity of the known writing. In the 1980s we had the problem of Hitler's Diary, which was accepted as genuine by one of the leading document examiners in the world. Michel and Baier, two of the German document examiners who were involved in exposing the Hitler forgery in an article in the *Journal of the Forensic Science Society*, pointed out some principles that should be used in examining documents. 'The reliable information on the point of origin of the material examined has to be obtained and inter-homogeneity of the documents cannot be over stressed.' Basically, you have to compare all of the known writings together to make sure how it breaks down into different groups. Can they be accounted for, or can they not be accounted for. The known writing of Casement should be crucial. In effect, as much time should be spent on examining the known writing as should be spent on the questioned writing.

Another problem which Michel and Baier pointed out is the need for the examiner to be familiar with the writing system. In Dr Giles' report she suggests that Roger Casement used a modified Civil Service system. She is referring to the English Civil Service system in Osborn's book. Osborn was one of the leading document examiners around the turn of the century and his book is still used as the leading text in the field. This is the system that Dr Giles suggests Casement was using or was in common use at the time. She points out a number of features in Roger Casement's writing, which she calls distinctive features, but when she describes them in the report she fails to give any examples. Using her descriptions I went through a letter that was given to me in the Home Office material, which was distributed at the Royal Irish Academy Casement Conference a few years ago. There are examples of writings taken from the British Consul in Norway. He sent a letter to the Home Office and basically he has the same general features that Dr Giles records in her report. I am not saying he wrote it but the features are similar. If I were examining writings from the turn of the century, I would have to collect a number of examples and analyse them to establish what was common and what was uncommon. Casement's writing of the 'd' was very pronounced in the way it swept up and back, but I noticed exactly the same feature not only in the Consul's writing but also in a number of other writings in other papers made available by the Home Office. So that was a common feature. A document examiner, then, has to decide after very thorough examination on exactly what emphasis should be put on various features.

Dr Giles did not do any chemical analysis of the ink or pencil. With modern analytical techniques, such as Ramon spectroscopy and X-ray Fluorescence, it may be possible to do non-destructive testing in the future to answer the questions about them.

The handwriting comparisons in the Giles Report are inadequately documented. As there were no charts in the report, I have no way of evaluating her handwriting comparisons. When I presented my paper 'How forensic science would approach the Casement Diaries' at the Royal Irish Academy Casement Conference I mentioned the possible use of 'Write On'. 'Write On' is a computer program developed in Canada by Pikaso Software. The way it works for a comparison is that each page of the document or documents to be examined is scanned into a computer and then the known and questioned documents are typed into the computer. This process enables you to select either words, letters, letter combinations or positions of the letters for display and study on the computer screen. Of course, this time-consuming method of scanning and typing involves much work, but I think that in the controversial case of the Black Diaries such a detailed analysis of the documents should have been employed. Such an approach would have produced comparison charts tracking every place Casement wrote 'the' in the questioned and known writing. This type of comprehensive analysis can stand up better to all vigorous challenges. Basically the forensic document examiner should work along the lines of presenting a case to a jury. In a handwriting comparison case, the jury should be taken through the evidence step by step; and charts are the best way of showing why this is the handwriting of X, why this is the handwriting of Y, and all the charts should reach the standard that when a jury looks at the charts they feel confident in reaching a well-informed judgement.

As editor of the *Journal of Forensic Sciences* and the *Journal of the American Society of Questioned Document Examiners*, I would NOT recommend publication of the Giles Report because the report does not show HOW its conclusion was reached.

Because of the controversial nature of the case Dr Giles should have been requested to prepare a detailed report that could be presented to a jury. To the question, 'Is the writing Roger Casement's?', on the basis of the Giles Report as it stands, my answer would have to be I cannot tell. In the fullness of time, there will emerge further illumination of the ink and pencil question. Very gradually we will draw closer towards convincing answers to most, if indeed not all, of the questions posed by the enigma of Casement's diaries.

Part 2—Diagnosis of deceit

4

Dis-covering Casement

It is today widely believed that between Casement's arrest and execution in 1916 the Black Diaries now held in the UK National Archives were clandestinely shown to influential persons in order to disarm appeals for his reprieve. This belief was once again articulated by law professor Seán McConville on 2 June 2016 at a Casement event in London, when he stated to a TV audience of millions that '... the diaries were circulated in London ... Blackwell ... was circulating these diaries at a time when Casement's fate had not finally been decided ...'. The original sources of this belief, however, are the books written by René MacColl, B.L. Reid, Roger Sawyer, Brian Inglis and Séamas Ó Síocháin. These volumes together comprise more than 2,000 pages and, at an average of two years for each study, represent around ten years' research. Strangely, in these 2,000 pages there is not a single verifiable recorded instance of the diaries in the UK National Archives being shown to anyone in that period. How can this be?

It is not to be believed that these authors after ten years of research overlooked this crucial aspect. If they found instances of the diaries being shown during that period, it would seem that they withheld that vital information from their readers. Since this is not credible, we must assume that none of them found any instance of the diaries being shown in that period. It is well attested that typescript pages were shown during that time and that a large quantity of these eventually found their way to Singleton-Gates, who published them in Paris in 1959. But Casement did not type those pages.

What would constitute a proof of authenticity of the diaries held in the National Archives? There are no witnesses to Casement's authorship, and no rigorous and impartial scientific tests have been carried out. The only evidence that has been adduced in favour of authenticity is a resemblance in handwriting. The attempts at corroboration in July 1916 are not evidence of authorship.

Perhaps, however, the question about authenticity is a false trail. In the period between 25 April and 3 August 1916 the British authorities claimed to be in possession of the five bound volumes now held in the UK National Archives, but there is no verifiable record that these volumes were shown to anyone in that period. Rather than show the diaries, the Intelligence chiefs had decided to prepare typescript pages and to show these to influential people—journalists, editors, politicians, churchmen and others. They told these persons that the typescript pages were authentic copies of original diaries written by Casement, but they failed to provide any proof that the typescript pages were copies of anything written by anyone. The proof that they did not provide would have been exhibition of the bound-volume diaries now in the UK National Archives. No explanation has ever been proposed for this failure.

Today there are five bound volumes in the UK National Archives, but their existence today does not prove their existence in the period 25 April–3 August 1916. That the bound-volume diaries were not shown during that time means that there was some impediment to showing them. The protagonists—Blackwell, Thomson, Hall, Smith and others—had the strongest of motives for showing the bound-volume diaries which they said had been discovered but they did not do so. The impediment certainly existed and it was such that these powerful men, whether jointly or singly, could not overcome it. Therefore it was beyond their *joint power* to show the bound-volume diaries *in that period.* This circumstance indicates that the impediment could not have been overcome by anyone in England at that time—not even by the monarch. In this regard these powerful men had touched the limit of their *human* power.

The question is therefore not about forgery or authenticity but about the material existence of the bound-volume diaries at that time. The absence of verifiable evidence that they existed before 3 August 1916 means that questions about authenticity are meaningless. What first requires to be proved is their existence in that period before 3 August. Those who claim that the typescripts were true copies have now had 100 years to produce evidence of the existence of the bound volumes in that period. That they have not done so indicates that they too have been unable to overcome the impediment that defeated their powerful predecessors, Thomson, Smith, Hall etc. In these circumstances an impartial court of law would decide to act as if the bound-volume diaries did not exist *at that time* and would dismiss a case for their authenticity as being untryable. The case for the typescripts being copies at that time could not be tested or proved without verifiable independent evidence that the bound volumes existed before August 3.

Documentary evidence establishes that there is no record of the bound volumes being shown in 1916. PRO HO 144/23455 contains some 200 pages relating to the deliberations of the Working Party that was responsible in 1958–9 for advising the cabinet on future policy concerning the Black Diaries. Among these pages is a long document dated 6 March 1959 and entitled 'Memorandum by the Secretary of State for the Home Department and Lord Privy Seal and the Secretary of State for Commonwealth Relations'. This document contains Annex 'A', which is entitled 'History of the Casement Diaries', and paragraph 4 of that Annex contains the following: 'There is no record on the Home Office papers of the diaries or the copies having been shown to anyone outside the Government service before Casement's trial'.

Thus the case in favour of the material existence of the bound-volume diaries before 3 August rests entirely on the word of Thomson, Hall, Blackwell, Smith and others, and these are the persons who at that time were showing typescripts which depicted Casement as 'addicted to the grossest sodomitical practices'. These men can only be considered as hostile and unreliable witnesses by virtue of their uncontested behaviour. There are no neutral witnesses who testified to seeing *at that time* any of the bound-volume diaries now in the UK National Archives. Absence of proof of existence of the bound volumes at that time entails that no proof of their authenticity can be derived. That no proof of authenticity can be derived means that the veracity or falsity of the typescripts cannot be considered until such proof of existence is provided. *Ei incumbit probatio qui dicit, non qui negat*: the onus of proof rests on the accuser, not on the defence.

If questions about authenticity are meaningless owing to lack of conclusive evidence after 100 years, claims favouring authenticity do not rest on verifiable facts or on independent testimony. Such claims therefore rest on an induction that excludes the normal apparatus of reasoned proof, a process that is indeterminate, untestable and unprovable, akin to that of faith.

That there is no independent witness to the existence of the bound volumes at any time before 3 August 1916 means that their continuous existence from 1903, 1910 and 1911 can only be presumed *because* it cannot be proven. That the Intelligence chiefs did not show the bound volumes to any independent witness during the three-month period up to 3 August is an extraordinary omission but it cannot have been an oversight, given their joint plan to destroy Casement's moral reputation. Therefore the *presumption* that the bound volumes existed before 3 August is groundless because unsupported by verifiable facts or the testimony of independent witnesses. That the bound-volume diaries are effectively 'date-stamped' proves only that they are date-stamped but does not constitute a verifiable fact that they existed on those dates. The anomalous behaviour of the Intelligence chiefs was nonetheless intentional, and intentional behaviour is that which is felt to be necessary. Therefore they felt it necessary to show typescripts rather than bound volumes. That necessity compelled them to exclude showing the bound volumes. Such a necessity indicates that there was no option; the bound volumes could not be shown by any of the Intelligence chiefs at any of the many recorded showings of the typescripts. An impartial person, indifferent to the political equations, would be irresistibly drawn to the conclusion that the bound volumes held in the UK National Archives could not be shown in that period because they did not exist before 3 August; therefore they cannot be authentic Casement writings. The search for reasonable alternative explanations being exhausted *after 100 years*, the impartial person would regard this as satisfying the 0.91 probability threshold required for proof beyond reasonable doubt.

5

An uncanny deception

'No man walks this earth at the moment who is more absolutely good and honest and noble-minded' (Herbert Ward, 1903).

In October 1914 Roger Casement was 49 years old. The ex-consul had worked and travelled in north and south America, Europe and Africa; his pioneering human rights investigations had made him world-famous and had brought him honours from the British Crown. A growing disaffection with imperial colonialism and the Home Rule crisis had led Casement to an active role in the cause of Irish independence. By 1914 he was on the Provisional Committee of the Irish Volunteers, a renegade to the Crown and a revolutionary plotter. On 29 October, 87 days had passed since George V had ordered Foreign Secretary Edward Grey to declare war on Germany; Casement was in Oslo for 39 hours *en route* to Berlin. Unbeknownst to Casement, a secret plot began on that evening of 29 October in the British legation at Oslo which would eventually lead him to a brief meeting with hangman John Ellis eighteen months later on the scaffold in Pentonville Prison. The germ of the plot to destroy Casement was written in a four-page memorandum marked 'top secret' and sent late that evening by diplomatic bag to Grey in London. This memo contained a brief, unfounded insinuation of 'unnatural vice'. The authors were Francis Lindley and Legation Minister Findlay.

In July 1913, after much deliberation, Casement had formally resigned from the consular service. During his years with the Foreign Office he had personally met and known dozens of high-ranking civil servants and ministers of state, diplomats both British and foreign, members of parliament, lawyers and journalists, police and judicial officers. Among these were Foreign Secretary Grey, Herbert Samuel, Louis Mallet, Lord Lansdowne, Gerard Spicer, William Tyrrell (head of the Political Intelligence Department), Charles Roberts MP, the journalist H.W.

Nevinson, Sydney Parry, J.H. Morgan (professor of Constitutional Law), E.D. Morel of the Congo Reform Association, Baron von Nordenflycht (German consul in Brazil) and King Leopold of Belgium. Among his close friends were Dick Morten, sculptor Herbert Ward, historian Alice Stopford Green, Irish-language pioneer Agnes O'Farrelly and the Cadbury family, in whose homes he had been a welcome guest. In Ireland he had spent much time with those involved in the Irish-language revival movement and later with the organisers of the Irish National Volunteers. In 1910, on his investigation in the Putumayo, Casement spent some three and a half months in the company of four English commissioners representing the Peruvian Amazon Company; their names were Bell, Gielgud, Barnes and Fox. The long list of notable people known personally to Casement included barrister Patrick Pearse, Sir Arthur Conan Doyle, political leader John Redmond, missionary John Harris, former ambassador James Bryce, Joseph Conrad and British Minister in Brazil Sir William Haggard.

On 18 July 1914 Casement arrived in New York. He spent 89 days in the US and visited Philadelphia, Buffalo, Virginia, Chicago, Baltimore and Long Island, where he addressed public meetings of Irish-Americans on the path to independence and the need for German support. During this period he spent time with most of the leaders of Clan na Gael, including the editor of *The Gaelic American*, John Devoy, and Philadelphia businessman Joseph McGarrity. Two pro-British lawyers, neither sympathetic to Clan na Gael, also befriended Casement: John Quinn, the renowned art collector, and Sligo-born Bourke Cockran, democratic Congressman and political mentor and friend of Winston Churchill. Casement was a house guest for three weeks in Quinn's New York home.

He also met painter John Butler Yeats, former US president and Nobel Peace Prize-winner Theodore Roosevelt, author Mary Colum and the German consul in the US, von Bernstorff. It was clear to British Intelligence even before Casement arrived in New York that he had 'turned' and had become 'a person of interest'. Anti-war and anti-recruitment declarations made abroad by a famous former Foreign Office consul could not be ignored. Casement was under British surveillance throughout his US sojourn and reports to Wiseman's SIS Section V were forwarded to London. Casement's activity also drew the attention of the IRB, some of whom were unconvinced that a well-connected former British official who had served the Crown for twenty years and had been knighted was indeed now an Irish revolutionary. His curriculum did not suggest deep, long-term revolutionary commitment. Indeed, his conversion to revolutionary plotting seemed difficult to understand. The IRB hired a detective to trail Casement in the US.

By 15 October 1914, when Casement sailed for Norway, he had been spied on for about fifteen months by RIC informers, by British agents in the US and by the IRB's detective. Neither these agents and informers nor the scores of persons he encountered during many years of consular service nor any of those he encountered in the US had noted or reported any sign of a disposition to 'unnatural vice'. On the contrary, the remarks made about his character for decades show a remarkable consistency with that made by Herbert Ward in 1903.

Nonetheless, the 1911 diary clearly shows a man with more than a mere disposition; it reveals a victim helplessly addicted to 'unnatural vice'. Therefore all those named above, along with all the informers and spies, must have been cleverly deceived by a man with the capacity of a Houdini.

On 31 October 1914 Casement arrived in Berlin, where he apparently continued a further and perhaps even more remarkable phase of systematic deception of German officials—state, police and military—for almost eighteen months. These officials included Zimmerman, von Wedel, Secretary of State Jugow, Professor Schiemann, Richard Meyer, von Nadolny, Isendahl, General de Graaff, Baron von Stumm, Baron von Lersner, Baron von Berckheim, Count Graf von Lutterich, Chancellor von Bethmann Hollweg and the Admiralty specialist in espionage Captain Hans W. Boehm. Also deceived were his personal friends US Consul St John Gaffney and Dr Charles Curry.

Spied on by both sides in the USA, Casement was to find himself again under police surveillance in Germany. Some elements in the military shared the same uneasiness as the IRB men in the US. They could not understand why so many state officials seemed to trust Casement so easily and to give him so much attention. Once again his curriculum and worldwide reputation raised suspicions that he might be a particularly audacious British spy ingeniously representing himself as an Irish revolutionary. The KV intelligence files in the UK National Archives show that British spies in Germany also followed his movements. By the time

Casement finally left Germany in April 1916, he had been constantly spied upon in Ireland, the USA, Norway and Germany for over two and a half years.

This, then, was a most remarkable and *uncanny* deception. The deceived listed here include top state officials, lawyers, prominent clergymen, high-ranking military staff and diplomats, academics, journalists, informers, spies and secret police, all of whom failed to perceive any sign of Casement's secret nature, which was nonetheless uncannily detected on 29 October by two British officials who had *never met or seen Casement*. They alone did not fall under his spell.

A deception on this scale, spanning many years in many places, is impossible to comprehend unless it is attributed to a strange blindness afflicting all these people, or else some kind of complicity. Neither of these explanations has any credibility, however. That Casement was indeed a master of concealment finds confirmation in a short article published in the *New York Herald* on 25 April 1916, which reported that eight months earlier he had plotted with German agents in Peru to facilitate the escape from jail of the Putumayo murderers, the very men whom he had indicted in his 1910 investigation.

> 'Prisoners ... held for three years for trial for the Putumayo atrocities, in August 1915, escaped from jail in Iquitos, Peru, and in canoes at hand fled down the Amazon ... led by Armando Normand, who, Sir Roger Casement declared at the time of his [Normand's] arrest, was the worst criminal in the world. In the escape of these prisoners evidences of German intrigue, with Sir Roger as the guiding genius, were apparent.'

Thus this master deceiver was also an accomplice in the murders he had denounced. This complicity was not self-protective; rather it revealed a criminal instinct of an almost diabolical nature, contrary to all justice and all civilised values. This instinct he had also concealed. And it was this evil instinct which guided his disposition to unnatural vice and which enabled him to deceive so many for so long, enabled him to conspire with the barbaric destroyers of civilisation in Germany and enabled him to secretly condone the murder of the innocents of Putumayo while denouncing the atrocity to the world. The treason with which he was charged seemed almost the least of the evils he had perpetrated.

Either the 55 persons named above (and dozens more unnamed) suffered from the same neurological dysfunction in the cortical zones of the brain which prevented them from decoding the signs of Casement's disposition or he was miraculously capable of totally concealing all such signs from everyone for many years. Or else there were no signs to conceal, therefore none to decode, and therefore no one was deceived except British officials Lindley and Findlay, who never set eyes on Casement—in which case it was they who accomplished the uncanny deception by 'deceiving' themselves.

6

Battle of the books

'Truth exists. Only falsehood has to be invented' (Georges Braque).

1

Since 1956 no fewer than eight authors have published books defending the Black Diaries as authentic, and a list of the *twenty* various editions shows that published support for authenticity has been consistently renewed every three years on average (see full list below). This is extraordinary by any standards and it seems strange that authenticity should need such consistent defence over the generations and through a period of such radical social and political changes. It is difficult to imagine a numerous readership for so many books about a figure from a century ago. In the 60 years since the first was published, the pop-cultural revolution of the 1960s and '70s ran its course, the Troubles exploded, the Falklands War took place, the Berlin Wall came down, the Soviet Union imploded, the Cold War ended, the digital generation arrived, 9/11 happened, the Peace Process began, the Iraq War began, followed by Wikileaks—and much else besides.

The works of five of these eight authors have enjoyed sixteen editions in Britain and the US. These are probably the most influential and accordingly they will be examined here to discover how each of them deals with some of the central questions in the Casement controversy. The questions selected are (i) provenance, (ii) the Oslo memo, (iii) the Findlay Affair and (iv) diary materials.

Provenance relates to various accounts of how and when the bound volumes allegedly came into police possession. The Oslo memo refers to a secret document of 29 October 1914 containing the seed of the scandal allegation of 1916. The much-disputed Findlay Affair concerns events in Oslo during and after Casement's brief stay *en route* to Berlin. From May to August 1916 diary materials were shown, but there is no evidence that the bound-volume diaries were shown.

René MacColl

René MacColl's 1956 book, the most hostile to Casement, went to four editions, with two of those being mass-market paperbacks. MacColl was a star journalist with the Beaverbrook press group and a name of some authority.

Provenance: MacColl accepts without question the official version of provenance and ignores the conflicting versions published by CID chief Basil Thomson.

The Oslo memo: He says nothing about this document, which was probably not available to him in 1956.

The Findlay Affair: He accepts Casement's version that Christensen was taken by British agents to the legation, where Findlay proposed the assassination of Casement and later offered a written bribe for information leading to his capture.

Diary materials: Since he fails to distinguish between the bound-volume diaries and the police typescripts, MacColl does not examine this aspect and fails to cite any instance of the volumes being shown to anyone in 1916.

Brian Inglis

Popular broadcaster, prolific author and editor of *The Spectator*, Inglis was another authoritative voice. His 1973 book, probably the most influential and subtle, enjoyed five editions between 1973 and 2002. His 1973 edition contains no source references whatsoever, these being deposited separately in the National Library of Ireland.

Provenance: He accepts the official version without question.

The Oslo memo: Inglis refers to this crucial document but he cites only the 57 words of the scandal innuendo and fails to reveal the anomalies and contradictions in the remainder that reveal it to be the invention of Findlay.

The Findlay Affair: Inglis creates his own subtle version, which contrasts totally with MacColl's. The Inglis version portrays a treacherous Christensen playing a double game, deceiving both Casement and Findlay.

To dispose of the earlier MacColl version, Inglis claims that the PRO files declassified in the late '60s 'told a different story'. Scrutiny of those files shows that they do not tell any story at all and contain nothing to contradict Casement's account of Christensen's being first contacted by British agents from the legation. The Inglis revisionist version is now treated as fact although the PRO files do not support it.

Diary materials: Since he fails to distinguish between the bound-volume diaries and the police typescripts, he does not examine this aspect and fails to cite any instance of the volumes being shown to anyone during Casement's lifetime.

B.L. Reid

Reid was an American professor of Literature. His *The lives of Roger Casement* was published by Yale University in 1976.

Provenance: Reid seems undecided as to how and when the trunks and diary/diaries came into police possession.

The Oslo memo: Reid was certainly aware of this document from Inglis's book, published three years earlier, but he does not mention it.

The Findlay Affair: Reid summarises both versions and favours the Inglis version of the double game. He does not mention that no betrayal took place in spite of Findlay's £5,000 written bribe, which document Christensen at once passed to Meyer in Berlin.

Diary materials: Reid creates confusion between the volumes and the typescripts but fails to cite any instance of the volumes being shown to anyone before the execution.

Roger Sawyer

Sawyer reports that he originally believed that the diaries were forgeries but around 1976 he converted to authenticity. His original interest in Casement stemmed from his study of anti-slavery movements. He was a council member of Anti-Slavery International and has written extensively on the subject.

Provenance: Sawyer disputes the official version and disagrees with the other authors; he claims that the trunk(s) and the diaries were found either in late 1914 or early 1915 and refers to evidence found in 1959 by Richard Crossman MP. Sawyer claims that Thomson's contradictory accounts were due to carelessness.

The Oslo memo: Sawyer mentions this document in his 1984 study but, like Inglis, cites only the allegation of scandal.

The Findlay Affair: Sawyer accepts the version invented by Inglis, which claims that Christensen intended to sell Casement to Findlay. He does not mention that no betrayal took place in spite of Findlay's £5,000 written bribe, which document Christensen at once passed to Meyer in Berlin.

Diary materials: Sawyer exploits confusion between the volumes and the typescripts, but in his 1984 book he claims that Clement Shorter was shown 'the originals by Basil Thomson'. He fails to cite any source reference or date for this event, which is unmentioned by any other author. This unverifiable claim is followed immediately by a claim that the rolled manuscript pages reported by US journalist Ben Allen were the 22 pages torn from the 1903 bound-volume diary. The pages shown to Allen, however, were five times larger than the 1903 pages; this falsehood appears to come from the Inglis book of 1973.

Séamas Ó Síocháin

Ó Síocháin was professor of Anthropology at Maynooth University. His 2008 book is the most detailed and he has enjoyed access to more Casement files than the other authors. He accepts the Giles Report as a definitive verification of authenticity.

Provenance: Ó Síocháin accepts the official government version without question.

The Oslo memo: He was certainly aware of this document from Inglis's 1973 book but he does not mention it.

The Findlay Affair: He cites Casement's version but favours the version invented by Inglis in his 1973 book. Like the other authors, he fails to inform his readers that no betrayal took place despite the written bribe, which Christensen surrendered at once to Meyer in Berlin.

Diary materials: Ó Síocháin exploits confusion between the volumes and the typescripts but fails to cite any verifiable instance of the volumes being shown to anyone before Casement's execution.

91

2

In the Inglis book there is a subtle process of transformation of conjecture and innuendo into facts, which are accepted by later authors to establish a standard version. Since all of these authors are guilty of misinformation, distortion and innuendo, it is legitimate to ask why they resort to duplicity when, as they claim, they are convinced of the authenticity of the diaries. Such deceptions ought not to be necessary if their convictions are sincere. It is unthinkable that these deceptions are unintentional, because in that case they would be self-deceptions or simple mistakes—and, if mistakes, that these authors should make so many mistakes in common is not credible. Since the misinformation, omissions and innuendo appear to follow a design, it is legitimate to ask whether the authenticity that the authors wish to uphold can be sustained only by means of systematic duplicity. Such duplicity betrays that their declared convictions are not sincere and that they are aware of the falsity of the diaries. Five random examples of duplicity will illustrate the point.

MacColl: He offers two anecdotes intended to corroborate the authenticity of the diaries. The first comes from an anonymous source in Cork and the second from Sullivan, Casement's defence lawyer, both of whom he interviewed in 1954. The anonymous Cork source refers to an earlier named source who in turn refers to an even earlier named source, both dead in 1954, hence no verification was possible. MacColl recounts a hearsay story of other black diaries being found after the execution and destroyed by a friend in Belfast. The Cork source of 1954 died in 1967 and was then identified by MacColl; once again no verification was possible. The statements attributed by MacColl to Sullivan were denied soon after by Sullivan. Sawyer also relies on MacColl's Cork anecdote.

Inglis: On page 439 of the 1974 paperback edition (appendix III) we find the following: 'The other [diary] was a copy of his Putumayo diary, which he made for the use of the Select Committee investigating the affair. As he told the chairman, he was sending the copy because "naturally there is in it [the original diary] something I should not wish anyone else to see".' Inglis claims that Casement sent a copy rather than the original to the chairman of the parliamentary Select Committee, Charles Roberts MP; this is false. It is very clear from Casement's correspondence with Roberts that he sent the original handwritten document of 142,000 words and excused its illegibility in parts and its personal, sometimes intemperate tone; it was not intended for others. The purpose of Inglis's deception here is to insinuate that Casement did not send the original document because it contained compromising material that he wished to conceal. Casement, however, did not tell the chairman that he was sending a copy, as Inglis states. Inglis lied in order to insinuate that the authentic document now in the National Library of Ireland is a 'cleaned-up' version of an earlier incriminating document. Roberts asked for the document by telegram on 24 January 1913 and Casement sent it on 27 January; it was received on 1 February.

Reid: On page 213 of his 1976 study we find the following: 'In his first account of these events, sent to Sir Edward Grey on 31 October 1914, Findlay wrote that Christensen had simply presented himself at the door of the British Legation at 79 Drammensvein in the *late afternoon of the twenty-ninth*' (emphasis added). Findlay did not write this at any time and Reid's assertion is false. Findlay's letter of 31 October does not contain this apparently paraphrased written statement attributed to him by Reid. Findlay's letter states: 'The man called at the Legation *about 11 a.m.* and asked to see me alone. He went over much the same ground as he had covered with Mr Lindley on Thursday evening' (emphasis added). There is no reference anywhere in this or in any other letter to Christensen's arrival at the legation on the afternoon of Thursday 29 October. Therefore Reid misinformed his readers by *falsely attributing* to Findlay his (Reid's) own false account of Christensen's arrival on the 29th. Reid's motive for this deception arises from his need to support the new Inglis version of Christensen's alleged treachery.

Sawyer: On page 140 of his 1984 book we find the following: 'Within a week, John Harris had read the diaries himself, at Dr Davidson's request and on his behalf'. This simple sentence can only mean that the diaries now held in the National Archives were shown to and read by Harris, but Sawyer knows very well that this is false. He knows that Harris was shown the police typescripts only and that this fact is verified by PRO HO 144/23481. Since Sawyer knows the facts, his misinformation is intentional duplicity. This instance is replicated many dozens of times throughout the works of all five authors, which indicates the adoption of a *common strategy* aimed at concealing from readers the absence of any evidence for the showing of the bound volumes during Casement's lifetime.

Ó Síocháin: For reasons that remain unclear, Basil Thomson solicited corroboration in July 1916 from Oslo hotel workers, a tax inspector and Christensen's mother. Ó Síocháin describes these statements as affidavits and they mainly concern allegations against Christensen. Ó Síocháin accepts these as true statements but he ignores Thomson's written dismissal of them as worthless; he also ignores the fact that the statements are technically not properly sworn affidavits and he does not reproduce them in his book. These spurious documents were not used in 1916 and they remained secret for decades. Sawyer also refers to these statements from Oslo.

3

For two reasons the Inglis book of 1973 merits special attention. In the first place this 448-page biography contains no source references. Secondly, it was the first study published after the restricted release of the bound volumes in 1959 and, more importantly, the first to appear after the release in 1967 of top-secret Foreign Office files.

Inglis claimed that cost made impossible the inclusion of source references. His publishers were Hodder and Stoughton, a major house with its head office in London and offices in Sydney, Auckland and Toronto. His book is approximately 200,000 words in length and contains 45 pages of appendices, bibliography and index. A note among those 45 pages informs readers that the source references can be found in the National Library of Ireland. The list of sources extends to 29 typed pages and contains approximately 1,100 references, which when typeset would have added some twenty pages to the book, increasing its length by a mere 2.24%. Rather than following standard publishing practice by including his sources in a controversial historical biography, Inglis preferred to include Casement's famous speech from the dock and an article by Shaw, which occupy thirteen pages. Both of these had already been published elsewhere, whereas his sources were not published. The claim about cost is simply not credible, given the resources of his publishers; its falsity is evident in the fact that none of the subsequent editions up to the most recent in 2017 contains the source references. Are we to believe that cost was a prohibitive factor in 1973 and remained so for the following 44 years while other publishers, large and small, did not allow the prohibitive costs to prevent them from including source references as normal practice in their books?

The exclusion of the sources in such a controversial work deserves to arouse the maximum suspicion. It is obvious that Inglis's decision makes it almost impossible for readers to check and verify what he has written. Given that Inglis was the first biographer to enjoy access to the 1967 released files in the Public Records Office, it is logical to suspect that exclusion of his sources is related to the content of those files. Inglis tells us that he attempted an 'acceptable compromise' by indicating the source within the text of the book so that the reader does not need separate source references—'… when quoting from a letter, by saying by whom and to whom it was written and when. Ordinarily this establishes where the original is to be found.' This is, of course, a *non sequitur* unless the reader is an experienced Casement researcher. Three examples of letters referred to in his book demonstrate that Inglis fails to keep his com-promise in these instances. (Page references are to the first edition of 1973.)

In the last four lines of page 278, with reference to the 3pm meeting on 30 October between Christensen and Findlay in the legation at Christiania, Inglis writes: 'But he [Findlay] transmitted Christensen's information to Whitehall, enclosing the material Christensen had handed over. It included a letter in which Casement described his servant. "I am glad I brought him, indeed—he is a treasure".' In these lines there are four deceits. Christensen did not hand over any material. Findlay did not take possession of any letter from Christensen. The letter that Inglis mentions had not yet been written. The letter mentioned does not state that 'he is a treasure'.

The letter referred to by Inglis, which has no addressee, was written in Berlin in November, some days—if not weeks—after it was allegedly handed over to Findlay on 30 October. This letter is also cited by MacColl and by Doerries, whose published version gives the date of 2 November. Internal evidence demonstrates that the letter was written later in November and was one of the 'fake letters' prepared by Casement for Christensen to show Findlay to mislead him. This ruse is explicitly confirmed by Casement's Berlin Diary entries for 17 and 24 November. Ostensibly Christensen was to post these letters from Christiania. The letter states: 'I will send this tonight by the man, who returns as I have said to visit his people'. Christensen left Berlin for Norway on 22 November and not on 2 November. Further internal evidence in the letter demonstrates that it was not written on Casement's second day in Berlin, 2 November.

In his *Prelude to the Easter Rising* (2000) Doerries states that a photocopy of this letter is held in the NLI with reference MS 14,914, Volume 1. He publishes the full text of this letter. However, the photocopy of the letter is now missing from that file in the NLI and it is not listed on the contents page of Volume 1. It appears, therefore, that someone removed the original volume containing the letter and replaced it with a manipulated volume at some time after the publication of Doerries's book in 1999. The purpose would be to avoid the possibility, however remote, that Inglis's deceptive citation might be detected. Paradoxically, Inglis himself refers to this NLI file on page 420 of his first edition as being copy material from German archives; this strongly indicates that he had seen the letter when researching in the NLI. And although he was certainly aware of the correct version of the letter published by MacColl in 1956, this did not deter Inglis from altering Casement's original text to obtain an innuendo that has deceived many thousands of readers for 46 years.

It is almost certain that Inglis saw this photocopy in the NLI, and he had certainly seen the version cited by MacColl. Nonetheless, he claims that Christensen handed the letter to Findlay *before it existed*. On page two of Findlay's 26 November account to Nicolson of his meeting with Christensen on that day, Findlay refers to this letter as a postscript to one of three letters shown to him by Christensen at that meeting (FO 95/776 038). Findlay states that he made copies and therefore did not take possession of the letters. On 4 December Findlay sent his copies of the fake letters to Nicolson. Findlay does not claim that material was 'handed over' and does not mention the phrase 'he is a treasure'. The phrase went unnoticed by Findlay but not by Inglis, who noted its potential for innuendo. Inglis changed the verb tense from past to present, which shifts the meaning from appreciation towards an innuendo of endearment. The version cited by both MacColl and Doerries differs significantly from Inglis: 'I am glad I brought him indeed—he *has been* a treasure'. The shift in meaning is so subtle as to escape most readers but it did not escape Inglis, who changed the meaning for the purpose of manipulating his readers' understanding. Doerries's source is the Political Archives in Bonn, and he reports that the letter is initialled by Count Adolf von Montgelas and Meyer of the Foreign Office.

In Inglis's source list in the NLI we find a page 278 reference to line 27. There are only 25 lines on that page. The line 27 reference says 'R.C. letter, 2 November (enclosed in Findlay memo)'. This must be the same letter and this curious reference demonstrates that Inglis knew that the letter did not exist on 30 October and therefore was not 'handed over' to Findlay. Further proof of Inglis's duplicity is that the relevant TNA file does not contain the letter allegedly 'handed over' and enclosed.

On page 337 line 28 Inglis states: 'Christensen wrote to the Foreign Office from the United States suggesting they might like to have his testimony against the traitor'. Once again we do not know when or to whom the alleged letter was written, although we can conclude that the original—if it existed—is among Foreign Office (FO) files. There is, however, no trace of any letter from Christensen in those files. Ó Síocháin and Reid give a different version. On page 444 Ó Síocháin writes: 'On 10 May ... word came to the FO from the US that Adler Christensen had made an offer to testify against Casement ...', and his source note reads 'Acting Consul General, Philadelphia, to Nicolson, 10/5/1916 PRO FO 95/776 and 5/6/1916 KV 2/9'. This indicates that it was the consul who wrote to the FO and not Christensen, as stated by Inglis. The present writer has been unable to locate this communication in either FO 95/776 or KV 2/9. In the latter file there is a police report dated 5 June 1916 of a purported interview with Christensen in Philadelphia. It can be concluded that Inglis's claim that Christensen wrote to the FO is false.

On page 282 line 24 Inglis refers to a letter from Casement to Eoin MacNeill in Dublin, which Inglis says went to the FO 'thanks to Christensen'. His source list refers to lines 8, 10 and 34 only and does not mention line 24. Casement's letter is dated 28 November and was written in Berlin. It concerns the German government's statement of goodwill towards Ireland. Inglis cites an extract from the letter but gives no source and no date either in his book or in his source list. From Inglis's comment 'thanks to Christensen' we are to assume once again that Christensen 'handed over' the letter to Findlay. Casement also wrote a letter to Devoy in the US on the same day; the subject was the same and the extract cited by Inglis from the MacNeill letter is repeated verbatim in the letter to

Devoy. This letter to Devoy is quoted in full by Doerries in his *Prelude to the Easter Rising* (1999), and his source is given as the Political Archives in Bonn. Doerries notes that the letter bears a comment by Richard Meyer of the German Foreign Office and the initials of Count Adolf von Montgelas, which makes it possible that the German authorities undertook transmission of this letter. It is possible that the MacNeill letter went by the same channel. The MacNeill letter was intercepted, however, as confirmed by Ó Síocháin in a source note: 'RDC to Eoin MacNeill, 28,11,1914, Documents Relative to the Sinn Féin Movement pp 4–5. The "channel" Casement used here for getting letters through was not as reliable as he thought since his letter to MacNeill was intercepted. For his references to it see NLI MS 1689, fols 24 & 18.'

Documents relative to the Sinn Féin movement was published by the British government and it confirms that the letter was not sent directly to MacNeill but was enclosed in an envelope addressed to 'a lady then in London'. There is no reason to doubt that this was Mrs Stopford Green; since she was a known associate of Casement, she too was suspected of potentially treasonable behaviour and her correspondence would have been censored by the police on instruction from the Home Office. That it was intercepted indicates that it was posted to London—probably from Rotterdam—and therefore was not 'handed over' to Findlay, as implied by Inglis.

That implication is wholly untenable, because Christensen left Berlin on 22 November, six days before the letter was written. He returned to Norway and remained there until 15 December. Findlay's correspondence confirms that he met Christensen in the legation on 26 November and 12 December during that period. The implication is even more untenable since there is no reference to the letter in Findlay's communications with the Foreign Office. Simply put, this letter was never in Christensen's possession and Inglis has once again misled his readers.

Each of these instances portrays Christensen as treacherous and this is not by chance. An integral part of Inglis's plan was to exploit the PRO files in such a way as to convince readers that at last the true story was emerging from his inspection of those files. Inglis's story did not, however, emerge intact from the files but from Inglis's own predetermined plan. The untrustworthiness of Christensen had to be solidly established and Inglis succeeded; it has become *de rigueur*. Portraying Christensen in an unsavoury light serves to cast doubt on the trust Casement placed in him, thus implying that this trust originated in aberrant instincts.

Inglis refers repeatedly to Christensen handing over material to Findlay as evidence of his double-dealing. To hand over means to physically give something into another's possession. At his first meeting with Lindley on 29 October nothing was handed over, according to both the Lindley memo and Christensen's account. At his first meeting with Findlay at 11am on 30 October Findlay confirms that nothing was handed over. At the 3pm meeting on 30 October Findlay confirms that nothing was handed over. At subsequent meetings in November and December Findlay confirms that *he himself copied* the documents shown by Christensen, and therefore they were not handed over. These were supplied to Christensen by Casement for the purpose of deceiving Findlay, which they succeeded in doing. Therefore Christensen's double-dealing was aimed exclusively at Findlay and was directed by Casement, but Inglis distorts the facts so that his readers will believe that Christensen was deceiving Casement and not Findlay.

Following Inglis's 'creative journalism', Ó Síocháin also deploys the deceitful locution of 'handed over'. On page 393 Ó Síocháin writes that at his meetings with Findlay on 30 October Christensen 'handed over documents given him by Casement for safekeeping during the encounter with HMS *Hibernia*'. The falsity of this assertion is demonstrated by three sources. First, the Lindley memo alleges that the letters shown were pencil copies of originals no longer in Christensen's possession. Second, Findlay's own accounts of his meeting with Christensen on 30 October state that he was shown pencil copies, which he himself then copied. Third, Casement was in possession of these letters when he first visited the German legation in Christiania on 29 October. Thus Findlay himself never claimed to have *taken possession* of original documents at either meeting on 30 October.

On several occasions Inglis cites his source as MacColl's 1956 book. Three of these are on page 276 lines 1–4, page 332 line 33 and page 333 line 18. MacColl's study does not contain any documentary source references whatsoever and therefore Inglis has no documentary sources for these assertions. One of these claims concerns Casement's defence lawyer, A.M. Sullivan, who, according to MacColl, had been told before the trial of the contents of the police typescripts but refused the offer to examine them. The second claim also concerns Sullivan, who, according to MacColl, told the journalist that Casement had glorified homosexuality at one of their 1916 prison meetings. Neither MacColl nor Inglis record the fact that Sullivan later corrected MacColl's version of that private interview when on 25 April 1956 he wrote to *The Irish Times* that 'Casement told me nothing about the diaries or about himself'. Neither of these claims have anything to support them apart from MacColl's word. The interview with the 83-year-old Sullivan took place in 1954 and there was no witness. Inglis has therefore relied on an unverifiable claim that he knew had been denied. Inglis's third reference to MacColl's book as source occurs on page 276 and concerns the sending of a message after an alleged identification of Casement by a German on the SS *Oscar II*. Although of less consequence, this instance cannot be verified either because no specific source is cited. Inglis's source list gives MacColl's page 141, but this page does not refer to any message or identification. The reference appears on page 144 of MacColl's book and it might have been sourced in German Foreign Office documents that MacColl consulted at St Anthony's College, Oxford; these were seized at the end of World War II.

Inglis makes a number of references to Cork City Coroner J.J. Horgan, who helped Casement in 1914 in an attempt to restore transatlantic shipping traffic to Cork. Horgan's 1949 memoir *From Parnell to Pearse* reveals that he had no sympathy with Casement's political aims despite having considerable respect for him.

The Inglis source list refers to lines 30 and 32 on page 240, but there is no line 32 on that page, which ends at line 30. The line 32 reference states 'Personal communication to the author', but Inglis does not say who wrote the personal communication or when, or what the communication stated. Inglis fails to mention that in his book Horgan expressed his confidence in Casement's moral rectitude and his conviction that British Intelligence was responsible for the diaries scandal: 'Yet no one who knew him could believe the vile, and utterly unproved suggestions which, with diabolical cleverness, were later made against his moral character by British propagandists' (page 140). Once again we have an example of selective framing, the systematic omission of that which might compromise the desired outcome.

Inglis states that his biographical narrative for the years 1903, 1910 and 1911 is based principally on the Black Diaries for those years, which means that he does not recognise them as questioned documents whose authenticity has never been established. For the 1910 narrative he relies on the Dollard diary and completely ignores the much more extensive 1910 Amazon Journal, which is the undisputed work of Casement. Therefore a genuine and highly detailed Casement document contributes nothing to Inglis's 1910 narrative and is not even mentioned, so that his readers would not know of the existence of this 140,000-word narrative. Yet Inglis was fully aware of it and briefly referred to it in an appendix to his 1974 paperback edition. It is axiomatic that serious history draws on undisputed sources. Historian Martin Mansergh made the point succinctly: 'But as a working historian, you cannot deploy as a source material whose authenticity is seriously disputed' ('Roger Casement and the idea of a broader nationalist tradition', in Daly 2005, 200). Nevertheless, Inglis ignored an authentic source document in order to privilege a controversial disputed document.

There are some who might conclude that Inglis's parsimony with the truth amounts to dishonesty. His use of selective framing, as demonstrated in these examples, is indicative of his desire to manipulate readers towards a predetermined conclusion, and this is evidence of bias. In the light of these examples and failing to find an alternative, readers would conclude that Inglis excluded sources from his book in order to deceive them.

4

The deception is not restricted to specific events or documents. It is uncovered also in narrative strategy, in how the biographical story evolves. Inglis developed a narrative strategy that became the standard model. He alters the chronology of his biographical account so that events that belong to 1916 are brought forward in the narrative sequence in order to condition the reader in advance. The reordered chronology mainly concerns the diaries, which entered the story only in 1916 after the arrest and were unknown in 1903, 1910 and 1911. By presenting these in the respective years of the principal chronological narrative, however, Inglis treats them as real events in Casement's life, on the same level as the ordinary events in his career. Thus he ignores the fact that nothing was heard of them until

1916. This chronological manipulation aims at progressively eroding the reader's perception of the absence of moral scandal in Casement's life before 1916. It poisons perception of Casement *in advance* so that the reader will accept the wholly remarkable 'coincidence' between the alleged discovery of the diary/diaries in 1916 and the arrest. Biographical narrative sets out verified events and facts in the original chronological sequence; the diaries were not verified facts in 1903, 1910 and 1911. The typescripts became *alleged facts* in 1916 and have remained so. Inglis altered their disputed status by embedding them in the undisputed reality of those earlier years, in the same way in which the police typescripts mingle compromising behaviour with routine innocuous behaviour so as to cast an aura of reality over both. Inglis's chronological manipulation of the narrative was essential in order to avoid offering readers a portrait of Casement's life over 30 years, which is totally free of moral scandal *until* he becomes a prisoner of the British. For the general reader, unwary and trusting, it has proved an effective strategy of deception, and it was adopted and further developed by Ó Síocháin.

The later works resort to a clumsy and amateurish psychology first presented by Inglis: 'He was a split personality … his personality was compartmentalised. Sections of it were cut off from each other …'. This reduces a complex *conscious* organism to little more than a malfunctioning contraption. Inglis then lists four main Casements, with others in attendance. Despite its inherent contradiction, this became a mantra repeated as a standard explanation by the other authors. The *reductio ad absurdum*, however, is that these various Casements acted together to *knowingly conceal* one of the group—'a cut-off section'—from all those who knew the remaining Casements, which would demonstrate a remarkable integrity or wholeness of personality over 30 years. In short, no one noticed that Casement had a 'split personality' until Inglis detected it in 1973, 57 years after Casement's death.

The Oslo memo is a critical piece of evidence in the Casement story and yet only two authors mention it, and then only to present the unsupported scandal allegation. The extensive literature on Casement *effectively suppressed* this document until 2016, when it was 'uncovered' in TNA by the present writer. A study of the four-page handwritten memo reveals that it has received so little attention because it is very clearly the invention of British Minister Findlay in Oslo. About 92% of its content is unverifiable; its improbable innuendo and contradiction explain why it was unused at the time and remained dormant even in 1916. This also explains why Inglis and Sawyer refer only to the scandal allegation—the seed that inspired the police typescripts. This false document is fully analysed for the first time in Chapter 11, 'Anatomy of a lie'.

The publication of so many works in favour of authenticity could be mistaken for propaganda, if only because it is difficult to distinguish from propaganda since the results are identical. It is more important to note, however, that the declared conviction shared by the authors is consistently compromised by their shared deployment of tactics of misinformation, omission, innuendo and confusion, which devices flow into one another smoothly. And it is of cardinal importance to note that these tactics are used principally when the authors are dealing with the questioned matters of provenance, the Oslo memo and the diary materials. These tactics play hardly any role when dealing with the verified facts of Casement's consular career, his growing involvement in Irish political and cultural affairs, his frustration with the Foreign Office, his health problems and the Home Rule crisis. Indeed, in these matters there is often balance, comprehension and sometimes even sympathy, which act to persuade the reader of the author's overall impartiality.

The 'battle of the books' was undertaken in order to guide public understanding of the story by establishing a definitive version for the future that would, in Sawyer's words, 'rebut a diabolical charge' of forgery. That battle, reinforced by a compliant media and by the Giles Report, has largely been successful owing to a shared strategy of 'information management' based on omission, distortion, deceit and innuendo; it is a strategy that the authors were constrained to adopt in defence of the alleged authenticity of the Black Diaries.

List of 21 editions by eight Casement authors, 1956–2017
The period covers three generations, each being supplied to the natural consumer level of market saturation but without flooding the market (h/b = hardback; p/b = paperback).

1956—MacColl, h/b UK

1957—MacColl, h/b US

1960—MacColl, mass-market p/b UK

1965—MacColl, mass-market p/b UK

1973—Inglis, h/b UK

1974—Inglis, p/b UK

1974—Inglis, h/b US

1976—Reid, h/b US

1984—Sawyer, h/b UK

1993—Inglis, p/b reprint

1997—Sawyer, p/b UK

1999—Sawyer, p/b UK reprint

2001—Weale, h/b UK

2002—Dudgeon, h/b Ireland/UK

2002—McCormack, h/b Ireland

2002—Inglis, p/b UK (5th edition)

2008—Ó Síocháin, h/b Ireland

2010—Sawyer, Kindle UK

2011—Ó Síocháin, Kindle Ireland

2016—Dudgeon, Kindle Ireland/UK (2nd edition)

2017—Inglis, Kindle UK

7
Invisible evidence

In the extensive literature on Casement there is at least one aspect that has gone unexamined and has been misunderstood. It is widely believed that the notorious diaries were shown to influential persons in 1916 in order to deflate the campaigns for Casement's reprieve. What follows is a scrutiny of the evidence for this belief. That 'diary materials' were exhibited in 1916 is undisputed, but what exactly were those materials? Among the many who saw 'diary materials' were the following persons.

Artemus Jones: Junior counsel to Casement's defence lawyer, Sullivan. Jones was passed typescripts by a junior counsel on instruction from Casement's prosecutor, F.E. Smith, and was told to pass them to Sullivan, who refused them. [1]

Alfred Noyes: Author and professor of Literature. While working in the Foreign Office, Noyes was briefly shown typescripts by Stephen Gaselee (Foreign Office). To Noyes's comments, published without his knowledge as propaganda in the US, was added a false statement of his authentication. [2]

F.E. Smith: Attorney general and politician. Casement's prosecutor was in possession of the typescripts before the trial and he passed these to Jones in the hope that Sullivan would allow them as evidence, thereby authenticating them, and then plead an insanity defence *in vain*. [3]

Ben Allen: US journalist in London. Allen was shown a roll of handwritten pages 'of almost legal size' by Captain Hall several times in May; later Hall showed him typescripts. Allen was sceptical because Hall declined to allow him to verify the matter with Casement. [4]

John Harris: Baptist missionary. Harris had known Casement in Congo. He was shown typescripts by Blackwell on 19 July. [5]

Henley Henson: Anglican bishop. Henson was shown typescripts in July by King George V. [6]

King George V: Typescripts were in the monarch's possession from May onwards, and he showed them to Henson in July. Most believe that

Smith left the typescripts with the monarch but this has not been confirmed. Others think that Hall's Room 40 colleague Herschell was responsible.[7]

Walter Page Hines: US ambassador in London. Hines, a close friend of President Wilson, was shown typescripts and given two photographs of the same by Thomson in London on 26 July.[8]

Cecil Spring Rice: UK ambassador to the US. Unspecified typescripts were sent by diplomatic bag on 21 July to Captain Gaunt for Spring Rice. On 28 July unspecified photographs of handwriting were sent by diplomatic bag to Spring Rice.[9]

Doctors Percy Smith and Maurice Craig: Psychiatrists. As part of the corroboration plan, they were shown the 1911 typescript and reported their medical opinion on Casement's mental state on 10 July.[10]

All of these people saw typescripts that had been typed by the Metropolitan Police; both ambassadors also saw photographs. Many other influential persons—including John Redmond, H.W. Nevinson, various MPs and leading journalists—were shown typescripts, but no evidence can be found which records the showing at that time of any of the bound-volume diaries now in the UK National Archives. On 17 July 1916 Ernley Blackwell, legal adviser to the Home Office, mentioned in a memorandum 'Casement's diaries and his ledger entries covering many pages of closely typed matter …', which is not a description of the bound volumes.[11] In 1959 the Home Office Working Party stated that it had no record of the bound volumes being shown at that time.[12] In 2017 officials at the UK National Archives confirmed that they do not know of any documents which record the showing of the bound volumes in 1916.[13]

It follows from these facts that no verified evidence of the showing of the bound volumes in 1916 has been produced in 100 years. Thus there is no evidence of their existence during Casement's lifetime. Since they certainly exist today, it is possible that at least two bound volumes *came into existence* after 1916 and before February 1922. The third bound-volume diary could not be found in Scotland Yard after an exhaustive search in 1921.[14] The first official description of the bound volumes came only on 23 July 1959, when Home Secretary Butler announced in parliament that 'The Casement Diaries consist of five volumes found in a trunk …'; moments later, he listed the dates of these volumes.

In a court of law, none of the above-listed persons could testify on oath that the typescripts they had seen were true copies of original documents unless they could also testify on oath that they had seen the original documents. Failing this latter, a court would demand that the original documents be produced for examination and authentication. The court would distinguish between belief and knowledge, between faith and evidence.

Any proof of the material existence of the bound volumes in 1916 must be of the same standard as the proof given for the existence of the typescripts at the same time: independent witness testimony. Without that testimony, belief in the contemporaneous existence of the bound volumes is merely a reasoned supposition based on an *untested* belief that the typescripts are copies. It is therefore necessary to identify the grounds for that untested belief and to determine the sufficiency of those grounds.

There are two principal grounds. Firstly, those showing the typescripts were officials in authority who spoke for the state. Secondly, the narrative in the typescripts contains detailed information that appears to illustrate Casement's experience recorded in diary form. The first ground can be dismissed as insufficient, since the word of those officials rested on blind trust and could not be verified. The second ground appears more convincing as a basis for belief that the typescripts are copies of authentic original diaries. The detail is such that scepticism is rendered difficult, and for many perhaps impossible.

Therefore the grounds for scepticism arise not from the detail in the typescripts but from the extraordinary fact that the intelligence chiefs did not show the bound volumes—or, more precisely, that they left themselves without any evidence of such showing and therefore without evidence of the volumes' existence. It is obvious that showing the bound volumes *at that time* would have crushed any possible scepticism about the typescripts.

It has been argued that absence of evidence is not evidence of absence—that is, absence of evidence does not *entail* that no evidence exists. It entails only that evidence has not been produced. Nevertheless, the wilful non-production of evidence requires explanation by those who *claim to possess the evidence*. In law, a court can demand disclosure. In the matter of the typescripts and bound volumes no explanation has been given by the intelligence chiefs *or by anyone else* for the non-production of the necessary evidence.

On the hypothesis that the bound volumes were in police possession in 1916, the following reasons can be proposed for the failure to disclose them:

(A) oversight—the intelligence chiefs forgot to show them;
(B) showing them was not considered necessary;
(C) there was a legal impediment;
(D) reasons of state security.

Only one of these has any credibility—(B)—but this reason would be the result of a decision predicated upon the calculated anticipation that proof would not be asked for. It remains to be explained why the intelligence chiefs would make that *quite unnecessary* calculated anticipation when they had irrefutable proof to hand, unless 'calculated anticipation' is a euphemism for 'hope'.

In order to further examine why the bound volumes were not shown, it is necessary to find credible reasons for the extraordinary decision to produce the typescripts rather than simply show the bound volumes. It is undisputed that the typing operation required several weeks during May and June, and that several Scotland Yard typists were employed in typing the many thousands of words. These typists had to decipher handwriting that is often cramped and difficult to read, with many words in foreign languages, all of which made errors inevitable. That this remarkable labour-intensive and time-consuming operation was undertaken *demands* explanation when one considers that the intelligence chiefs had two alternative options. The first was to show the bound volumes, pure and simple, which would have been both the easiest solution and the most immediately effective. The second option was simple photography of the bound-volume pages, which would have occupied one photographer for a day or two at most. The advantages of photography are obvious: photographs can be reproduced as required, and photographs reveal an image both of the original handwriting and of the material reality of the original page. Casement himself used photographs in his investigations to record the reality of the experiences he was reporting. Despite the fact that photography is easier, faster, more economical, more reliable and more *convincing*, the intelligence chiefs *rejected* that second option as they had inexplicably rejected the first. They decided that only typescripts would be prepared and shown.

Of all those who saw 'diary materials' it appears that only John Quinn was shown photographs of handwriting. This unique event took place on 23 August, when the influential New York lawyer was shown one or more photographs by Captain Gaunt of Naval Intelligence; this was three weeks after Casement's execution and some ten days after Quinn had published a four-page eulogy of the deceased in the *New York Times Magazine*. Quinn's own letters of 24 August testify to the showing but give no details of what he saw.[15] Quinn reported that the very small handwriting in the photographs bore a resemblance to Casement's hand, and this resemblance shocked and confused him. Nonetheless, that resemblance was not sufficient and Quinn wrote: 'I don't want to be quoted to anybody as vouching for the authenticity of the diary … I am going to put a handwriting expert on the photographic copies'. No expert ever set eyes on the handwriting, however, because Gaunt informed Quinn that he was already in breach of Grey's explicit veto against showing diary materials. So far as can be determined, these photos have never been seen since that day.

Quinn's letters reveal his overconfidence, firstly in thinking that it would be easy for him to identify the handwriting as forged and secondly in imagining that Gaunt would allow him possession of the photos for expert inspection. In his letter of 24 August to Spring Rice, Quinn penned eight lines of admiration for Gaunt, whose charisma had proven effective; a man spontaneously liked and respected does not stoop to deception. Quinn's earlier certainty was confused by a double *resemblance*—that of Gaunt to a clean, decent person and that of the photographed handwriting to Casement's hand. Having convinced Quinn of his integrity, Gaunt's task was complete. That task was to confuse Quinn, not to convert him; out of his depth, Quinn forgot that Gaunt was one of those who, as Quinn wrote on 22 August, 'pretend to be gentlemen' but who 'go to the sewers for their arguments'. It was too late for Quinn to recover from the error of viewing the photographs in the first place. Gaunt, head of an intelligence network, duly interpreted Quinn's confusion as a tacit authentication sufficient for immediate purposes.

Nevertheless, an important dimension emerged from the event. On

21 August Quinn wrote to Godkin: 'I am going to see the British Naval Attaché in a day or two by appointment at his request. I am told that he has certain pages of the alleged diary or what purport to be photographic copies of it. Of course they are forgeries. ... I am told that London has had this alleged diary for months, *since shortly after he went to Germany.* Then was the time to use it ... it would have alienated Irish sympathy from him ... would have kept him out of Ireland. Then it would indeed have made him a man without a country. But they did not use it then ... If I can get the photographic copies of the diary, I will submit them to a handwriting expert here, because I have plenty of genuine specimens' (emphasis added). On 24 August Quinn wrote to Spring Rice: 'Why the thing [the diary] wasn't used when he was in Germany, which would have kept him there, is a mystery'.

The use of the locution 'I am told' in the letter to Godkin indicates that the unnamed informant is a third person, not Godkin. The absence of that locution in the letter to Spring Rice on the 24th indicates that the recipient already knows the identity of the source, who need not be referred to because the source is the recipient—Spring Rice. The secret nature of the information, true or false, is not the scandal about Casement but concerns the *significance* of when a diary was found. This highly reserved information would only be revealed on a need-to-know basis, for example to convince an influential person hostile to the scandal. Quinn had known Casement personally and consistently vouched for his moral integrity. He was on good terms with Spring Rice and both had sought a reprieve for Casement. It is unthinkable that Quinn had heard this reserved information and Ambassador Spring Rice had not. Thus Quinn's letter to Spring Rice on 24 August indicates already *shared* knowledge requiring no explanation: 'Why the thing wasn't used when he was in Germany ... is a mystery'. The 'mystery' is predicated upon the following: at the time of writing to Spring Rice, Quinn *believed that a diary existed and had been shown in London* and that the photos shown to him in New York were evidence of this, although *he still suspected forgery.* Nevertheless, Quinn could not understand why the diary, even if forged, had not been exposed in 1915 to neutralise Casement and render him 'a man without a country'. Quinn assumed that a handwritten diary, *forged or genuine,* had been shown in London, but in 100 years no evidence has been produced which records the showing of any of the bound volumes before 24 August 1916.

That Quinn remained unconvinced is evident in his 9 September letter to Gavan Duffy, ignored by the biographers: '... I was finally shown what purported to be photographic copies of his diary and the handwriting looked like his ... the Naval Attaché told me that he had received a peremptory cable from Gray [*sic*] under no circumstances to show the diary'.

There is no way of knowing what the photographs showed. The archive files refer to them as 'photographic reproductions of parts of Casement's diary' without specifying exactly what the images displayed.[16] Quinn failed to take note of the content, and without knowledge of the content no facts about this writing can be determined, so that the event leads only to further conjecture and questions.

It cannot be determined whether these photographs were destroyed or have been withheld, perhaps unrecorded, by British intelligence or are today in a private collection. Whether concealed or destroyed, they are no longer available for inspection and none of the principal biographers claim to have seen them or *to have enquired for them*. If they have seen the photographs viewed by Quinn, they do not record the fact. More precisely, they do not record having seen the evidence upon which they place so much faith.

And this leads to a crucial consideration. It is the destruction or concealment of the photos that is indicative of deception. If the photos shown to Quinn were of compromising Casement *diary* handwriting, they were evidence for the authenticity of both the photos and the diaries; there was no reason to destroy authentic evidence that would have constituted solid proof of the diaries' existence at that time. The typescripts were kept, although they were weaker evidence of the diaries' existence. The photos were destroyed (or concealed permanently) so that they could at no future time be checked against the *bound volumes*. Since the archives testify both to the existence of the photos and to *the use made of them* to denigrate Casement after his death, it is not plausible to argue that they were destroyed in order to eliminate evidence of their use. The archive files clearly reveal that intention and the preservation of those files exposes the destruction of the photos to which they refer. Thus these photos, by virtue of their disappearance, become invisible evidence.

Hence the photos were not evidence of the volumes *at that time,* whether or not they were photos of Casement's handwriting. In short, if the photos had been authentic images of scandalous Casement diary writings, there was a very *strong motive for their preservation as evidence*, even stronger than the motive for preserving the typescripts as alleged copies of the bound-volume diaries. If there was good reason to destroy the photographs, there was even more reason to destroy the typescripts that were proof positive of the smear campaign. The typescripts had to be preserved, however, since they contained the texts to be later forged into the bound volumes. There was no other reason to preserve them. The destruction of evidence is always suspicious; the destruction or concealment of allegedly *conclusive photographic evidence* that proves one's case can only be explained by a need to conceal the falsity of that evidence. To paraphrase Inglis, '… no person or persons in their right mind' destroys or conceals the conclusive evidence that proves their own case.[17] That the evidence was destroyed or concealed by state officials in their right minds demonstrates that the photos were not authentic.

If the bound volumes are considered primary evidence, the typescripts are secondary evidence. By definition, however, evidence must be seen, and since the bound volumes were not seen they cannot constitute evidence, unless the surreal concept of 'invisible evidence' is accepted. Therefore the typescripts were the real primary and only evidence. It remains unexplained why the intelligence chiefs based their smear campaign exclusively on this primary evidence; it also remains unexplained why typescripts were produced rather than photographs of the bound volumes. None of the principal biographers (Inglis, Sawyer, Reid etc.) have addressed either of these questions.

The decision having been taken, the laborious typing process began and the first typescripts were shown to journalists in late May by Captain Reginald Hall, head of Naval Intelligence. Before then the smear campaign had spread like an uncontrollable viral infection, transmitted by rumour, gossip and whispering, but the showing of the lethal typescripts was a tightly controlled exercise aimed at corrupting specific influential persons in both Britain and America.

Casement was condemned to death on 29 June but there remained three possibilities of reprieve: an appeal to the Court of Criminal Appeal, an appeal to the House of Lords and lastly the Royal Prerogative. The first failed on 18 July and Smith refused the second. The third depended formally on a request to the monarch from the cabinet, which was under pressure from both Smith and Blackwell to 'allow the law to take its course'.[18]

At this point the attitude of the US administration became critical; a Senate appeal for reprieve seemed probable, and a negative response might consolidate or prolong US neutrality in the war. In this delicate situation the two ambassadors, Page and Spring Rice, had to be 'handled' with care. Page was a personal friend of President Wilson and Spring Rice believed that a reprieve would be to Britain's advantage.

Casement's life was still in the balance when US Ambassador Page asked to see diary materials. On Wednesday 26 July he met Thomson, who provided two photographs of extracts from the 1911 typescript.[19] On 21 July unspecified typescript material was sent by diplomatic bag to Captain Gaunt for UK Ambassador Spring Rice in Washington, and on 28 July unspecified photographs of handwriting were sent by diplomatic bag to the ambassador.[20] Almost incredibly, yet again the intelligence chiefs rejected the option of showing the bound volumes or photographed pages from these. The typescripts had sufficed for the monarch and they (plus two photos of handwriting) would have to satisfy US opinion. And it would be better if no Senate appeal were made.

It is exceedingly strange in view of what was at stake—a possible end of US neutrality—that this second opportunity in late July to photograph for the ambassadors a few original pages of one of the bound volumes was also rejected; perhaps the same 'inhibition' which had excluded photography of the bound volumes in May was still mysteriously effective almost three months later. This inhibition seems to have been of an *absolute nature*, a kind of taboo—unthinkable—or even an impossibility. If indeed impossible, the search for credible reasons has led to the only explanation that commends itself to common sense: it is impossible to photograph something that does not exist.

Notes

[1] PRO HO 144/23481-199. Papers of Artemus Jones, Bangor University, BMSS/28093-28094; letter to W. Maloney, 1 March 1933.

[2] Noyes 1957.

[3] PRO HO 144/23481-199. Papers of Artemus Jones, Bangor University, BMSS/28093-28094; letter to W. Maloney, 1 March 1933.

4   Affidavit by Allen dated 19 August 1960, NLI MS 13,452; letter from Allen to Maloney, 2 December 1932, NLI MS 17,601(1).

5   PRO HO 144/1636 … 3A.

6   Letter from Inge to Alfred Noyes, 24 December 1953, cited in MacColl 1958, 280.

7   *Ibid.*

8   PRO HO 144/23481, History of the Casement Diaries, March 1959, Home Office Working Party.

9   PRO FO 395,43.

10 PRO HO 144/23481-202.

11 PRO HO 144/1636, 15 and 17 July 1916.

12 PRO HO 144/23481, History of the Casement Diaries, para. 4, March 1959, Home Office Working Party.

13 Communications to the author from TNA officials in August and September 2017.

14 A facsimile copy of the Gaselee letter in MEPO 2/10672 from TNA contains Carter's handwritten note; also available on-line.

15 Quinn's letters here cited are held in the Quinn Papers at New York Public Library.

16 References to various PRO files can be found in Reid 1976, 421.

17 Inglis 1973.

18 Memorandum of 19 July to cabinet cited by Reid (1976, 418).

19 PRO HO 144/23481. 'The Ambassador was given photographs of two passages from the typescript.' History of the Casement Diaries, March 1959, Home Office Working Party.

20 References to various PRO files can be found in Reid 1976, 421.

8
Thinking the unthinkable

'Have you got some trunks at 50 Ebury Street? I propose having them down and examined.'

These sentences were not written by the master of absurdist drama Eugène Ionesco but by the London Metropolitan Police. They appear on page 3 of the official transcript of Casement's third interrogation on 25 April 1916. The purported speaker is Assistant Chief Commissioner Basil Thomson, and his question is the first reference to the controversial trunks that allegedly contained the scandalous diaries. Thomson might as well have continued, '... examined to see whether there are any scandalous diaries'. The inept question betrays that the existence and location of the trunks are already known to the speaker. The purpose of the question in the transcript is to conceal police possession of the trunks; it clearly fails to do so, since the question content is predicated upon foreknowledge of their existence and location. An impartial observer would ask why the police wanted to conceal that foreknowledge. The answer is that they wished to officially record a false date for possession of the trunks.

That the official date is false is now widely accepted by many experts, including a leading Casement authority Roger Sawyer, who as long ago as 1997 wrote: 'It is unthinkable that his luggage would have remained untouched while his every move was being monitored' (Sawyer 1997, 8). Casement's every move was being monitored when he was in the USA, even before he left for Norway on 15 October 1914. Sawyer is a firm believer in the authenticity of the diaries and therefore his comment demonstrates that he believes that the diaries were in police hands long before Casement's arrest. He does not, however, attempt to explain the deception in the police transcript.

Sawyer is not alone in his conviction. Perhaps the most prominent believer in authenticity, CID chief Basil Thomson himself, also agrees that the trunks were located before arrest, as he wrote in 1922: 'Some months earlier, when we first had evidence of Casement's treachery, his London lodgings had been visited and his locked trunks removed to Scotland Yard'. And there are others: Unionist MP Montgomery Hyde, a former MI6 agent, barrister and prolific author (*Trial of Sir Roger Casement* (1960)), agrees that the diaries were found long before the arrest, as he stated twice to parliament. Highly regarded journalist and editor of *The Daily Telegraph* Donald McLachlan, also a former intelligence officer, investigated the matter in 1959 for Richard Crossman MP and reported that the chief of Naval Intelligence, Captain Reginald Hall, had located the trunks some eighteen months before the arrest.

Sawyer reports: ' ... it seemed wise to approach Richard Crossman who, as British Director of Political Warfare against the Enemy and Satellites or as Assistant Chief of the Psychological Warfare Division of SHAEF, might reasonably have been expected to inherit whatever machinery was used in the previous war. He elicited help from Donald McLachlan, who had held a number of propaganda posts which came loosely under the heading "Naval Intelligence" ... it was his guidance which led to the discovery that Hall had heard of Casement's alleged proclivities twenty-one months before the execution, and not long afterwards Hall discovered the whereabouts of the traitor's personal luggage' (Sawyer 1984, 137). The discovery quickly followed the circulation of the secret Findlay memo in early November 1914. This manifestly false document contained the first allegation of scandal. Another scholar, Professor Seán McConville, also holds that the trunks were found long before the arrest: 'I think they [the diaries] were in British possession for quite a long while ... they had these trunks from the moment that Casement started issuing pro-German pamphlets ...' (talk at the Irish Embassy, London, 2 June 2016).

These informed individuals believe that the diaries are authentic and were found in the trunks many months before Casement's arrest. It is undisputed that British Intelligence investigated Casement's bank accounts in early 1915 and that German communications with the USA were being intercepted and decoded by Room 40 at this time. In this context Sawyer is right: it is not credible (thinkable) that his former lodgings were ignored until the third day of his interrogation in April 1916.

In the latter months of 1914 the priority for British Intelligence was Casement's capture, and this might be achieved if he attempted to return to Ireland. In early December 1914, Hall secretly chartered the ocean-going 600-ton *Sayonara* and selected a 50-man undercover crew. She sailed in mid-December to patrol the west coast of Ireland, gathering information and spreading disinformation. On 19 January 1915 the costly mission was abandoned when it became known that Casement was still in Germany and had no plans to leave. By mid-1915 there was no end to the war in sight and no prospect of Casement's capture while he remained in Germany. The KV intelligence files in TNA refer to the consideration of a plot in August and September 1915, if *evidence could be manufactured*, to 'unmask' Casement in Germany as a British spy; this plot would have been unnecessary if they already possessed the incriminating diaries.

It is a remarkable fact that no one has attempted to explain why the diaries allegedly found in the trunks in 1914/15 were not *at once* used against Casement. Obviously the scandalous diaries represented a potent weapon and their exposure at that time would have meant the prompt and definitive end of the Casement predicament. Besides being a triumph for British Intelligence, exposure would have been a *devastating blow* against nationalism in Ireland and the USA, which in turn would have led to increased Irish recruitment to the war effort. Revelation of the shocking evidence would have destroyed Casement everywhere, above all in Germany, and would probably have induced his suicide. The intelligence chiefs had an immediate solution in their hands but they held back the evidence for up to eighteen months.

It is unthinkable that none of the experts in the Sawyer camp sought to explain this long silence; the absence of an explanation indicates that the experts failed to find one that was credible without compromising their belief in authenticity. It is even more unthinkable that Thomson and Hall would have *intentionally refrained* from showing the bound-volume diaries to anyone after Casement's arrest. That they did not show them is verified by the complete absence of any record of such a showing; all records of diary materials being shown refer to typescripts or photographs of those typescripts. There is no record of bound-volume diaries being shown before February 1922.

It is undisputed that the typescripts were completed after the arrest and the text had only two possible sources: either the text was copy-typed from genuine Casement diaries found in the trunks in 1914/15 or it came from the imagination and diligence of the intelligence services. The first lemma generates three crucial questions. Why were the diaries kept secret for up to eighteen months? Why, when the authorities possessed the diaries, were typescripts made after the arrest? Why was no one shown the diaries *after* the arrest? The second lemma raises only one question: why was the typescript text concocted? It is obvious that the first three questions lead to speculative answers, whereas the fourth question gives an answer that agrees with the recorded facts of the smear campaign. That answer fully satisfies the question but does not prove that the text was concocted. The question, however, also serves as an answer to the three crucial questions. Because no incriminating diaries had been found and kept secret for up to eighteen months, the text was concocted. The text was concocted so that it could be typed for the smear campaign.

Some might consider it thinkable that the best answers to the three crucial questions are that the intelligence chiefs wished to *protect* Casement's reputation for as long as possible, that they felt it somehow more *convincing* to show typescripts and that they simply *forgot* to show the bound-volume diaries. If, however, these answers are unthinkable (not credible), it follows that no incriminating diaries were found in the trunks *at any time*.

The hypothesis that Sawyer *et al.* are correct about the *diaries* being in police possession in 1914/15 renders the authenticity position incoherent. The hypothesis is that by late 1914 or early 1915 the intelligence services had not only sufficient evidence of Casement's treason but also devastating *material* evidence in the diaries of his moral infamy. The problem, then, is twofold: how to explain why the intelligence officers kept that explosive material evidence secret, thereby protecting Casement's reputation, and how to explain the absence of any reference to diaries in the KV intelligence files. Those same files, however, do mention the alleged sources of both the trunks and the diaries: W.P. Germain of 50 Ebury Street is mentioned on 16 January 1915 and W.J. Allison & Co., Farringdon Road, is mentioned on 12 February 1915.

None of the Sawyer group even pose these obvious questions. Failure to ask the questions indicates that the most logical answer compromises the claim that the diaries were found long before the arrest. Since it is unthinkable that his luggage 'remained untouched', it is unthinkable that the scandalous diaries were kept secret for so long. It is even more unthinkable, in the light of Major Frank Hall's 4 November typed version of the Findlay memo alleging 'unnatural relations', that the diaries confirming the allegation remained a secret. Since there is no reference in the secret KV files to the finding of scandalous diaries, the intelligence officers not only kept it secret from their political masters in government but also *kept it secret from each other*. This manifest incoherence requires a modification of the Sawyer hypothesis to allow the 1914 finding of the trunks and the postponement of their opening until April 1916. Even this modification, however, negates Sawyer's claim that 'It is unthinkable that his luggage would have remained *untouched*' and makes the unthinkable necessarily thinkable. The only purpose of possessing the trunks was to open them. To avoid this collapse into contradiction, Sawyer must accept the logical answer, which is that no compromising diaries were found in the trunks. This is the most coherent answer that corresponds to logic and common sense and it would be accepted by any impartial person.

In the 21 days between 21 April and 12 May 1916, three events occurred which radically changed the context of Hall's original plan to use official police typescripts to undermine Casement in Germany: Casement's arrest, the Easter Rising and the subsequent executions of the leaders. Casement's fate was in British hands at last, so it was no longer necessary to neutralise him in Germany. The evidence of the failed arms shipment and the Rising increased his guilt as a traitor. The executions, however, profoundly altered the political climate by raising Casement to potential martyr status. The new priority became how to execute him without creating another martyr. Thus the defamatory texts were an even more essential and urgent instrument.

Having initially destined him for a military trial and probably death by firing squad, the authorities hesitated too long with Casement. Probably the most famous Irishman of the time, whose name had long been associated with humanitarian compassion, he was also a former British consul and a knight of the realm who personally knew dozens of distinguished and influential people throughout Britain. Never before had the authorities faced an adversary with such a formidable curriculum. While they hesitated, fifteen Rising leaders were shot in Ireland, the last on 12 May. On 15 May Casement was removed from military custody in the Tower of London and returned to Brixton Prison to await a civil trial—a strategic political decision but too late. A prompt military execution would have made Hall's typescripts unnecessary and embarrassing. And Hall had pre-empted matters on 3 May when he began his campaign by showing unidentified handwritten incriminating pages to US journalists in the Admiralty. He continued to show these pages at the weekly press meetings until 24 May, when they vanished forever and the first typescripts appeared.

Since no plausible explanation can be found for the long silence about the alleged finding of *incriminating* diaries in 1914/15, the claimed discovery has no foundation in verifiable facts. That no such incriminating material was found in the trunks sufficiently explains why there is no record of the discovery at that time or later. Although the detail of Findlay's obviously false memo had wisely been ignored in 1914, its essential allegation of 'unnatural relations' indicated to Hall and Thomson a possible defamatory strategy aimed initially at destroying Casement's credibility in Germany.

Thomson later claimed that, while Casement was in Germany, informer and fraudster Maundy Gregory suggested the use of diaries, and Thomson also consistently claimed to have found one diary only—for the year 1903. This is the diary that gave rise to the 'wealth of detail' argument for authenticity, and the 1903 typescript does indeed contain much detail that appears authentic. It would have been obvious and attractive to Thomson and Hall that very little preparation was needed for the narrative of the 1903 typescript; it required only the interpolation of a limited number of incriminating references. The operation mostly involved copy-typing of the original innocuous entries.

They also foresaw that the original 1903 Casement diary could never be shown to prove that the typescript was a true copy. This awkward fact, however, was sidestepped when Hall realised that the impossibility of showing one diary as proof meant that no proofs need be produced for further diary typescripts. Thus further narratives could be invented since none would need to be proven by showing the originals. Indeed, more was preferable to less, because more meant more apparently authentic innocuous detail. Expanding the scale from one diary typescript to three served to *increase* the deceptive authenticity of detail and thereby render scepticism more difficult.

During the preparation of the narratives for the 1910 and 1911 typescripts, the forging of bound volumes was not contemplated, since they would not be necessary for the original purpose of destroying Casement's reputation in Germany and damaging it in the USA. Hall, a master of deception, correctly foresaw that the 'wealth of detail' in official typescripts would be sufficiently convincing.

The principal source of the text for the 1910 typescript was the officially typed copy of Casement's personal account (the Amazon Journal) of his 75-day 1910 investigation, which had been held by the Foreign Office since 1913. Preparation of this narrative was a considerable undertaking and probably required several months, compared to a relatively brief time for the 1903 narrative. There was no single source for the 1911 narrative text, which explains why the reduced quantity of authentic detail was compensated for by a greatly increased amount of highly explicit incriminating material—about 45%.

At 4pm on 24 April 1916, Hall made a courtesy visit to King George V at Windsor Castle to inform him of Casement's capture prior to the press announcement on the 25th. To coincide with that announcement, a grey propaganda story had already reached the *New York Herald* for publication the following morning. The 'fake news' that it reported on page 2, column 1, was already *eight months old*. 'Prisoners ... held for three years for trial for the Putumayo atrocities, in August 1915, escaped from jail in Iquitos, Peru, and in canoes at hand fled down the Amazon ... led by Armando Normand, who, Sir Roger Casement declared at the time of his (Normand's) arrest, was the worst criminal in the world. In the escape of these prisoners evidences of German intrigue, with Sir Roger as the guiding genius, were apparent.'

The 24 April entry in the monarch's personal diary records Hall's visit but does not mention diaries. Only days later, however, Hall was showing incriminating papers to journalists. Later in May the king was given typescripts—most think that Attorney General Smith was responsible—which he retained and showed to Bishop Henson in July.

Described by his *admirers* as ' ... the coldest-hearted proposition that ever was—he'd eat a man's heart and hand it back to him' (Edward Bell, US attaché) and as ruthless and cunning, Hall was a master of deception and a maverick. His was undoubtedly the brain guiding the diary plot.

In 1926 Hall began to write his autobiography; having completed some 25 chapters by 1932, he was refused permission to publish by the Admiralty, and it is claimed rather improbably that some sixteen chapters were destroyed. Today only seven chapters remain in the Churchill Archives at Cambridge, deposited there by Hall's son Richard in 1974. Chapter 5 is extant and deals with the *Sayonara* cruise in December 1914. There is no mention of the diaries in that chapter (or in the other surviving chapters 1, 2, 3, 6, 7 or 25). It is unthinkable that Hall omitted to mention the diaries in one of the missing chapters, but whatever he wrote about them he was prevented from publishing. That there was something that had to be concealed in 1933 does not entail that it must be concealed today, some 84 years later. That it was 'destroyed' suggests that it referred to facts and circumstances which compromise the alleged authenticity of the TNA diaries. Hall's book contained information that is still so sensitive that it is not published in the 2017 first edition of his autobiography from the History Press (*A clear case of genius: room 40's code-breaking pioneer*). This unpublished material, if not destroyed, would therefore be among the still-classified Casement files. It cannot be excluded that Hall's 'destroyed' chapters were the source seen in 1959 by Donald McLachlan that allowed him to confirm Hall's finding of the trunks in 1914/15.

Something that is unthinkable can be made thinkable by unlocking the mystery. Two keys unlock the 'unthinkable' and make it thinkable. Disposal of the alleged discovery of diaries in 1916 is the first key that opens the puzzle. Disposal of the *presumed* existence of the bound-volume diaries in 1916 is the second key.

The unthinkable turns out to be the impossible. It was Casement's friend and supporter Conan Doyle who wrote in *The Sign of Four*, '… when you have eliminated the impossible, whatever remains, *however improbable*, must be the truth'. Thinking the unthinkable leads inexorably to the conclusion that no incriminating diaries were ever found and that the Black Diaries were fabricated after Casement's execution.

9

Manufactured evidence

The Millar entries in the 1910 Black Diary have attracted much attention from Casement's biographers and have been cited as irrefutable evidence of the diary's authenticity. In brief, the entries for late May 1910 relate an ongoing affair between Casement and someone called Millar. Corroboration of the Millar relationship appeared possible because the entries allege a continuing liaison on 'home ground' and on specific dates rather than a casual encounter; moreover, the typescript ledger for June 1911 alleges that Casement paid a large sum to gift a motorcycle to Millar. Although the diary entries are quite explicit, they reveal no personal details about Millar.

Rather than being evidence of authenticity, the following scrutiny demonstrates how the Millar evidence was manufactured early in 1915 and then secretly 'verified' in 1916, and thereafter the purported verification was locked in official silence for another 82 years, almost *40 years longer* than the Black Diaries. Only in 1995 was Millar's identity revealed and only in 1998 were details of the motorcycle revealed. That manufactured evidence was routine practice is verified by the report proposed to British Intelligence by an unnamed agent in Germany dated 8.8.15 cited in Chapter 11, 'Anatomy of a lie'.

That Millar was a real person is undisputed; he was born in Larne in 1890 and died in Dublin in 1956. That he knew Casement is also undisputed, although there is no evidence outside the diary and ledger that he knew Casement in 1910 or 1911. The external evidence for his acquaintance with Casement consists of a letter that he wrote to Casement in November 1913; this letter is now in the National Library of Ireland.[1] This external evidence is, significantly, not mentioned by Major Frank Hall of Military Intelligence in his secret letter to the cabinet legal adviser Ernley Blackwell, dated 31 July 1916, which 'confirmed' the identification of Millar as J.M. Gordon, a bank employee resident in Belfast. The text of the 1913 letter is entirely innocuous (see Appendix) and refers to Millar's purchase of two watercolours on Casement's behalf at a Belfast gallery exhibition of paintings by his friend Ada MacNeill. That the original letter is now in the National Library of Ireland indicates that it was deposited there by Gertrude Parry as part of her 1950 donation of Casement papers. That it was in her possession indicates that she received it from Gavan Duffy in 1916 after the execution, when Basil Thomson sent Casement's possessions to him; '… when we had returned everything *except a diary and a cash book* to his solicitors, they wrote to complain that some of his property had been detained'.[2] That it was in Thomson's possession indicates that it was found in one of Casement's trunks in police custody from early 1915.

It was Frank Hall's responsibility to report on all of Casement's known contacts in Ireland. He began his investigations in early November 1914, within days of Casement's arrival in Berlin. It will be demonstrated here that Hall used the 1913 letter and not, as he claimed, the ledger entries for the identification of Millar. Phase 1 of Hall's operation began with the finding of the Millar letter in Casement's trunks early in 1915. Phase 2 led quickly to the identification of J.M. Gordon in Belfast and his motorcycle. Phase 3 followed with Hall's discovery from the registers held by Essex County Council that Cyril Corbally of Bishop's Stortford was registered as a previous owner of the motorcycle in May 1910. Phase 4 comprised the manufacture of the liaison for the diary typescript and the linking of Casement and Corbally for the typescript ledger. Phase 5 came in 1916 after the police typescripts had been shown, when Hall wrote to Blackwell to 'verify' those entries by identifying the enigmatic Millar.

These are the 1911 ledger entries:

June 3—'Cyril Corbally and his motor bike for Millar. 25.0.0'
June 8—'Carriage of Motor Bike to dear Millar. 18/3.'

It is at once evident that these entries alone do not contain enough information to lead Hall to the motorcycle registration F3044 cited in his letter to Blackwell. The motorcycle itself had to be located in Belfast and that could not be done *without already knowing Millar's full name*, since J.M. Gordon alone used that machine. Therefore, *even if the ledger was an authentic document in Hall's possession*, it could not have led to the identification of Millar as J.M. Gordon; this was achieved via the 1913 letter and the art gallery. It would have been a routine matter to identify the gallery in Belfast that hosted the 1913 exhibition. An inspection of the gallery's sales register for the Ada MacNeill exhibition would reveal the full name and address of the purchaser of the two pictures named in Millar's letter to Casement. Normal police enquiries would thereafter establish Millar's age, his bank employment, his single status and that he owned a motorcycle. Upon identification of Millar, Hall would note the motorcycle's Essex registration number and obtain from Essex County Council the name of Corbally as a previous owner and details of the 3.5hp Triumph registered to him in 1910. Therefore Hall's claim in his letter that Millar was identified through the motorcycle is false; only when Millar had been identified from the 1913 letter was the motorcycle identified.

Hall would not have missed the fact that Millar is a middle name and not the surname. Millar would at once be cleared of any suspicion of subversive sympathies, especially since he was a signatory of the Ulster Covenant in 1912 against Home Rule. Hall would not miss the fact that he now had irrefutable evidence that Casement was on friendly terms with a young single man in Belfast in 1913 who nonetheless appeared to have no political ground in common with him; this would naturally lead him to ponder the nature of the relationship between the 48-year-old Sir Roger (in 1913) and the unknown 23-year-old bank clerk. In November 1914 Hall had written with reference to the allegation in Findlay's 'memo': 'I am awaiting further information on this point, and also as to his habits (natural & un-natural!)'. This clearly indicates the direction of his enquiries and of his thinking.[3] An intelligence officer's natural suspicion and Hall's clear conviction of Casement's 'un-natural' habits would dispose him to perceive this unexplained relationship with young Millar as being exactly what he was hoping to find. The absence of evidence concerning the nature of the relationship could be overcome by the manufacture of suitable evidence, a process already under way with the invention of the diary narratives for the typescripts.

The advantage of framing Millar as a Casement partner was that Hall *and only Hall* could identify him as a living person with a verifiable Belfast address and occupation, but, most importantly, Millar could not be identified from the diary entries. From the 1913 letter Hall could not know that Millar was not a surname but only a middle name. Only when Gordon was identified would Hall understand this, and that identification could not be made from a middle name only. Once identified, Hall would note that Gordon's use of his middle name offered a degree of anonymity and therefore security. Gordon would not be identifiable in the diary or ledger from the name Millar. The framing of Millar (and therefore of Casement) was thus achieved without revealing his full identity as J.M. Gordon. The identification of J.M. Gordon could only be made via the 1913 letter that unambiguously reported his transaction in a Belfast art gallery.

Vehicle registration documents at Essex County Council record the date of transfer of the motorcycle to J.M. Gordon as 10 July 1911.[4] This is the date given to the Essex motor registry office by the person who transferred ownership of the motorcycle to Millar. There is no evidence that Corbally sold the vehicle to Millar. Indeed, extensive research has not determined how Millar located the machine for sale or the identity of the vendor. Most probably the unknown vendor advertised in one of the popular motorcycle magazines of the period. There are no private adverts bearing Corbally's name for such a motorcycle in those publications in the period April to early July, although there are several from motor traders in that period.[5] Motor traders do not advertise the name of the previous owner because the vehicle *when advertised* belongs to the trader. If Millar's motorcycle was sold by a trader, Corbally's name would not appear and Millar would not see his name until after the transaction was completed, when he would receive the vehicle logbook listing Corbally's name and address. At a date soon after 10 July, Millar received the motorcycle in Belfast and only then wrote his own full name and address into the logbook and posted it to Essex for registration as required by law; 10 July defines the day on which the motorcycle left the unknown vendor's care and responsibility.

The 8 June ledger entry shows a specific sum of 18/3 allegedly paid for transport of the machine to Belfast. This is approximately £102 sterling today and it indicates that *whoever* wrote that figure in the typescript ledger knew that there was a considerable distance between the vendor and Millar. Since Corbally's address in the Essex register is the Bishop's Stortford golf club, where he was secretary from 1910 (when he acquired the motorcycle), it can be inferred that the machine was dispatched to Millar from a location within Corbally's area, including London. The machine did not leave the unknown vendor until 10 July, however, which leaves an unexplained delay of a full month after the alleged payment in June.

Having served as the means of identifying Millar, the innocuous letter of 1913 was of no further interest to Hall and would have been returned to Casement's possessions in Thomson's custody. J.M. Gordon died in 1956 and thus never knew that his middle name had been secretly used in the campaign against Casement. Nor would anyone else until 1995. That apparently mysterious identity as Millar in the 1910 typescript diary and ledger would enjoy a fake but secret verification one day before Casement's hanging, precisely timed for the last cabinet meeting and intended to overcome hesitancy about the political expediency of an execution. The false verification passed to Blackwell in 1916 was known to some of Casement's biographers from a brief unsigned summary accompanying Hall's letter, but his original letter remained secret until 1998. The text of Hall's letter cites the five dates of the typescript entries concerning Millar but, significantly, *it does not cite the precise date* of the transfer of the motorcycle.

> 'Dear Sir Ernley, re Casement's diary: I have ascertained that the individual referred to as "dear Millar" in the entries under date May 28th/29th 1910, May 13th/14th & June 3rd 1911 is a young man named JOSEPH MILLAR GORDON aged 26, a clerk in the Donegall Sq. Branch of the Belfast Bank who resides with his mother at CARNSTROAN—Myrtlefield Park Belfast. We traced him through the Motor Cycle which Casement gave him. (One Cyril Corbally registered a TRIUMPH Motor Cycle F3044 in 1910 and in 1911 the number was transferred to J.M. Gordon.) Gordon has not been interviewed but if it was considered advisable to approach him on the subject we could easily arrange to have it done discreetly. Yours very truly, Frank Hall' (TNA HO/144/1637/139).

Hall was a native of Warrenpoint, Co. Down, a former secretary of the UVF and a key conspirator in the successful secret gunrunning operation to arm loyalists in 1914. The 1910 entries concerning Millar show a familiarity both with idiomatic speech and with locations in Northern

Ireland, which Hall certainly possessed. Two of the most disputed diary entries, those of 28–29 May, refer to alleged episodes in his native Warrenpoint, a fact which perhaps amused Hall, as if he wished to leave some evidence of authorship. Hall's interest in the Casement matter was inevitably personal and not confined to intelligence-gathering; he was also present at the 1916 Scotland Yard interrogation.

Thus the Millar story in the typescript diary and ledger had the unique virtue of being tailor-made for 'authentication' by means of verified facts about J.M. Gordon and his motorcycle. Outside the typescript diary and ledger, however, there is no evidence that Casement knew Millar in 1910 or 1911 and no evidence that such a substantial gift was ever made. Millar's innocuous 1913 letter indicates that Casement knew Millar's mother and that Casement's request to acquire the paintings discreetly was addressed to the mother and not to the son. This in turn suggests that Millar's mother might have been a friend or acquaintance of Casement's friend Ada MacNeill, someone who understood the delicacy of Casement's relations with MacNeill.[6] In short, Casement knew the Gordon family, mother and son, through Ada MacNeill.

The second sentence in Hall's letter contains eleven words, of which only the first three are true. '*We traced him* through the Motor Cycle // which Casement gave him.' While both clauses are false, the first would have been sufficient, although partly true and partly false, but Hall added the second clause to insinuate his silent meaning, which was that the ledger entries were true. Yet Hall did not witness Casement making any payment and did not witness Casement writing the ledger entries. Nor did Hall trace Gordon through the motorcycle, as has been demonstrated. Therefore Hall deceived Blackwell, who in turn misled the cabinet. That Hall felt it necessary to deceive Blackwell in August 1916 indicates that his letter was the outcome of a plan that he had initiated at an earlier time, a plan to which he was fully committed. His 1916 letter was the fulfilment of his decision in early 1915 to frame Millar.

Two further important considerations reveal the Millar story to be manufactured evidence. Hall had one simple option for a definitive verification of the ledger entries; he did not interview Millar in Belfast for obvious reasons, but he could easily have obtained confirmation of the alleged payment from Corbally himself in nearby Bishop's Stortford. It can be excluded that the omission of this obvious step was an oversight by a senior intelligence officer. In addition, Hall had access to Casement's bank account, where evidence of such a substantial payment would be recorded, but he did not produce bank evidence of the alleged payment.[7] Such evidence would also have been definitive.

To conceal one thing, two things must be concealed. First, the primary item itself must be concealed; second, that anything has been concealed must also be concealed—the cover-up must be covered up. The primary item was the 1913 letter and the second phase was the replacement of the concealed letter by the ledger entries. By concealing the 1913 letter as the true source of Millar's identification, however, Hall betrayed his intent to deceive Blackwell and the cabinet. The deception was necessary because it privileged the ledger as the only possible source of the verified fact of Millar's real existence. Since truth cannot be derived from falsity, Hall attributed the illusion of truth to the typescript ledger, but his concealment of the true source is Hall's inadvertent acknowledgement that Corbally's name in the ledger plays a deceptive role.

The Millar story is a textbook set piece of manufactured evidence, with the false and the true poised in an illusory equilibrium. The illusion derives from failure to perceive that the verified fact does not entail what it appears to entail. Millar's ownership of the motorcycle, verified by the Essex document, does not entail that any gift was made; it merely shows that Millar owned a specific motorcycle. Any determination about this alleged gift with unknown motivation must exclude the typescript ledger as evidence, because it is the only document alleging that a gift was made and the authenticity of the ledger is questioned. In short, a disputed document cannot corroborate an undetermined circumstance. Without the questioned ledger, nothing testifies to a gift ever having been made. The suppression and disposal of the Millar letter of 1913 indicates the necessary concealment of the crucial document that led Hall to Gordon's identification, which inspired the false Millar story.

In conclusion, the following balance sheet presents the facts discovered in the above analysis of the Millar evidence.

In favour of authenticity:
- Handwriting resemblance and Hall's word in his 1916 letter.

Against authenticity:

- No external evidence to support the transaction reported in the ledger.
- No confirmation from Corbally of receipt of money from Casement.
- No confirmation of payment from Casement's bank accounts in the possession of British Intelligence.
- Evidence of Hall's hostile motivation.
- Hall's opportunity to manufacture evidence over many months.
- Hall's concealment of how he identified Millar.
- Unexplained delay of motorcycle transfer after alleged payment on 3 June until 10 July.
- Hall's letter kept secret until 1998.

A balance sheet reports verified facts, not opinions or conjectures. The impartial reader is invited to assess the above facts and to decide whether the typescript ledger entries are true or false. The impartial reader should bear in mind the Inglis dictum of 1973: '... and if one was forged, all of them were ...'.

Notes

[1] There are also two postcards from Millar to Casement, dated early September 1913, in the Maloney Papers in NYPL. Both are innocuous. Hall would not have seen these, since they probably arrived in the US with Casement on his visit in July 1914.

[2] Article by Basil Thomson published in *English Life* (March 1925).

[3] TNA KV-2-6.

[4] The Essex Records Office holds the original registration of the 1908 Triumph motorcycle F3044. Hall omits any reference to this document.

[5] The largest market for new and used motorcycles within easy reach of Corbally at the time was London. The most widely circulated publications carrying weekly advertisements were *The Motor Cycle* and *Motor Cycling*; the very popular *Exchange & Mart* also carried weekly motorcycle adverts. These periodicals are available in the British Library under LOU.LD80 and LOU.LD81.

[6] Ada MacNeill had strong romantic feelings for Casement, which were not reciprocated.

[7] The KV files in TNA reveal the extent of Hall's probes into Casement's bank accounts in London and Dublin. There is no trace of any payment to either Millar or Corbally among those files.

Appendix: Text of 1913 Millar letter

'*My dear Sir Roger,*

I went to the exhibition about the pictures and have secured a pair by Miss MacNeill which I think will please you. There were none of hers above £2=2=0 in price, most of them being small ones from 10/6 up to £1.1.0, but there was this pair and another pair each picture being £2.2.0 so by taking two I was able to approximate to the amount you mentioned. The titles of the two pictures are "Evening on the Moor" and "A Grey Day in the Glen", both extremely nice & the tone very well done, probably the dull effect in each case suggested by the titles. They are both Irish scenes and I shall find out the exact places and let you know. The man in the place was not sure of that but can find out.

The other two pictures were "White Lines on a Sullen Sea"—an impression of a rough bit of sea with a rocky shore & the waves coming in with white crests—and some coast scene in India. They told me Miss MacNeill had been in India some little time ago and painted this while there. I chose the other pair for two reasons: first the scenes are Irish and I know you would like that best & second the frames and mount are much nicer, being gilt & well finished whereas the others are stained wood of some kind and rather coarse.

The pictures must remain in the Exhibition till 15 Dec. as if everyone took away his picture as he bought it towards the end there wouldn't be any exhibition! But I suppose you are not in any particular hurry for them & you can just let me know where you want them sent to & I'll look after them you may be sure. It's a jolly nice show, quite small you know, but some very nice little pieces of work. There are one or two little Egyptian scenes, I forget by whom at the moment, one of a bridge of boats, which is very nice. There are also some bas reliefs or mouldings apparently of some kind of clay. There are an astonishing number of works sold already, a red star on each one sold, & you may be surprised at the number of red stars.

Mother was unfortunately not able to go with me as some friends arrived unexpectedly and prevented her, but I told her all about it &

she concurs with what I have done. Excuse the writing but I am doing this down town. With every kind thought & hoping this will please you. Of course I did not give your name, but my own.

Ever yrs, affectionately
Millar.'

Part 3—Pathology of deceit

10

The Casement secret

'A wise man proportions his belief to the evidence' (David Hume).[1]

Premiss: *There is no record of the bound-volume diaries now held in the UK National Archives being shown to anyone in 1916. CID chief Basil Thomson stated that he found one diary only and a cash ledger.*[2]

The passing of what has been criticised as 'conservative Catholic Ireland' and the arrival of the digital era with the 'Celtic Tiger' and now the Facebook generation coincided with the emergence of an entire culture of 'Casement the homosexual martyr', which is ultimately based upon the unproven authenticity of the diaries. Since no scientific or other credible proof has been found for authenticity, it is clear that socio-cultural factors have played a major role in the general acceptance of the authenticity of the diaries. And among these factors are widespread and radical changes in attitudes to sexuality.

The number of people who have studied the Casement story *in depth and impartially* is probably less than 50, and their judgements on authenticity are probably equally balanced each way. A much larger number have read at least some of the books and have seen the TV documentaries and the many press reports. This larger number has been tutored by a small number of authors and journalists to reach a rather superficial consensus. Nonetheless, certain basic facts remain: there is no 'hard science' proof that Casement wrote the diaries; there is no witness to Casement's authorship; there is no evidence that the National Archives diaries were shown in 1916; there is no certain provenance for the diaries held in TNA.[3]

This latter fact is of fundamental importance. It is axiomatic in law and in common sense that the provenance of incriminating evidence must be above doubt. The crucial evidence cannot be conjured out of a hat at a convenient moment. No prosecutor would enter court without incontrovertible proof of the provenance of his incriminating evidence. The principle in law is *ei incumbit probatio qui dicit, non qui negat*, often translated as 'innocent until proven guilty' but better understood as meaning that the onus of proof rests on the accuser, not on the defence. It is therefore for those who claim authenticity to prove beyond doubt the provenance of the diaries. This has not been done in 100 years. The authors of the principal studies of Casement—Reid, Inglis, Sawyer and Ó Síocháin—have not provided proof of provenance and have preferred not to dwell on this delicate anomaly whilst acknowledging its existence.

There are today no less than six versions of provenance, none of which agrees with the others. Four of these conflicting versions have a single source—CID chief Basil Thomson. The other two versions are contained in official documents held by TNA: the interrogation transcript and the police list of the alleged contents of Casement's trunks. From these six versions it is *impossible* to ascertain whether diaries were found, when diaries were found or whether the diaries found are the NA diaries. It is possible to ascertain that trunks were found but not how or when. None of the six versions answers the most basic questions convincingly. Collectively, the six versions confirm only the existence of trunks in police custody.

Whispers, rumours, secrets
The fatal error is one of conflation: 'the diaries were shown to …' is simply false; 'typescript pages were shown to …' is true.

In June 1916, before Casement's trial, rumours were circulating of a secret diary with unspeakable content. His solicitors, Duffy and Doyle, attempted to trace the source and to see the typed pages that had caused the rumours. They spoke to officials and journalists but none admitted ever seeing the typed papers and no material trace of them could be found. It looked like a conspiracy to defame, but the conspirators were invisible. Just as Duffy and Doyle failed ever to set eyes on the mysterious papers, others who had seen those typed pages failed to set eyes on the secret diary. Of the many journalists, diplomats, editors, officials and influential figures of the day who had indeed seen the typed pages, none ever recorded seeing the diaries now held in TNA. Not even King George V was shown the diary; he too had to be content with the alleged typed copies.[4] Someone was keeping tight control over an operation which was obviously a defamatory campaign based on whispering, innuendo and insinuation. It was, in short, a masterpiece of black propaganda. Secrecy is 'an instrument of conspiracy',[5] but what was being kept secret?

One hundred years have passed since those days; many books have been written and read, much research carried out, many conferences held and many once-secret documents revealed. An information revolution has taken place, but that century-old secret remains intact.

Six versions of provenance

> 'The conscious and intelligent manipulation of the … opinions of the masses is an important element in democratic society. Those who manipulate this unseen mechanism … constitute an invisible government which is the true ruling power. … We are governed, our minds are molded … largely by men we have never heard of … who understand the mental processes … of the masses' (Edward Bernays).[6]

- Version 1—published in *The Times* (21 November 1921) by Basil Thomson.
- Version 2—published in *Queer people* (1922) by Basil Thomson.
- Version 3—published in *English Life* (March 1925) by Basil Thomson.
- Version 4—published in *The scene changes* (1939) by Basil Thomson.
- Version 5—interrogation transcript HO 144/1636 Ref. 20261; incomplete.
- Version 6—MEPO 2/10672, official but incomplete list of the contents of the trunks.

Clearly, as head of CID and as Casement's principal interrogator, Thomson is a key figure in the creation of the conflicting versions. Versions 1–4 were published after his forced resignation in November 1921. The reasons for his resignation are often given as a dispute with Lloyd George; on 4 March 1921 Home Secretary Edward Shortt admitted to the House of Commons that government officials had forged copies of *Pravda*. Thomson's Scotland Yard department was believed to be involved.

The six versions make sixteen distinct statements and yield some 56 instances of contradiction from the four basic contradictions, which are (i) the date of police possession of the trunks, (ii) how the trunks came into the possession of the police, (iii) the request for keys and (iv) the finding of the diary/diaries.

The conflict between the versions involves every aspect of the alleged discovery of the diary or diaries, including when, how and where. Two versions give 25 April as the date when the police took possession of the trunks. Four versions give alternative dates, ranging from late 1914 to 23 April 1916. Version 6 states that the trunks were delivered to Scotland Yard by a former landlord, whereas Version 2 states that the police seized the trunks from Casement's former lodgings in Ebury Street. One version records events that do not appear in the transcript. Version 6 is dated a full three months after the alleged delivery on 25 April. The transcript contradicts three versions concerning alleged requests for keys to the trunks. It also contradicts four versions concerning both dates and diaries. Most importantly, Thomson's four versions record the alleged finding of *one diary only*—that of 1903.

Since four of the versions come from the pen of Thomson himself, these must be scrutinised. That there are four conflicting versions of the *timing* of possession of the trunks—and therefore, presumably, possession of the diary or diaries—would strongly indicate to an impartial observer that important facts are being withheld and concealed. The most important fact relates not to *how* the trunks were found and brought into police custody but *when* this happened. Thomson offers three versions of this event: 'when we first had evidence of Casement's treachery' (late 1914); 'some months earlier' (1915–16); and the first interrogation (23 April 1916). A fourth version, cited in official records of the interrogation and the list of contents of the trunks, gives the date as the last interrogation (25 April).

Thomson's inconsistency regards the possession of the trunks, not what he claimed to have found in the trunks. In this he is strangely consistent: he found only one diary, although the official police list, dated three months later, records three diaries found in Trunk No. 1. In all four of Thomson's versions he claims to have found one diary and at no time ever mentions three diaries. And yet there are three diaries in TNA today.

What can explain Thomson's repeated references to the single 1903 diary and the absence of any reference to the 1910 and 1911 diaries *in any form*? In 1922 Thomson possessed the 1910 typescript but he never referred to this version in writing at any time. To answer this question we can turn to the principal authors on Casement: Inglis, Reid, Sawyer and Ó Síocháin.[7]

Inglis, perhaps the most widely read Casement author, completely ignores Thomson's versions. So does MacColl. Sawyer refers to the question but dismisses it as errors by a careless author. Reid refers to the question but carefully edits his quotations from Thomson's versions in order to conceal the gravity of the contradictions. None of these authors had access to MEPO 2/10672, released in 2001. Ó Síocháin had access to MEPO 2/10672 and to more sources than any earlier author; he mentions Thomson's versions but appears to agree with Sawyer.

That five of the principal Casement authors chose to avoid the question of provenance requires explanation. The most salient point ignored or overlooked by all these authors is, strangely, the only consistent aspect of Thomson's versions: that Thomson records the alleged finding of *only one diary* in the trunks, that for 1903. Nowhere does he mention the 1910 or 1911 diaries. That this single aspect of one diary is consistent in Thomson's versions of provenance lends it an aura of credibility that is entirely dependent on the non-discovery of the other two diaries listed in MEPO 2/10672 as being in the same trunk. More precisely, it is not credible that Thomson found three diaries but chose to state *four times* that he had found only one. To this must be added that part of Thomson's 1925 statement suppressed by author B.L. Reid: 'He must have remembered afterwards that there was something more than clothes in the trunks, for when we had returned everything *except a diary and a cash book* to his solicitors, they wrote to complain that some of his property had been detained'. If we are to believe that the 1910 and 1911 diaries had also been found in the trunk, we must also believe that they had not been read and we must believe that they were duly sent to Casement's solicitors after the list was dated on 28 July. This in turn constrains us to believe that Gavan Duffy later returned these incriminating diaries to the Metropolitan Police, where they allegedly remained until 1925, after which they passed to the Home Office until 1959. No impartial and intelligent person would believe this four-part sequence. No impartial and intelligent person would believe any part of this absurd sequence. Either *only one diary* was found or none were found in the trunk.

It is highly improbable that *all aspects* of Thomson's four versions are false. Two aspects have a higher veridical probability: (a) that the trunks were in police possession some months before the arrest, and (b) that a 1903 diary (and no other) was found in one of the trunks. That these aspects are asserted six times in the four versions favours the probability that they are true but does not guarantee their veracity. If they are true, the other aspects are false, as are the interrogation transcript and MEPO 2/10672.

Since both the interrogation transcript and the police list of contents assert 25 April as the date of possession of the trunks, this deserves some scrutiny. The transcript reveals the following anomaly.

The interrogation of 25 April contains 1,719 spoken words, which occupy from 8.6 to 17.2 minutes depending on rate of speech. An average estimate would calculate 12.9 minutes as the duration of the interrogation. There are two references only to trunks, both by Thomson; the first occurs after 5.37 minutes and the second after 12.37 minutes, leaving only seven minutes between them. Here are the verbatim references to the trunks:

Reference 1
'A.C.C.: Have you got some trunks at 50 Ebury Street? I propose having them down and examined.
Sir R.C.: There's nothing in them.'

Reference 2
'A.C.C.: Sir Roger, your trunks are here but there are no keys.
Sir R.C.: Break them open.'

These 34 words are the only reference to trunks in the transcript and there are no references to diaries. Two aspects of these references are cause for grave suspicion.

Aspect 1: The first reference demonstrates that there are trunks at Ebury Street belonging to Casement and which Thomson intends to obtain for examination. The second reference demonstrates that the trunks are now in Scotland Yard, locked and without keys, and that Casement has given permission to force them open. The anomaly is that only seven minutes have passed between the first reference and the second, which means that the trunks have been located, seized and brought to Scotland Yard within seven minutes. This is an impossibility.

Aspect 2: The first reference also indicates that Thomson is aware of the existence and location of the trunks *before* he purportedly orders their seizure. That he specifies 'trunks' rather than possessions or property indicates either that he has knowledge of the trunks from an earlier police visit or that he has already taken possession of the trunks from an earlier police seizure. In both cases there is obvious knowledge of the trunks that can only have come from an earlier police visit.

It is verified both by the transcript itself and by Thomson later that the shorthand writer was dismissed at some point or points during the three-day interrogation. The transcript is therefore incomplete and the last interrogation is headed 'excerpt'.[8] The question-and-answer dialogue in that interrogation appears logically intact, however, so that both references to trunks seem out of place and irrelevant to the discussion.

The false elements of Thomson's versions might be those concerning the date and modality of the finding of the trunks. It is highly improbable, however, that after finding three incriminating diaries Thomson would forget or deny what he had found and later falsely record *four times* (1921, 1922, 1925, 1939) that he had found only one diary. The probability of denial can be eliminated, since no reasonable motivation can be adduced. The probability of forgetting such a find can be regarded as utterly remote. And if Thomson read one diary, as claimed, he certainly did not leave the other two unread, any more than he read them and sent them to Gavan Duffy.

In June 1930 Home Secretary J.R. Clynes referred to Thomson's published statements about the alleged finding of the diary as being unauthorised.[9] This was certainly true, since Thomson was no longer CID chief and had left the Metropolitan Police in late 1921. The comment tends to suggest that Thomson's writings were unreliable because unauthorised by the government. In turn, this suggests that government statements are reliable by virtue of being issued by the government. This equation of integrity with government will convince very few inside or outside government.

A reasonable explanation for the avoidance by the principal Casement authors of the provenance/discovery anomaly must take account of the possible answers that arise from openly confronting those questions. A reasonable explanation would be one which conforms to common sense and is supported by verified facts and which extinguishes further doubt on the matter. That five authors do not offer a satisfactory explanation indicates either that they considered this to be of little importance or that they were unable to construct such an explanation based on facts and common sense without compromising their shared thesis that the TsNA diaries are authentic. Only one author makes an attempt; it can speak for itself:

> 'Later the trail was to be both revealed and confused by Thomson's contradictory statements about how this material came into his hands. The reason is almost too simple to be grasped; he was a prolific author, and his writings abound with errors of detail' (Sawyer 1984, 141).

> 'What then of Sir Basil Thomson's contradictory accounts of how he came by the diaries? Anyone familiar with the reminiscences of senior civil servants and politicians will not be surprised to find numerous errors in their utterances. *Had Thomson had much to hide during this part of his life, he would have taken great care to be consistent in his recollections;* as it was, he wrote too much and took too little care' (Sawyer 1997, 25 [emphasis added]).

'Errors of detail' owing to 'too little care' are proposed as an explanation for the former chief of the CID forgetting that he had found three incriminating diaries by the world-famous Sir Roger Casement. Not only did Thomson forget this crucial detail in 1921 but he also continued to forget it over the following eighteen years. If this is convincing, then the term requires generous redefinition. The reason given by Sawyer is indeed too simple to be grasped or *believed* by any impartial person. Thomson's 'amnesia' affected not only the number of diaries allegedly found but also when they were found and how he came to possess the trunks. Having been on the famous renegade's trail for some eighteen months, having been advised months before Casement's capture by his informer Maundy

Gregory that it would be useful to find such diaries and having triumphed in April 1916, he thereafter becomes confused and cannot quite recall how it all happened. According to Sawyer, the fact that Thomson's recollections are inconsistent somehow attests to his integrity—he has nothing to hide. Therefore, if Thomson is hiding nothing, he is telling the truth that he found only one diary. And he tells that truth four times, consistently. This is further supported by his attestation that *only one diary* was retained when the property was sent to solicitor Duffy. PRO HO 144/1637/311643/178 refers to the property returned—no diaries were returned.

Thomson's alleged amnesia—allowing him to forget that he had discovered three incriminating diaries rather than one—is equivalent to forgetting that three burglars were arrested rather than only one. These alleged 'errors of detail' require deeper scrutiny in order to reveal what they conceal. Invariably and of necessity every cover-up requires that truth be mixed with falsehood, because this confounds the investigation more effectively than a cover-up composed entirely of lies. On this common-sense basis, Thomson's versions should contain some truth, which can be discovered by evaluating the motives for the falsehoods. All aspects of Thomson's four published accounts are potentially false. Here are the aspects of his versions:

- Regarding the date of possession of the trunks: any time between late 1914 and 23 April 1916.
- Regarding how the trunks were possessed: delivered by Germain or seized by police.
- Regarding when the trunks were opened: first interrogation (23 April) or later.
- Regarding the number of diaries found: one 1903 diary.

The first three relate to the trunks. The fourth relates to a diary. This last is the more important because it evokes the weakest motive for falsehood. The first two contain falsehood. The last two might contain truth. The first three versions offer many more possibilities for confusion and falsehood. More possibilities of falsehood imply more motives for concealment of the truth. Less possibility of falsehood implies fewer motives for concealment.

It follows that the first three above should contain more falsehoods than the fourth, which remains unchanged, whereas each aspect of the first three changes in each published version. The first three are inconsistent and the fourth is consistent. Inconsistency, by its nature, is an indicator of concealment. Inconsistency is as distinct from error as the intentional is distinct from the unintentional. On this basis, Thomson's intentional concealment would concern when the trunks were found and opened. The motive for this concealment is directly connected to *when* the alleged finding of one or three diaries took place. From this concealment derives the story of locked trunks and no keys, as reported both by Thomson and by the incomplete interrogation transcript. Locked trunks and no keys are essential to the timing of the alleged finding of one or three diaries. The timing is crucial, because less time between the finding and the first showing of the typescript pages enhances the probability that the typed pages are authentic copies. Conversely, a greater span of time between finding and showing decreases that probability. In plain terms, a three-month delay might be sufficient for the invention of the narrative in the alleged typed copies, whereas a two-week period is almost certainly insufficient. This equation provides the motivation for the story of locked trunks and no keys and, in turn, the *raison d'être* of the story is to counteract the earlier finding of the trunks—months before Casement's arrest. The story of the locked trunks has *no function* unless the trunks were already in police possession months before the arrest. For this reason the story is *awkwardly inserted* into the last page of the incomplete interrogation transcript—and inserted some time *after* the last interrogation, when the shorthand record was decoded into plain English. That the story appears in the transcript does not prove that it appeared in the original shorthand record.

With regard to one or three diaries, both assertions can be false but only one can be true. It is necessary, therefore, to adduce a credible motive for falsehood by Thomson. More precisely, if his published claim from 1921 onwards of finding only one diary was false it was nonetheless motivated. Lies are intended to conceal facts from others. The version that Thomson might have been tempted to relate in 1921 was that he had found three diaries when, in truth, he had found none or only one. A motive must be adduced for his not relating—ever—that he had found three diaries. Even if untrue, it would have been a lie that no one would have refuted in 1921 or later. That he was not so tempted indicates that the option was not available to him rather than his choice being a matter of integrity. If the option of a three-diary version was not available to him in 1921 and later, it entails that he did not know of three bound-volume diaries. He knew at most of one bound-volume diary only. If he did not know of three bound-volume diaries in 1921, he did not know of them in 1916.[10] To this must be added, yet again, that there is no record of anyone being shown three bound-volume diaries in 1916.

The number of people who saw the alleged copy typescripts in 1916 can only be guessed but probably amounted to more than 30, including journalists, civil servants, ambassadors, cabinet ministers, religious, political and legal figures. It is not credible that none of these people noted the absence of the bound-volume diaries as conclusive evidence, and therefore it is highly probable that some of them were not fully convinced by the alleged copies alone. In July and later, in order to counterbalance this lack of conviction, several attempts at corroboration were provided.[11] Principally these were a number of 'affidavits' sworn at the British legation in Christiania (Oslo) by seven or eight Norwegians before British Vice-Consul Henry Charles Dick between 11 and 21 July.[12] A second attempt was made by consulting two psychiatrists, who examined the typed pages dated 1911 and gave their opinions on 10 July. A third attempt was a post-mortem anal probe by the prison medical officer, who declared certain proof of the signs of sodomy. Obviously it would have been simpler and more conclusive if the bound-volume diaries had been produced to convince the sceptics, but they were not produced. The corroboration attempts had no function other than to reinforce the case for authenticity of the *unseen* bound-volume diaries, rendering it 'unnecessary' for them to be seen.

The first viewing

'... after the trial of Sir Roger Casement I threatened to resign from the Cabinet unless this traitor was executed ... I gave them choice of Casement or myself. Nothing gave me greater delight than the execution of Casement' (F.E. Smith, Lord Birkenhead, attorney general, in the *Boston Post*, 14 January 1918).

In 1916 Stephen Gaselee was an FO official, one of those responsible for showing the alleged typed copies of the diary materials allegedly found in Casement's trunks. Among others, he showed them to Alfred Noyes, who was convinced without *ever* seeing any bound-volume diaries. Many years later Noyes realised how he had been manipulated by his colleagues.[13]

On 7 December 1921, one day after the signing of the Treaty, Gaselee wrote the following letter from the FO to Lt. Colonel Carter at New Scotland Yard:[14]

'Dear Carter,

We have seen with interest that there will shortly begin in the New York "Nation" what is said to be the hitherto unpublished manuscript of the personal diary of Sir Roger Casement. It is said to begin at the time of Casement's mission to Germany in 1914, but contains a retrospect of the period from 1904 to 1914.

This naturally should interest us a good deal, and we shall watch the instalments carefully. The object of this letter is to ask whether you still have in your possession the original diary about which we were in correspondence with your department at the end of July and the beginning of August 1916.

Considering the nature of the diary, I trust there will be no necessity to refer to it, but if this new publication contains anything outrageously untrue about Casement's activities in those years, it might be necessary to check it by that which was formerly in your possession.

Yours sincerely.'

There is a handwritten note from Carter at the top:

'Spoke to – Gaselee + told him I had made exhaustive enquiries + everything pointed to the Diary being here, but that it had probably been put away very carefully + it could not at present be traced. 12/12/21 (Note: C.I.D. are looking also)'

There are several things to note about this letter and its note of a *verbal* response: (a) it refers to a single diary, (b) which was purportedly held in New Scotland Yard from 1916 to 1921 (c) but after *exhaustive enquiries* (d) could not be traced. Note also that Gaselee does not identify the diary by year but that Carter knows which diary is referred to. Note, too, that Gaselee is seeking one diary and not three. Further, he is not seeking a typed version but the original.

The reason given for Gaselee's request is tenuous, if not false: the original diary is not needed in order to check details in the New York publication since a typed version would serve this purpose just as well, if not better. Further, it is unclear how the events of ten years could be cross-checked with the events in a single-year diary, especially if that diary relates to a year prior to the period 1904–14. Certainly all three diaries would enable him to check a longer period, but he does not ask for all three diaries. It follows either that Gaselee knows that the other two diaries are located elsewhere and he already has access to them or that he does not know of the existence of the other two diaries *as bound volumes*. Which diary is he seeking and for what purpose? The answer might lie in the following fact: two months after the date of this letter, on 6 February 1922, two bound-volume diaries were shown to Michael Collins in the House of Lords by 'arrangement' with Birkenhead, Casement's prosecutor.[15] From their description as 'common office diaries' it would seem that these were the 1910 and the 1911 diaries.[16] If Gaselee knew in December of their location in the Lords, it follows that he was seeking the 1903 diary at Scotland Yard. If in December he did not know of their existence, it still follows that he was seeking the 1903 diary. If the 1903 diary could not be found at Scotland Yard after 'exhaustive enquiries', then it seems highly improbable that Carter would have been able to trace the 1910 or the 1911 diary in the Metropolitan Police HQ had he been asked. That Gaselee did not ask for either the 1910 or the 1911 indicates that he either knew their true location or did not know of their existence. Officially, however, throughout this period after 1916, all three diaries were held at Scotland Yard until 1925. Nevertheless, obviously all three were not at Scotland Yard.

Carter's 'exhaustive enquiries' did not produce the 1910 or 1911 bound volumes either, nor does he even mention them. The previous correspondence of July/August 1916 referred to by Gaselee also concerned only the 1903 diary. If all three bound volumes existed in 1916, it is highly probable that they would have been kept together in a secure place. There is no reason to think that one diary was more important than the others, and no reason why they should be separated and kept in different places, but in 1921/22 they *were* in different places. Since there was no reason to separate them, it can be inferred that they were not separated because they were never together in the period 1916–22. This means that they were not found together in the same trunk on any date. Therefore the MEPO 2/10672 list is false. More than false, it is incomplete, fails to account for four trunks and is unsigned. These circumstances support the argument that Thomson never knew of the 1910 and 1911 bound volumes in 1916. Nor did he learn of them in the years following.[17]

That Gaselee required the original rather than an officially typed 'copy' links his request to Birkenhead's arrangement to show Collins the diary or diaries. It is therefore reasonable to deduce that Birkenhead instigated the request for the 1903 diary as part of his plan to manipulate Collins and, through him, the new Free State government. That he succeeded is clear not only from the later silence of that government on this topic but also from Collins's own remarks of 6 December 1921: 'I believe Birkenhead may have said an end to his political life. With him it has been my honour to work.'[18] That Collins found it an honour to work with Birkenhead is perplexing, because in 1916 Birkenhead was the most influential figure in the destruction of Casement and publicly boasted of his role.

Therefore *Collins was favoured over the monarch* with a viewing of two bound volumes. If the typescript pages shown to the king were not genuine copies of Casement diaries, it follows that the king was misled by a government conspiracy to deceive him. The only way in 1916 to verify the authenticity of the typescript pages was to examine the bound-volume diaries. There is no record that anyone did this. At any time, however, the king might have demanded to see the bound volumes, and his demand could not easily have been refused. Apprehension about this possibility provides a substantial part of the motivation for the fabrication of the bound-volume diaries now held in TNA.

Collins did not and could not have demanded to see the bound-volume diaries. The *offer* to see them came from Birkenhead at an opportune moment. Collins accepted and viewed two volumes but left no written comment. Six months later Collins was dead.

There is no record that the king ever demanded to see the bound-volume diaries. There is a record that Collins viewed the 1910 and 1911 diaries. That Collins left no written comment after the viewing means that he did not formally refute them. Equally he did not authenticate them. The absence of a Collins refutation conditioned the Free State government to shun the question of authenticity as of lower priority when crippled by a civil war, serious economic and administrative problems, and anxiety over partition and the Boundary Commission.

Why was Collins shown the diaries and not the monarch? Which of them was the greater danger to the conspiracy? The king could be trusted to act within an established constitutional tradition and was duty-bound to protect the reputation of his country and his government. Collins was an experienced conspirator with a network of spies and informers; he had contacts and sympathisers within the British establishment. He had evaded capture with a price on his head for at least two years. He had organised the destruction of the British intelligence apparatus in Ireland. In short, Collins was, even in 1922, potentially still a dangerous man. He represented to Birkenhead the greatest future danger to the conspiracy over the diaries, and that is why Birkenhead *offered* to Collins that which was not felt necessary to offer to the king. Birkenhead gambled on obtaining Collins's silence after seeing the diaries and he won. The bullets that killed Collins on 22 August 1922 removed the danger definitively.

A second viewing

The destruction of Casement was not completed at his bodily execution; the meaning of his destruction continued to resonate for decades after 1916. On 23 or 24 January 1925 a second viewing of the diaries took place.[19] Peter Singleton-Gates, a young and relatively unknown Fleet Street journalist, was allowed the same privilege as Michael Collins three years earlier. Again two diaries were shown but this time the location was probably Scotland Yard, since the proposal to show was made and fulfilled by Wyndam Childs, Thomson's successor at the CID. Singleton-Gates was in possession of alleged typescript copies of two diaries that had been given to him in 1922 by Thomson, and by 1925 he had prepared these for book publication. A day after the showing of the alleged originals, Birkenhead blocked publication by threatening publishers with prosecution under the Official Secrets Act. A week later the home of Singleton-Gates was searched for the typescript papers, which he had already concealed elsewhere. Singleton-Gates had to wait 34 years before he could publish his version of the 'Black Diaries' in Paris, an event that 'induced' the British government to transfer their diaries to the PRO and to allow very restricted access under controlled conditions.

The government's action in blocking publication[20] and attempting to confiscate the typed papers has a self-evident motive. Publication of the alleged copies was a threat to the long-term plan of concealment. Publication in 1925 would have led to questions in Britain and in Ireland concerning the bound-volume diaries, and to demands to see them. Having generously circulated the typed papers in 1916, the same authorities later determined that the bound-volume diaries would remain totally under their control.

A paradigm shift

A paradigm crisis occurs when anomalies in an established explanatory model can no longer be ignored as before and its credibility is threatened. A paradigm shift occurs when a new explanatory model is found which not only resolves the anomalies but also offers greater probative power.[21]

The dominant paradigm has been that the typescript papers were authentic copies of the diaries now in the National Archives. The thesis outlined here requires a paradigm shift: the bound-volume diaries are copies of the typescript papers.

Secrecy is the lifeblood of conspiracy. The many secrets around the Casement story have generated an atmosphere of conspiracy for 100 years. The authors who engineered consensus on the Casement narrative have, despite their efforts, signally failed to dispel this atmosphere. Their failure is due to their over-reliance on innuendo and insinuation so as to avoid answering the most basic questions.

That there was a plan to destroy Casement's reputation is undisputed even by those who believe that his execution was morally and legally justified. That the plan involved top-ranking security and government officials is not disputed. That the plan helped to ensure his execution is not disputed. That this plan was founded on truth is, however, disputed. The plan involved the covert showing of typed papers incriminating Casement, and it was orchestrated by agents of the British government. If these *papers* were proved false, then this plan was and remains a conspiracy, which is a criminal offence. These typed papers have never been proved to be authentic inside or outside any court of law.

The paradigm shift enables an impartial enquirer to engage with what appear to be valid questions but are in fact duplicitous rhetorical devices signalling a familiar defensive strategy to protect a paradigm in crisis—the false question framed to intimidate response. Ó Síocháin,[22] like Inglis *et al.*, cannot resist the resort to such a worn-out strategy. Here are his 'questions'.

(1) Is it credible that the British authorities would have begun forging such a corpus as early as 1914, when they first got an indication of Casement's homosexuality, in the absence of any indication of the likely progress of the war or of his subsequent movements?

Answer: Yes, it is entirely credible, but the forging of the bound-volume diaries took place *after* his execution. The invented narratives were prepared before his arrest and then typed for the vital smear campaign.

(2) Could they possibly have forged such elaborate documents in the short time between the date given for the confiscation of the trunks in 1916 and the circulation of diary material?

Answer: No, the bound-volume diaries were not forged in that short time. They were forged later and over a longer timespan.

(3) Is it credible that limited resources would have been allocated to such a complex enterprise at any of the times mentioned?

Answer: Yes, it is perfectly credible. Vast sums and intensive efforts were spent on all forms of propaganda throughout the war; these included highly skilled forgery in several languages.[23] Resources were not limited; Britain, with the largest empire in human history, was not a poor country. Casement's was a major showpiece state trial intended to demonstrate the *entire rationale* for WWI—the preservation of the British Empire. His destruction had to be achieved at all costs because it represented the destruction of all that threatened that empire.

When the dominant paradigm is stripped of its supporting chicanery and verbal legerdemain, what remains is a very unstable structure resting on insecure foundations. A thesis that cannot withstand logical investigation is a false thesis, even if believed by many. A thesis that mixes innuendo with facts has no integrity.

Innuendo, misinformation, fallacy

David Hume's 'wise man' measures his belief according to the evidence. Innuendo and gossip are not evidence but they are essential when the evidence is weak or absent. In lieu of evidence and reasoned argument, the engineers of consent offer a toxic blend of innuendo, misinformation and fallacy to drug the reader into confusion. Thus intoxicated, the mind loses all critical power, forgets the toxic blend and then believes. Shakespeare defined the state:

> 'And all their minds transfigur'd so together,
> More witnesseth than fancy's images,
> And grows to something of great constancy'.[24]

These rhetorical strategies are not arguments and therefore are unworthy of mention, but since they play a key role in the deception they will be mentioned briefly solely to demonstrate their falsity. Here are a few examples of the ingredients in this duplicitous cocktail.

Innuendo

At the close of the 2002 BBC TV documentary *The Secret of the Black Diaries*, an image is shown of a letter written on 6 June by Casement to an uncle. A voice-over reads the following extract: 'Some day a rather interesting account of my doings will see the light I hope, although I shall not be able to revise the proofs. But it will show a side to the picture that people in this jaundiced time don't understand. I have left a pretty full record.'

This letter is held in the Public Records Office of Northern Ireland (PRONI), reference T3787/19. The text of the complete letter makes it very clear that Casement is referring to his German writings of 1914–16, which were published in 1922 in Munich by Dr Charles Curry and in the USA by *The Nation*. Despite the clear references in the full letter, BBC producer Paul Tilzey selected an extract that, in the biased context of the broadcast, would easily convince viewers that the references were to the infamous diaries and that this extract is a veiled confession. The innuendo is intentional.[25]

Inglis's innuendo regarding Casement's German diary has been mentioned in the Introduction and his prolific duplicity is demonstrated in Chapter 6, where readers will find a further example of his 'verbal legerdemain' when he refers to the innocuous Amazon Journal of 1910.

Sawyer cannot resist innuendo and on page 7 of his 1997 edition of the 1910 diaries he claims that Casement had a scandalous reputation in Rio, where he was consul. At the point of his claim he provides no evidence or source, so the unwary reader is unable to verify and the idea is unopposed.

> 'Although Casement's sexuality had prompted *much gossip* when he was serving as Consul-General in Rio de Janeiro from 1908 to 1910, it did not interest British Intelligence ...' [emphasis added].

Of this *abundant* gossip Sawyer offers not one example, but elsewhere, when the suggestion has been securely planted, he does indicate its source. A single anecdote published 'verbatim' 28 years after 1910 by Ernest Hambloch, Casement's vice-consul in Rio, appears to be the source of 'much gossip'. Hambloch worked with Casement for only three weeks. Inglis also mentions this anecdote, so that its residue remains as an inference, but then he wipes his hands on the reader by adopting a sceptical distance. In Hambloch's 1938 book[26] the trivial anecdote is rendered in direct speech to give it an authentic freshness retrieved intact decades later from the deep freeze of an extraordinary memory. Gossip and hearsay replace evidence.

Sawyer also insinuates that British Intelligence was aware of this alleged reputation in 1910 but that it was not of importance to them *at that time*. To be aware of something implies that the thing has a real existence, that the gossip was based on verifiable facts. Naturally Sawyer gives no evidence of this alleged awareness, but the unsupported insinuation, once made, goes unquestioned. The insinuation is effected by *implication*, an inferred meaning rather than a logical entailment.

Misinformation

When innuendo is too weak, Sawyer turns to misinformation: on page 140 of *Roger Casement: the flawed hero* he gives a false source for the alleged diary pages shown by Hall to Ben Allen in 1916:[27]

> 'The original rolled manuscript shown to the Associated Press representative ... was later found to have been twenty-two pages torn out of the 1903 diary'.

Sawyer knows very well that Allen described the pages shown to him as of almost legal size (216mm x 356mm), whereas the 1903 diary pages measure 90mm x 150mm, so that the former are 5.7 times larger than the latter. He also knows that none of his readers will cross-check his 'facts'.

B.L. Reid's misinformation takes the form of calculated confusion. Lack of precision in referring to the diary or diaries or typescript pages or photographs is Reid's tactic of confusion by conflation. On page after page each reference varies, so that the confused reader concludes that there is no substantive difference between the referents. Here are some random examples of this effective tactic:

pp 381–4: eight references to diaries (plural);

pp 458–9: six references to diary, diaries, photographed pages/facsimiles;

pp 474–5: six references to diary, diaries;

pp 477–8: five references to diaries, photographic copies, typed copy;

p. 490: six references to diary, diaries.

This amounts to 34 references in only eleven pages to variant forms of the material shown. There are 23 references to diaries (plural), six to diary (singular), four to photographs and one to typed 'copy'. There are 29 references to diary/diaries and *only one mention* of the alleged typed copies. Six of the 29 references are to Reid's own examination of the bound volumes in TNA. Therefore the remaining 23 references must be to the alleged typed copies, which, nonetheless, he identifies only once. There is no record anywhere in Reid's 532-page book of those bound-volume diaries being shown to anyone in 1916.

When the reader sees 'diary' or 'diaries' he/she assumes that this refers to the bound-volume diaries now in TNA. The result is that the tiring reader, in order to reach some understanding, believes that the bound-volume diaries were widely shown, when in fact Reid does not cite a single verifiable instance of this happening. Since Reid was a professor of English who criticised Thomson for slovenly writing, these 'confusions' cannot be other than a strategy intended to deceive the ordinary reader.

Fallacy

Sawyer claims that the continued survival of the TNA diaries testifies to their authenticity:

> '... the diaries obviously had to be preserved as the only wholly acceptable evidence for refuting the charge of forgery ... that they exist today must be attributed to the perpetuation of a continuing wish to rebut a diabolical charge'[28]

—they could have been destroyed while in that limbo of official silence but were preserved *because* they were authentic. Certainly their destruction before 1959 would have convinced many of their falsity, but here again we have the proposition that because an event did not happen to an object it establishes the quality of that surviving object. That George did not eat the banana does not show that the banana was a delicious banana. Therefore the preservation of the diaries *in total secrecy* demonstrates nothing about their veridical quality. Their preservation even in secrecy had a specific motive: if we destroy the diaries we also destroy our credibility and can never hope to convince anyone that they *were* authentic; in order *to claim* their authenticity we cannot risk destroying them. They do not become authentic because they were not destroyed. Destruction of evidence is suspicious; non-destruction of evidence does not validate the evidence.

The wise man

The Casement secret was born in a frenzy of hate and vengeance for the deep embarrassment caused by Casement to imperial pride. For 43 years the secret was officially silenced, and then for a further 57 years it was protected by selective access, by the unscientific opinions of selected experts and by publications that carefully and cynically engineered consent.

Hume's wise man asks to see the evidence and finds only a resemblance in handwriting; he looks at the quantity of innuendo and false information and shakes his head, incredulous. He asks for more verified facts and finds only a few. He asks for proof and is given none. He sees confusion, ambiguity, speculation and inexplicable anomalies everywhere in the long story; he sees secrecy, collusion, denial and manipulation, the ingredients of conspiracy. He notes that authenticity cannot be proved by logical arguments but that it can be disproved by such arguments. Finally and slowly the wise man begins to proportion his belief.

Notes

1   David Hume, *A treatise of human nature* (1738).
2   Thomson claimed to have found a diary for 1903 and a cash ledger for 1911. Sometimes this latter is also mistakenly referred to as a diary. To avoid confusion, the present chapter focuses on diaries only.
3   The UK National Archives, abbreviated as TNA or NA throughout.
4   In the various books no date is given for the king's viewing of diary materials; his reaction is not reported, nor is the identity of the person responsible revealed.
5   'Secrecy, being an instrument of conspiracy, ought never to be the system of a regular government'—Jeremy Bentham, *Introduction to the principles of morals and legislation* (1780).
6   Edward Bernays, *Propaganda* (New York, 1928). Considered the father of modern public relations, Bernays sought to 'rehabilitate' propaganda as a respectable profession after WWI. His phrase 'the engineering of consent' has been here adapted to 'the engineers of consent/consensus'.
7   Ó Síocháin 2008.
8   Both documents are incomplete. The three-page MEPO lists effects allegedly found in only five trunks, but the last numbered trunk is No. 9. Four trunks are therefore not accounted for. The interrogation transcript confirms the absence of the shorthand typist, and Thomson explained in his writings elsewhere that Casement was reticent when he knew that a record was being made.
9   *The Daily Telegraph*, 17 November 1930. Clyne's letter dated June 1930 was published in Gwynn 1930.
10 A handwritten letter from Thomson to Blackwell of 26 July 1916 refers to 'the diary' (singular); HO 144 1637 311643 140.
11 The three main corroboration attempts are dealt with more fully in *Lost to History*, Breac, Easter 2016, <breac.nd.edu>.
12 Affidavits: HO 144/1637/311643/140 ref. 20261. An excerpt of only one of the eight 'affidavits' is printed in Ó Síocháin 2008, 493. See *Lost to History* and also in Breac, Easter 2016, <breac.nd.edu>, for scrutiny of this 'evidence'. See also Appendix below for a brief account of the desperate chicanery behind these statements.
13 Noyes 1957.
14 Facsimile copy of the Gaselee letter in MEPO 2/10672 from the UK National Archives; also available on-line.
15 Cited in Taylor 1970, 176.
16 Cited in Maloney 1936, 217: ' "Collins told me it was in two volumes, each a common office diary," states a letter of Senator Gogarty's in the Casement Collection of the National Library of Ireland.' Duggan's statement in the NLI also confirms the large format of the diaries.
17 It would be surprising if the nucleus of conspirators excluded Reginald Hall, Smith and Blackwell; Gaselee and MI5 officer Frank Hall might also have participated. Thomson was probably excluded from awareness of the full plot since he had contacts with too many informers.
18 Cited in Taylor 1970, 152.

[19] Cited in Sawyer 1997, 13–16.

[20] In 1966 Singleton-Gates was again prevented from publishing a 240-page typescript entitled 'Casement: A Summing Up'. See Sawyer 1997, 22. No reasons for the prohibition are given.

[21] Thomas Kuhn, *The structure of scientific revolutions* (Chicago, 1962). Kuhn's lengthy and influential exposition is here presented in synoptic form.

[22] Ó Síocháin 2008, 491.

[23] Campbell Stuart's *Secrets of Crewe House* (1922) gives a retrospective, detailed account of the extent and expertise of British propaganda during WWI.

[24] William Shakespeare, *A Midsummer Night's Dream*, Act V, Sc. 1.

[25] *The Secret of the Black Diaries*, produced for BBC TV by Paul Tilzey and broadcast in March 2002 to consolidate the results of the Giles Report announced on 12 March.

[26] Cited in Hambloch 1938, 74.

[27] Cited in Reid 1976, 382, 383. Allen's account is very widely reported in the Casement literature.

[28] Cited in Sawyer 1997, 24.

Appendix

'Among the papers released to the Public Records Office in 1994 was a series of affidavits, eight in all, which testified to Casement's homosexual behavior in October 1914. The affidavits were forwarded to London and sent by Thomson to Blackwell on 26th and 27th July 1916. The statements were taken between 11 July and 21 July …' (Ó Síocháin 2008, 493).

Ó Síocháin places considerable faith in these 'affidavits', which he neither reproduces nor analyses but accepts uncritically. Nor does he comment on what purpose these were to serve *after* the trial. His satisfaction with the so-called affidavits is more significant when compared to CID chief Basil Thomson's *dissatisfaction* with them at the time, as expressed in his handwritten letter to Blackwell of 26 July 1916: 'Not much in them' (HO 144 1637 311643 140). That Ó Síocháin did not cite this letter is also significant. What Ó Síocháin does not tell his readers is that these are not affidavits at all. By misinforming his readers in this way he seeks to give legal weight to these unverified statements. An affidavit is a *sworn statement of facts made under oath* and under penalty of perjury in person before a legally authorised person. None of the statements contain such an oath *by the deponent* and therefore they *testify* to nothing. Despite describing these as affidavits, Ó Síocháin is careful not to present them to his readers, preferring to selectively paraphrase parts of one only, and thus he conceals what would be evident to any perceptive reader—that these are no better than gossip. Indeed, one of them announces itself as gossip heard that morning. The statement by Christensen's mother confirms that she does not know whether her son is homosexual since she has not seen him since 1906.

Even Basil Thomson concedes in the above-mentioned letter that some of the statements are unsworn; if unsworn, they cannot qualify as affidavits. A number were 'sworn' by the British vice-consul at Christiania (Oslo), Henry Charles Dick, who was not competent to give an oath on *behalf of the deponent*; his responsibility was simply to identify the deponent in his presence and witness the signature. It is the deponent who swears an oath *in writing* to attest the veracity of his/her own statement.

It appears that the alleged affidavits by two hotel porters were not, in fact, made by them at all; instead, a single statement was sworn on oath by Jacobsen as being his 'true account' of what he claimed the porters knew but refused to testify in writing. The statement attributed to Korth is also made 'under oath' but not by Korth; it was made on 19 July 1916 and refers to gossip heard again by Jacobsen *on that date* and not in 1914.

An affidavit is not a statement of opinion, hearsay or gossip but of witnessed material facts made under oath by the person who witnessed the facts. Four statements have the hand of Jacobsen on them, acting as proxy guarantor of authenticity, and three of these are hearsay. The vice-consul never took statements from four of the eight Norwegians. Degerud's statement in Norwegian expresses no oath but the official translation claims that it was made under oath.

Perhaps it was Ó Síocháin's awareness of the Monty Python aspect of these absurd statements that induced him not to reproduce them in his very detailed book.

11

Anatomy of a lie

Report to British Intelligence by unnamed agent in Germany, dated 8.8.15 (TNA KV-2/6):

<u>'Sir Roger Casement</u>
There is a curious though ... persistent feeling among quite important persons in Germany, that the above is in the pay of the British Government. ... arguments for this are the following:

> ... it is noticed that he is received into the best circles both officially and personally ...

> ... it is noticed that he appears to devote his chief attention to persons who influence ... either the public opinion or relations with Foreign Powers. That he is kept informed to an extraordinary degree, as to movements, both prospective and in execution, of the troops on all fronts.

> It is generally considered ... that the whole story of his attempted assassination is an extremely well-laid scheme, as is proved by the fact that the individual responsible still remains at his post.

> As a reward ... he will be given a high position in the English Government ... and ... be allowed to carry out with success a law sanctioning Home Rule.

... would you sanction a scheme ... whereby the matter could be so arranged *that **evidence could be manufactured** by which the position of the man would be rendered untenable.* If you wish for the names of the persons in Germany who are interested, I can furnish them at short notice' [emphasis added].

The 'memo'

On the night of 29 October 1914, Mansfeldt de Cardonnel Findlay,[1] minister to the British legation in Christiania, placed a four-page handwritten document into the diplomatic bag, along with a short covering letter addressed to Foreign Minister Edward Grey. The sealed diplomatic bag was collected that night by Hugh Gurney from the Copenhagen legation.

Findlay's document and covering letter reached Grey the following day and were passed to British Intelligence. The letter described the four-page document as a memorandum written on 29 October by Francis Lindley,[2] who had interviewed Adler Christensen, Casement's servant, that afternoon. The text stated that Christensen showed copied documents and revealed that his unnamed master was travelling to Germany 'about trouble in Ireland' and that he was an English nobleman who had been decorated by the king. The 'memo' also included the following: 'I understood that his relations with the Englishman were of an improper character'.

The 'memo' sent to the Foreign Office by Findlay on 29 October contains handwriting which is often illegible, with letter and word formation compromised; the document looks untidy and improvised, with many cancellations, interpolations and corrections. It is not addressed to anyone and the term 'memorandum' does not appear. Overall, it is very unprofessional and does not look like the work of an Oxford-educated diplomat. In the bottom right-hand corner of the last page, squeezed into the margin, there appear to be Lindley's initials—F.O.L.—with the date, but written in a different ink or perhaps in pencil.[3]

Despite its improvised appearance, the so-called 'memo' was written by the Winchester- and Oxford-educated diplomat and future ambassador Francis Lindley. Within days it was in the hands of Major Frank Hall, former secretary of the UVF, who prepared a typed version for circulation.[4] Hall was born in Warrenpoint, Co. Down, and had been one of the masterminds behind the illegal 1914 Ulster gunrunning from Germany that aimed to militarily defy the UK parliament over Home Rule. He had become a high-ranking British Intelligence officer with special responsibility for Ireland. With reference to the 'memo', Hall wrote: 'I am awaiting further information on this point, and also as to his habits (natural & un-natural!)'. The 'memo' had arrived precisely where Findlay had intended—in the hands of Casement's sworn enemies.

Neither Hall, Lindley or Findlay had ever met or even seen Casement, but with these thirteen fateful words the conspiracy began: 'I understood that his relations with the Englishman were of an improper character'.

Scrutiny of the 'memo' reveals seventeen cancellations and 21 interpolations, some in a lighter ink or in pencil. Several parts have been squeezed in after composition was completed. The document is not addressed to anyone and bears no heading as memorandum. Many words are scribbled and almost illegible owing to poor or non-existent letter formation. Overall, the visual impression is of hastily improvised and untidy work. It would be reasonable to think it improbable that a diplomat would produce such a document for presentation to his superior. It is inexplicable that any Crown official would send such a shoddy, partly illegible document to a famous cabinet minister. Improbable and inexplicable—but that is what happened. An analysis of the circumstances of the creation of the document will illuminate why and how it happened.

In the first place, the document, which is mentioned by only one Casement author (Inglis),[5] is extremely difficult to find in the National Archives because it does not resemble what is usually called a memorandum with the conventional identifiers 'From X' and 'To Y'. Indeed, it was located only after the personal intervention of a specialist at TNA. It cannot be confirmed that Casement's biographers have not seen this document; if they have seen it, however, they chose (with the exception of Inglis) not to mention it. Given that this document contains the first ever reference to the homosexual dimension, it is significant that it has not received the attention it deserves. When it is examined, anomalies, incongruities and a major contradiction emerge.

Lindley met Christensen at around 2pm on 29 October in the British legation. Christensen returned to the Grand Hotel after the meeting and informed Casement. Accounts suggest that the meeting was relatively short, perhaps 30 minutes.

In the 'memo' the crucial words are 'I understood that his relations with the Englishman were of an improper character. It is just possible I may have been wrong in this, but I don't think so.' The second sentence has been cancelled with single strokes on each line. Casement's biographers have interpreted the first sentence as the result of an implication made by Christensen to Lindley, but none have offered any explanation of why he might have made a self-incriminating implication to a complete stranger. The construal by the biographers is also based upon later remarks made by Findlay, who on 30 October wrote 'with whom he evidently has unnatural relations'[6] and on 31 October wrote 'He implied that their relations were of an unnatural nature ...'.[7] Later, on 24 February, he converted this *alleged implication into statements* made by Christensen, when he wrote '... informer stated the unnatural character of their relations to myself and Lindley'.[8] Findlay conjured the initial innuendo in the 'memo' into an implication the following day and then into a statement without any evidence for such implication or statement.

The first sentence, however, makes no reference to any speech, act or gesture by Christensen that might constitute an implication. Lindley does not say that Christensen made any implication; he says 'I understood ...', which refers to his own mental process during or after the encounter. He attributes nothing to Christensen. The sentence merely reports a subjective mental impression without explanatory evidence to give it context. The second qualifying sentence indicates that Lindley perceived no clear signals. Both sentences require analysis.

The concept of implicature developed by H.P. Grice allows a deeper understanding of how these sentences function logically and semantically.[9] 'Implicature' is a technical term in linguistics that refers to what is suggested in an utterance, even though neither expressed nor strictly implied. For example, 'John is meeting a woman this evening' suggests that the unidentified woman is not his mother, sister or wife. By not identifying the woman, the speaker tacitly invites the hearer to *assume* that John is involved with the woman. By contrast, the statement 'John is meeting his wife this evening' *entails* that John is married. If John is not married the statement is false. The truth of the statement is predicated upon John's being married.

Entailment statements cannot be qualified or cancelled without compromising their truth value. Implicature statements can be cancelled and can be qualified. The two sentences in the 'memo' constitute an implicature in which the second sentence qualifies the first sentence and then is cancelled in order to disguise that together they function as an implicature—a suggestion, an innuendo unsupported by facts or evidence. The truth value of implicature statements cannot be determined from the statements themselves. Entailment statements convey bare information, whereas implicature statements convey *unstated meanings* that require external verification. Therefore the 'memo' sentences have no intrinsic truth value until verified by external evidence. They have the same status as gossip.

Lindley's 'I understood …' is a self-referential report that precludes external verification of that which is reported. Nothing can verify Lindley's report of a mental impression because his words refer to an exclusively subjective invisible state rather than to a fact in the tangible world. The written words do not *entail* the experience reported. Therefore nothing can establish the truth or falsity of those words. Statements that cannot be verified or falsified cannot contribute to the determination of facts. Lindley's sentence does not refer to facts or even to alleged facts; it is innuendo, but on the basis of this innuendo a defamatory conspiracy was founded.

Further scrutiny of the 'memo' reveals incongruities that indicate that the plot began in Oslo on the evening of 29 October 1914. By definition, conspiracy requires at least two persons and scrutiny indicates that Findlay was co-author of the 'memo'.

A highly significant anomaly is the verb tense used in the qualifying sentence—'I may *have been* wrong …'—which indicates that the words were written in a later time-frame, distinct from the time of the meeting. If these words had been written in the same time-frame as the event, it would have been more natural to write 'I may be wrong …' . For precision, the two time-frames are (a) the meeting at around 2pm and the minutes after and (b) later that evening of the 29th, several hours after the meeting. The tense used strongly indicates the evening time-frame as the time of the hasty composition of the document. Since the document, despite its improvised look, was placed in the diplomatic bag that evening by Findlay along with *his* brief covering letter, Findlay's presence *during composition* that evening is a near certainty. The many interpolations and corrections strongly indicate the intervention of a second person assisting with composition before final approval. It is reasonable to deduce that the document is the joint work of Lindley and Findlay, improvised in haste for immediate dispatch. This deduction explains why the so-called memorandum lacks the normal identifiers 'From' and 'To'. It never was a memorandum in any normal sense of the term. This deduction is further supported by Findlay in his letter of 31 October to Grey: 'He [Christensen] went over much the same ground as he had covered with Mr Lindley on Thursday *evening*[10] (emphasis added). It is undisputed that Christensen met Lindley in the early afternoon. The 'ground' referred to in Findlay's letter is that covered by himself and Lindley *that evening* when they composed the four-page document.

The grounds for holding that the 'memo' was composed in the evening as a joint effort outweigh the grounds for believing that it was written by Lindley alone earlier that day. Evening composition means that it is not a memorandum at all, since both supposed sender and recipient were involved in its composition. The fact that such an unkempt *bout de papier* was sent that evening to the Foreign Office indicates that it was composed for that specific purpose and in a hurry. This is supported by the fact that no fair copy was written out or typed up, as would be professional and correct when sending legation documents for the attention of Foreign Secretary Edward Grey. To this must be added the observation that Lindley did not need to write any 'memo' to a colleague in the same office whom he would in any case see in person later that same day. (See Appendix II.)

On 30 and 31 October Findlay wrote two drafts and two letters to Grey at the Foreign Office, three of which refer to the 'memo'. It is clear from Findlay's unfinished short draft of 30 October that this was written after the 11am meeting with Christensen and before the 3pm meeting, but it does not refer to any implication by Christensen to him at that 11am meeting. In that draft Findlay wrote 'with whom he *evidently* has unnatural relations', which refers only to the 'memo' of the 29th, since *this allegation would not be 'evident' to Grey except* from the 'memo' already sent to him. Therefore this idea of a confirming implication made at the 11am meeting on the 30th came to Findlay *after* he had written the incomplete draft letter following that 11am meeting. The implication allegedly made by Christensen on the 30th appears only on the 31st, when Findlay wrote the longer draft letter to Grey. Neither the draft of the 30th nor the first short letter of the 31st mentions any implication made by Christensen at either meeting on the 30th. For greater precision: Findlay's *first two written records* after his meetings with Christensen do not record any implication about unnatural relations *made to him*. Since the *short letter* of the 31st was written after both meetings on the 30th and omits any implication, a rational person would deduce that no implication was made at either meeting.

In his second and much longer letter to Grey on the 31st, however, Findlay wrote: 'He implied that their relations were of an *unnatural nature* and that consequently he had great power over this man who trusted him absolutely' (emphasis added). It is not clear which meeting is referred to. On page 4 of the eight-page draft of that letter Findlay's first version of the above sentence reveals three corrections, including 'their relations were improper' with the word 'improper' inexplicably cancelled and replaced by the incongruous 'of an unnatural nature'. By this 'correction' Findlay avoided repetition of the word 'improper' previously used in the 'memo'.

The 'memo' contains detail on page 4 which is attributed to Christensen as the source but which it is extremely improbable that he could possibly have known: that there were eight German officers travelling on the SS *Oscar II* with false passports. It is not credible that these officers would have revealed such compromising information to anyone on board, far less to an unknown Norwegian travelling second-class. The true source of this information was Emile Voska, a Czech spymaster in New York, who obtained a list of German reservists living in the US who had bought false passports in order to return to Germany for war service. The list was passed to Captain Gaunt of British Naval Intelligence in the US, who passed it to Hall in London, who in turn sent it to the Foreign Office. From there the list was sent to legations and embassies in Europe and thus to Findlay in Oslo, who fed the information to the Norwegian police with hopes that the returning officers could be arrested for possession of false identity documents. (See Appendix III.)

Most importantly, there is a contradiction in the 'memo' itself that can only be explained as an oversight owing to the haste of its composition. This concerns two pencil-copy letters allegedly shown to Lindley, one addressed to the German chancellor 'outside' and one to Harden,[11] both in Berlin. Another two letters allegedly mentioned by Christensen *had not been copied* and therefore were not shown to Lindley. But on page 4 the 'memo' mentions the two copied letters (to the chancellor and to Harden) allegedly shown and then refers to a third letter 'addressed to the G. Minister *here*, which I *also* saw in copy ...' (emphasis added); this refers to the minister at the German legation in Oslo and not to the chancellor in Berlin. Yet the memo states clearly on page 2 that only two letters were allegedly copied and shown: 'There were four letters and my informant steamed them open (before returning them) and ~~had~~ made pencil copies (of two) which he showed me' (parentheses added to indicate interpolations). The page 4 affirmation contradicts the alleged fact on page 2. This means that Lindley claims to have seen a third copied letter which he also states did not exist. Page 2 and page 4 cannot both be true but both can be false. Page 2 was written *before* page 4, and whether page 2 is false or true it *follows that page 4 is false*. The affirmations on page 4 refer to three copied letters allegedly shown. The demonstrated falsity of page 4 entails the falsity of page 2. Therefore no copied letters were shown.

This contradiction has implications that reach beyond the veridical status of the 'memo' itself, and those implications compromise the drafts and letters subsequently written by Findlay in support of the 'memo'. The detail about copied letters in the 'memo' amounts to 56% of the overall length of 463 words, and that detail has been demonstrated as false. (Word count of the 'memo' includes all cancelled and interpolated words.)

That 56% of the document is false does not entail that the remaining 44% is also false; 7.56% of the document is certainly true and is undisputed. These are the 35 words on page 1 which refer to Christensen's afternoon presence in the legation, his being Norwegian and that he arrived from the US on the *Oscar II*. The remaining 36.29% is, however, compromised, if only because it cannot be verified and therefore no facts can be derived. This includes the innuendo on pages 1 and 2. Therefore 92.44% of the document contains text that is either false or compromised. Only a lawyer who wished to commit professional suicide would present the 'memo' as evidence in a court of law. Only those in a severe state of cognitive dissonance would insist that the 'memo' is authentic.

The scrutiny above represents the first and only analysis of this *faux* memorandum in 102 years. The fact that the principal Casement authors have avoided it cannot be due to negligence, since it is a fundamental document in the Casement story. It constitutes the birth of the conspiracy, which will pass through further phases of development in the hands of Findlay and of British Intelligence.

The extensive unverifiable references to copied letters and to German officers with false passports are intended to furnish illusory authentic detail as a supportive framework for the innuendo.

The probability of Findlay's claims that Christensen made a self-incriminating implication (later a statement) of homosexual conduct can be safely left to the impartial reader's judgement, based on his/her knowledge of human nature and on common sense. Equally, the probability judgement can be based on the record of Findlay's overall integrity *vis-à-vis* the false 'memo' and his later attempts to corroborate this.

Olsen

In March 1915 Findlay sent a letter to Arthur Nicolson at the Foreign Office that contained his account of events on the night of Casement's arrival in the Grand Hotel on 29 October 1914.[12] Findlay was not present in the hotel but he reported his source as an unnamed informant, a person with 'private interests' who would identify himself only 'if absolutely necessary'. According to Findlay, the informant was witness to compromising behaviour in Casement's room at around 2am on 29 October 1914. Christensen was present.

On 21 July 1916, Findlay's informant identified himself before Inspector Sandercock at New Scotland Yard as Gustav Olsen, former chief reception clerk at the hotel, and he signed a typescript account of the events of that night 21 months earlier.[13] In general terms the accounts coincide, but in detail they differ significantly. B.L. Reid in his 1976 book reports the earlier version but is not wholly convinced of its truth.[14] The second version is one of the so-called affidavits solicited in 1916 by Thomson as corroboration, but the statement signed by Olsen contains no oath and is therefore not an affidavit.

Findlay's 1915 account tells of a 'German Secretary' repeatedly asking for James Landy (Casement) in the hotel for two days before his arrival. At 2am on 28/29 October the German asked again, and Findlay's anonymous informant went to the room and entered *without knocking* to find Casement and Christensen sitting on the bed, embracing but fully dressed. The German was shown up and remained in the room until 6.30am.

The account that Olsen signed in 1916 tells of a German 'Naval Attaché', Hans Hilmers, seeking James Landy (Casement) urgently at 2am on the 28th/29th, whereupon Olsen went to the room, knocked and, 'without waiting for an answer', entered to find Casement and Christensen 'half-naked' and in a sexually compromising position over the bed. Casement asked Olsen to show the German up, and the latter remained in the room until early morning.

Casement's account states that Hilmers 'from the German Legation' arrived to see him at midnight, but on 29/30 October, to advise him to remain in the hotel during the following day.[15] Hilmers returned at 6.30–7am on the morning of 30 October to inform Casement that travel arrangements were being made and that Count von Oberndorff would visit at midday.

The significant variation in detail between the 1915 and 1916 versions might be explained as follows: the first version was prepared by Findlay in person in a handwritten letter marked 'Private and Secret' and therefore without the informant having seen it; the second version was revised and typed by Scotland Yard and then signed by Olsen in person in London some 21 months after the alleged events. The second version was created by the Metropolitan Police as corroboration for the ongoing campaign against Casement. Therefore this police version was 'inspired' by the first, which Olsen *had never seen*.

Despite allegedly witnessing this criminal behaviour in the hotel, Olsen did not report it to his superiors or to the police; instead, he allowed both men to stay a further night and had no qualms about welcoming Christensen back to the hotel on 26 November for two nights and again on 5 December for two nights, according to his 1916 statement, and on 12 December and yet again on 2 January, and as late as 20 October 1915.[16]

That B.L. Reid, who *always* favours the official version, had doubts about the Olsen story is not surprising. The weakest link in both versions of the story is the German secretary or naval attaché, without whom Olsen had no reason to disturb Casement at 2am. The alleged *insistence* of the German is the tell-tale mechanism. The 'urgency' indicates something important, but there is no record of such an urgent meeting on the night of the 28th/29th in Casement's writings. That the urgent information could not wait a few hours until morning indicates the inherent implausibility of the Olsen story, since *urgent information implies immediate action*, but there was no action that Casement could possibly have taken at 2am—and indeed, by Olsen's account, he took no action but remained in his room until morning.

That Hilmers allegedly remained in the room for *four hours* delivering his urgent information is not credible; he was supposedly resident in the same hotel and might have returned to sleep. That the chief reception clerk was on night duty rather than a night porter is peculiar. That Olsen knew when Hilmers left Casement's room is also strange.

The police version of 1916 is above all founded on an uncanny sense of timing—Olsen entered the *unlocked* room just when the unambiguous act was about to occur. Olsen records neither any protest by Casement nor any shock at what he allegedly witnessed. This is not credible.

MacColl's 1956 book does not mention the Olsen story at all and he gives a different time for Casement's arrival at the hotel. MacColl quotes directly from Casement's own account: he left the ship at 1.30am and arrived at the hotel at nearly 2am.[17] By the 1916 police account Casement arrived at the hotel 'just after midnight'. The SS *Oscar II* docked at midnight, however; 2am is after midnight but not *just after* midnight. By this account Olsen's 'uncanny sense of timing' failed him.

Inglis (1973) does not mention the Olsen story, nor is it mentioned by Sawyer. Ó Síocháin briefly refers to Reid's account of the Findlay version of 1915 without mentioning Reid's scepticism.

There are the following discrepancies between Findlay's 1915 version and the police version signed by Olsen in 1916:

> Findlay version—unnamed German secretary / police version—named naval attaché;
> Findlay version—Olsen entered without knocking / police version—Olsen knocked and entered without waiting for a reply;
> Findlay version—'not undressed' / police version—'half-naked';
> Findlay version—sitting on bed / police version—in compromising position over bed.

Another anomaly is Findlay's later description of Christensen as 'fleshy and of dissipated appearance', while the police version describes him as 'good looking'. When these discrepancies are added to the other unexplained aspects, such as the four-month delay before the story's appearance, the different timing of Casement's arrival at the hotel and the vital insistence of Hilmers a day early, both versions of the story are seen to require a generous credulity that most level-headed persons would be unable to find. Either one version is true or both are false. The second version is an 'upgraded' but contradictory version of the first. For both to be true they must agree in all details, which they do not. *Whether the first is false or true, the second is false since the versions contain contradictory details.* Upgrading cannot convert falsity into truth. Therefore the second version signed by Olsen is false and this falsity compromises the possible truth of the Findlay version, which Olsen had not seen.

The Olsen story

It may seem paradoxical but the 'Olsen story' was probably not told by Olsen at all, since the first version was written by Findlay and the second was typed by the Metropolitan Police for his signature.

Here is the relevant extract from page 2 of Findlay's handwritten letter of 13 March, marked 'Private & Secret', to Nicolson at the Foreign Office.

'I have received the following information from an independent Norwegian source. My informant would be prepared to come forward if *absolutely necessary*, but as his private interests would suffer may not wish to do so.

For two days before Casement's arrival on Oct. 28, a German Secretary who had been living at the Grand Hotel enquired repeatedly for Mr James Landy under which name Casement was passing.

Casement & Christensen arrived at Christiania at midnight & asked for rooms near each other. At 2. a.m. the German Secretary turned up & insisted on seeing 'James Landy' at once. My informant (who is a respectable man) was asked to go himself to Landy's room; he consented, & found Casement & Christensen sitting on Casement's bed with their arms round each other. They were not undressed but the nature of their relations was evident. The German Secretary remained with them from 2. a.m. till 6.30 a.m. and the waiter warned my informant that Casement and his friend or servant were evidently spies. This appears valuable corroboration of fact that German Legation had been warned to expect them and of the nature of their relations. It strengthens our case ...'

Findlay ends this letter by repeating an earlier request of 21 February for

information about the reason for Casement's leaving the consular service—
'Was it sodomy?'—and whether he was known 'to be addicted to sodomy'.
Answers to those questions might have had relevance three weeks earlier,
before the Olsen story, but at this point on 13 March, having just revealed
his *witnessed evidence* of 'unnatural relations', Findlay no longer needed
those answers, since they could add nothing to what he had already
allegedly learned from his informant. Nevertheless, he automatically
repeated the request as if he was unwittingly signalling the falsity of the
account he had just set out.

It is clear from the grammar of the opening sentence of the above
extract from Findlay's letter that he did not possess the informant's story
much before 13 March 1915, some four and a half months after the alleged
events. Again ineptly, he does not explain how he obtained the story,
although it is clear that the informant is a male hotel employee on night
duty who knows where guests are located. It is not clear how the
informant's 'personal interests' might suffer but possibly he feared
prosecution. If Findlay had possessed the Olsen story in October or early
November he inexplicably kept it quiet for an unaccountable length of time,
yet in late February he was still seeking confirmation about 'unnatural
relations', whereas earlier knowledge of Olsen's story would have made
confirmation unnecessary.

On 13 March 1915 Findlay sent this account of the Olsen story to
London. That such a delay occurred between the alleged event of 29
October and Findlay's report of it to London indicates that he did not have
the Olsen story before March 1915 despite claiming in writing that
Christensen had made an implication of 'unnatural relations' as early as 30
October. These facts support the argument that the Olsen story originated
in new circumstances after the written promise of 3 January and when
Findlay was aware not only that he had been duped and humiliated but
that he faced the threat of a criminal lawsuit in the Norwegian courts. That
Findlay did not report the Olsen story in October indicates that either
Olsen or Findlay kept the matter quiet until March or it was invented in
March. That Findlay had nothing more substantial than an alleged
implication in late February 1915 is clearly demonstrated in his
communications with London. Therefore Findlay 'found' the Olsen story
after 24 February 1915. It was Findlay rather than Olsen who had motive

to invent the story—to defend himself from a prosecution by Casement over his written bribe.

The Findlay version of 1915 does not rest upon a single verifiable fact, and when considered in the context of Findlay's distressed mental state its inherent implausibility compels one to regard it as a poisonous fiction. The poison was concocted by Findlay in late February or early March and was transmitted to London. An anonymous story from a reluctant 'witness' and without demonstrable proof could not, however, be safely used against a free Casement in Germany without risk of a strong legal reaction that would publicly verify Findlay's bribe on behalf of the British government— his prime motive for the poisonous fiction.

That the Foreign Office and the Intelligence chiefs appeared to overlook Findlay's story in March and the following months suggests that either they perceived its inherent implausibility and shared Reid's later scepticism or they felt it was too weak legally (being anonymous and uncorroborated) to be used against Casement at that time without risk of a court action for slander. British Intelligence would prefer tangible, visible and incontrovertible evidence to stand as 'self-sufficient proof' of the behaviour that Findlay had clumsily invented for them. Ideally, Casement should damn himself. Thomson's discussion (reported in his 1922 book *Queer people*) with his informer Maundy Gregory, a professional expert on sexual scandal in high places, introduced the idea of compromising diaries. In the absence of such diaries, the self-damning evidence would have to be manufactured when the time came.

On 24 February Findlay wrote to Nicolson: 'Casement is evidently unaware that informer stated the unnatural character of their relations to myself and Lindley'.[18] Neither the false 'memo' nor Findlay's letters of 31 October mention any such statement made by Christensen, but by 24 February the alleged implication had become for Findlay an unambiguous affirmation of fact. From this self-deluding position Findlay moved towards the invention of his informant's story for 13 March.

In March Findlay converted these unverified insinuations into alleged facts as a self-defence tactic by engaging an anonymous informant in the hotel. In the light of his earlier generous offer to Christensen, it is highly probable that Olsen, his anonymous informant, had also received a generous offer, especially when, by his own admission, Findlay was accustomed to paying informers for information. Therefore Findlay's curious locution that 'his private interests would suffer' was code for the price of Olsen's false testimony, which he duly provided in July 1916 when it was safe to do so after Casement's conviction.

Oslo—two versions

In his 1956 book René MacColl wrote: '... the British Minister in Norway, the late M. de C. Findlay, made a fairly spirited attempt to have Casement kidnapped. British agents got hold of Christensen and took him to see Findlay, who tried to bribe him to deliver Casement into British hands ... Christensen seems to have been loyal to Casement in everything having to do with this affair ... He promptly reported back to Casement ...' .[19]

Later authors give a very different version of these events in which Christensen is the villain. The now-standard version invented by Inglis, Reid etc. from 1973 onwards is that Christensen went on his own initiative to the British legation on 29 October with a proposal to betray Casement, but the evidence in the Foreign Office documents for his alleged treachery comes from one man—Findlay. The few verifiable facts do not sustain the version based on Findlay's incomplete account, which MacColl had not seen. Some might consider it ironic that MacColl's book, which is certainly hostile to Casement, might contain a more honest version. That MacColl found the Christensen version credible indicates that he believed Findlay capable of plotting to capture Casement by bribing Christensen, and this seems confirmed by Nicolson's later letters warning Findlay that no physical harm must come to Casement. Later authors describe the Christensen version as a preposterous pulp fiction emanating from a vulgar imagination but it was *believed and published* by MacColl, the distinguished journalist and jewel of the Beaverbrook empire. It was also believed by thousands of readers who, like MacColl, did not find it preposterous. When an alternative, more comfortable Findlay version was released to the Public Records Office in late 1967, however, the version *believed* by MacColl necessarily became a pulp fiction.

A great mistake

Findlay's judgement had already caused grave concern in Britain for his involvement in the Dinshawai controversy in Egypt in 1906 and his

173

authorisation of a summary court hearing which led to the hanging or flogging and incarceration of eighteen peasant villagers accused of the alleged murder of a British officer. Despite being reprimanded for his gross over-reaction and his justification of the retaliatory punishments, it was Pro-Consul Lord Cromer who paid the price with his resignation shortly after. It is difficult to imagine that Findlay would hesitate to take whatever retaliatory measures he felt necessary against Casement, the renegade and traitor.

On 3 January 1915 Findlay issued Christensen an undated one-page note written on legation notepaper, promising him on behalf of the British government a reward of £5,000 for information leading to the capture of Casement.[20] This note was to play a key role in determining subsequent events. The sum offered had been approved by the Foreign Office on 27 November, but Findlay was at once rebuked by Nicolson for having personally given a signed, written undertaking to Christensen. Findlay apologised. When Casement heard of the bribe, he determined on a legal action against Findlay in the Norwegian courts that he believed would provoke a diplomatic scandal; so began what has been called 'the Findlay Affair'.

Over the following weeks Findlay was to suffer for that written promise. After Nicolson's immediate rebuke, Findlay wrote on 6 January: 'I regret you should disapprove of my action ... I would never have done so in time of peace'.[21] As his mood darkened on account of the failure of his plan to trap Casement, he wrote again on 14 January to Nicolson: 'I need hardly say that the failure of the coup ... has distressed me greatly and I could not forgive myself if it was due to mismanagement on my part ... I cannot see how I could have acted otherwise than I did ... I am sorry if I was wrong in doing so ...'.[22]

In seeking to defend himself to London, Findlay erred again by describing his written promise as simply an offer of reward for information such as might be posted in any police station. Such public reward offers do not name the recipient of the reward in advance, however, nor do they offer immunity and free passage to another jurisdiction. Findlay's promise was a bribe made to a specific person.

The full extent of Findlay's humiliation was revealed in late February in a letter from Nicolson, which made clear the degree to which a man of low intelligence, a 'loathsome beast', had succeeded for months in duping His Majesty's Minister Findlay.[23]

> 'I enclose a copy of a letter which has been received from Casement … You will see that Christensen was playing a double game … merely a ruse to obtain something from you in writing. You made a great mistake in giving it … I have no doubt that Casement and his German friends will make the most of it. If Casement carries out his threat of exposing the whole story in Norway you should immediately see the Minister for Foreign Affairs and put the best light on the case by telling him frankly the main outlines.'

To this humiliation was added the threat of full exposure by Casement in the courts, and therefore a diplomatic scandal and a consequent risk to Findlay's entire career. It was by then clear to Findlay and to his superiors that Casement had masterminded the deception and that Christensen had played his role loyally.

Findlay had been 'dirtied' and humiliated by his contacts with Christensen, and his response was to intensify his plot against Casement. The chemistry of Findlay's anger fermented hurt pride into personal vendetta. Insinuations, however insidious, are not facts, but even insinuations can be made to *perform as facts* with the creative touch of lies. On 13 March, out of the blue, four and a half months after the 'memo', Findlay produced the story from his anonymous informant. The poisoned bait had been set in the October 'memo' by Findlay, who, by then intoxicated and desperate, transformed it ineptly into the Olsen lie, which in turn fed the vengeful plans of Thomson and Hall.

Those vengeful plans were formed soon after the arrival of the Findlay 'memo' when the trunks were found. The information that the trunks were found long before Casement's arrest comes, surprisingly, from Sawyer (1984, 137), who cites Hall as hearing of the homosexual scandal '21 months before the execution' and locating the trunks then.[24] The scandal heard by Hall obviously comes directly from the Findlay memo sent to London in late October, but Sawyer astutely does not mention Findlay or the memo. It is perfectly credible that Hall knew of the scandal in December 1914 since it was known to Grey and to Frank Hall of MI5, who prepared a typed copy of the memo for circulation.

After questions in parliament by Emrys Hughes MP in July 1959, Richard Crossman was asked to investigate. Crossman had no motive for inventing Hall's location of the trunks. Since Hall's only motive for locating the trunks would be to investigate their contents, he had no motive for ignoring them for nineteen months. Moreover, he would certainly have been told by Thomson of Maundy Gregory's advice regarding the use of diaries to defame Casement. It can be reasonably deduced (and many commentators have agreed) that the trunks came into police possession in December 1914 and that they were opened and their contents examined. From this deduction it follows that both the interrogation transcript and the police list of contents are false, since both attest possession on 25 April 1916.

No reasonable person will ask an impartial observer to believe that the police found the TNA bound volumes in December 1914 and decided to keep these explosive diaries secret for nineteen months, thus *protecting the reputation* of the renegade whom they were actively pursuing. From this it follows that the TNA diaries were not found in the trunks. This is supported by the absence of any evidence that the bound volumes were shown to anyone during Casement's lifetime. Thus the two false police documents attest to the start of the diary plot in late 1914, which allows sufficient time for the preparation of the narratives that later became the typescripts.

Verified facts

It is essential to indicate the few facts that are not in dispute:

- Christensen was at the legation once on 29 October and twice on 30 October.
- Christensen told Casement about the first visit at once.
- After Christensen met Findlay in person at 11am on 30 October, Casement instructed him to return that afternoon as invited by Findlay. Christensen returned and met Findlay again.
- Christensen did not tell Findlay on either visit that Casement already knew of his earlier visits.
- Christensen received the written bribe on 3 January and gave the document to Meyer on the 5th.

The most improbable aspect of the 'official' version that Christensen went uninvited on 29 October, intent on betrayal, is the fact that Christensen informed Casement of that first visit. The second most improbable aspect is Christensen's allegedly making a self-incriminating implication to Findlay. The source of the first aspect is not Findlay but Brian Inglis *et al.* The source of the second aspect is Findlay. *A rational explanation for both of these improbable aspects must be predicated on the truth or falsity of the alleged betrayal plan.* That there was no betrayal plan is verified by Nicolson's letter, which informed Findlay that Christensen had deceived him.[25] There never was a genuine betrayal plan instigated by Christensen. From this fact it is reasonable to conclude that Christensen did not go to the legation uninvited on 29 October, as alleged not by Findlay but by Inglis *et al.* From this it is reasonable to conclude that Christensen was indeed contacted by Findlay's agents, as per his account to Casement on his return. From this conclusion it follows that Findlay authorised that first contact and therefore knew of the presence of 'Landy' and Christensen in the hotel on 29 October. This knowledge implies an informer in the hotel, and that informer was later identified in July 1916 as Olsen. It is also verified by Findlay himself that his legation colleague Goff was resident in the hotel and had seen both Casement and Christensen there.

In his letter to Grey of 31 October Findlay stated on page 3 that he had identified Landy as Casement, and he attributed that identification to Christensen at the meeting on the 30th. The attribution cannot be verified. The only aspects of Findlay's version that can be verified are that on 29 and 30 October Christensen was in the legation, where he met Lindley and Findlay separately, and that Findlay had identified Casement by 30 October.

The verified facts above seriously undermine the biographers' version of the Christensen meetings on 29 and 30 October. When these facts are placed alongside the fact that Olsen was Findlay's hotel informer, the version believed and published by MacColl has greater credibility than the version invented for Findlay by the later biographers. To the proven falsity of the 'memo' must be added Findlay's dishonesty in the Olsen story of 13 March, with the result that the balance sheet for his integrity displays a painful shortfall. He predicated his Casement strategy from the beginning on 'unnatural relations' for which he possessed no verifiable evidence but which he could not renounce. When Nicolson exposed his deception by Christensen, his strategy was in crisis; soon after, Findlay *manufactured the evidence* of the Olsen story to save face and to protect himself.

The fatal nexus

When Christensen visited the British legation on 29 and 30 October, a kind of chain reaction was started which eventually led to the diary conspiracy and to Casement's destruction. With the 'memo' in the hands of his enemies, that lie quickly infiltrated the state security organs long before his arrest. The growing conspiracy created the degenerate traitor and the necessary evidence was manufactured in order to take revenge. Like all revenge, it was personal—very personal. Empire had honoured his name so that the empire's honour might be seen in his person, and he, the empire's hero, had openly defied the honour of the largest empire in history. The fatal nexus between treachery and 'unnatural relations' forged by Findlay in the 'memo' was also a malediction that uncannily prophesied the shape of things to come: his lies bound others into an uncontrollable vortex of deceit that endures to the present day. Evil is prolific and by its nature fertile; otherwise it would not exist. The poisonous lie invented by *one man* in 1914 still exerts its toxic effect a century later.

Believing is seeing

The falsity of the 'memo' and of the subsequent Olsen story has been demonstrated. The fact that Findlay never explained how first contact was made with Christensen compromises the versions published by post-1973 biographers. Two verified facts remain: (a) Casement was informed of the visits and (b) no betrayal took place.

It is undisputed that Christensen, following Casement's instructions, systematically duped Findlay to obtain the written bribe. The verified fact remains that Christensen did not sell Casement to Findlay *in spite of the bribe*, and that on 19 February 1915 he spoke to a German newspaper about the bribe and the Findlay plot.

The falsity of the Inglis version of first contact reinstates the MacColl version, which is the Christensen version. The demonstration that Findlay made first contact also produces a second confirmation of the falsity of the Olsen story; possession of that story on 29 or 30 October would have induced Findlay to exploit it immediately and not *four months later*. Such an immediate exploitation would also have made the alleged implication totally unnecessary.

It remains to demonstrate the relationship of the 'memo' to the defamatory typescripts shown in 1916. To establish a causal link in law an agency must be demonstrated to act as a *substantial factor* in the harmful outcome in order to be considered a cause of it. Agency and outcome must be intimately and obviously linked. The criterion for the existence of causal connection *in law* is that the cause must possess a specific feature in relation to the consequence in order to demonstrate causal connection. In the case of the Findlay 'memo' and the defamatory typescripts this special feature is *identity of allegation,* which acted as substantial and sufficient factor in the harmful outcome. Both 'memo' and typescripts were intended to destroy Casement's reputation with the same allegation and they achieved this shared objective.

That link is reinforced by the fact that the allegation in the typescripts *was not determined* by the 'memo' but was *freely chosen* as an extension of the same strategy and intent to defame. This free choice linked the 'memo' and the typescripts into a single continuous allegation bonded by a single intent. Within the parameters of *legal causation,* the 'memo' is the sufficient indirect cause and the typescripts are the direct cause of the harmful outcome.

With regard to the veridical status of the documents, it has been demonstrated that the 'memo' is untrue. From this there follow two considerations. (A) Accepting that the memo is demonstrably false makes it impossible for a rational person to believe that the typescripts are true copies of Casement writings. The impossibility arises from accepting that those who composed the 'memo' acted dishonestly while also believing that those who prepared and showed the typescripts acted honestly. No rational person can believe this because the *reductio ad absurdum* is obvious—both parties made the same basic allegation, which is therefore both true and false. (B) The 'memo' as sufficient indirect cause of the harmful outcome cannot be the cause of the alleged authenticity of the typescripts. If the typescripts are genuine copies, their authenticity derives from other factors and not from the false 'memo'. Those other factors are the claims of Findlay's government colleagues who circulated the false 'memo' and showed the defamatory typescripts without any evidence of their veracity. It is undisputed that, *whether genuine copies or not*, the typescripts were shown in order to defame. Those colleagues are therefore accessories to the crime of defamation inspired by Findlay.[26] Their testimony can only be admitted if it serves to prove that the allegations are true. The accessories did not seek or provide material or witness evidence as to the veracity of either 'memo' or typescripts *before* their showing. There were no 'other factors' to verify the typescripts, which fact signifies that they were not demonstrated to contain true facts before being shown. Because they are an integral part of the defamation initiated by Findlay's 'memo', their claim to be factual is without foundation, and it follows that the allegation in the typescripts must be deemed as false as the same allegation made in their originating source. To hold that the typescripts are genuine copies is to hold that truth can be brought into being by falsity. A simple analogy illustrates this: Findlay alleged that Casement was a Martian and, acting on this unsupported allegation, his colleagues produced diary typescripts to reveal his Martian origins. If truth can be derived from falsehood, then the categories are meaningless because they cannot be distinguished. If the typescripts are genuine copies it follows that Findlay's 'memo' is also factually true. Conversely, proof of 'memo' falsehood is also proof of the falsity of the typescripts.

It is undisputed that those who produced the 'memo' and the typescripts *acted* with a common malicious purpose. If the two phases are unrelated despite sharing the same basic allegation, then this was a most remarkable coincidence. Both phases so closely resemble conspiracies that an impartial observer might deploy Occam's razor and conclude that there was one conspiracy since there was one outcome that was reasonably foreseeable from the start. Coincidences do happen but, by definition, they cannot be made to happen.

Had it not been for his fear of a threatened lawsuit, Findlay would not have felt it necessary to invent the Olsen story. By late February, when Findlay realised that he had been duped and made to look foolish, these toxic ingredients fermented in his mind to become the poison that resulted in the Olsen story, which *only then* he transmitted to London. There the poison was incubated for future use. The destruction of the world-famous renegade knight required much more than an anonymous and improbable yarn by an unknown hotel employee in a foreign city, but the poison lost none of its lethal potency over the following year and even before Casement's arrest British Intelligence had decided how it could best be used. From Findlay's lies and insinuations there grew the plan to destroy Casement as a moral degenerate with the 'self-damning' diary typescripts. The smear campaign was essential to ensure that there would be no reprieve once Casement was condemned.

The initial success of the smear campaign with the typescripts bound the British authorities to maintain authenticity indefinitely. Governments do not admit that they have lied to everyone for a century. Thus in 1916 the typescripts were sufficient and necessary for the immediate task. Today the bound-volume diaries in TNA are still essential because they act to protect the typescripts, the original lie repeated by successive governments. This was always a lie that would have to be maintained no matter the circumstances. Paradoxically, radically altered attitudes to sexuality have made the lie easier to maintain—there is no slur today, despite the original intention.

Thus was born in the troubled and duplicitous mind of *one man* who had never met Casement the lethal virus that was used by Thomson and British Intelligence to rapidly infect the British establishment with a visceral hatred for a man whom all had honoured only a few years before. Findlay's 'memo' in the 'right hands' evolved directly into the diary plot that guaranteed Casement's destruction.

Upon this single document *without evidential value* an entire edifice of deception and innuendo was constructed, with Findlay laying the first lie in the 'memo' and then a second in the Olsen story, followed by another by British Intelligence which was taken up by Scotland Yard and the press and the agents of state propaganda. Within this Escher-like structure of illusions moved the main players in Casement's destruction, leading the bewildered through new perspectives of belief which spin lies into truths, distorting and controlling perception so that common sense is lost as in a trance, cause and effect are compounded and *believing is seeing*. A new generation of illusionists posing as impartial scholars and biographers shored up the edifice of lies for decades. In the art of deception they were as skilled and successful as their predecessors Findlay, Thomson, Hall, Blackwell etc. Of these scholars, one only risked a tentative reference to that single document of October 1914. These word-juggling alchemists convinced tens of thousands that their research had produced truth—not a difficult task but one they considered necessary because they knew that the illusory structure might crumble at any time. The hypnotic power of mass media broadcasting completed the task of disinformation and extinguished the possibility of doubt—and, with it, the possibility of truth.

Notes

[1] Findlay (1861–1932), minister at Christiania from 1913 to 1923, was knighted in 1916.

[2] Francis Oswald Lindley (1872–1950) succeeded Findlay in 1923; a future ambassador to Austria, Greece, Portugal and Japan, he was knighted in 1926. His memoirs, *A diplomat off duty*, were published in 1928.

[3] PRO FO 337/107.

[4] TNA KV-2-6.

[5] Brian Inglis, *Roger Casement* (Coronet, 1974). Strangely, this study contains no source references whatsoever.

[6] TNA FO 337/107.

[7] TNA FO 337/107.

[8] PRO FO 95,776.

[9] In linguistic pragmatics H.P. Grice (1913–88), the philosopher of language, developed a theory of meaning that involved the concept of 'implicature'. Among his principal works is *Studies in the way of words* (Harvard University Press, 1989).

[10] TNA FO 337/107.

[11] Maximilian Harden (1861–1927), influential and controversial German editor and journalist. Born Felix Ernst Witowski, he damaged the reputation of the Hohenzollern caste by exposing the Eulenburg homosexual scandal in 1906.

[12] Letter from Findlay to Nicolson, 13 March 1915 (PRO FO 95,776).

[13] Typed statement signed by Olsen, 21 July 1916 (PRO HO 144 1637 311643 140).

[14] Reid 1976, 212, footnote b.

[15] Curry 1922, 48.

[16] Christensen stayed in the Grand Hotel on 20 October 1915 when he arrived from New York with Monteith, as related by the latter in *Casement's last adventure* (Chicago, 1932).

[17] MacColl 1956, 140–1.

[18] Letter from Findlay to Nicolson, 24 February 1915 (PRO FO 95,776).

[19] MacColl 1956, 141.

[20] Findlay's handwritten bribe to Christensen, undated and issued on 3 January 1915 (UCD Archives, Boehm/Casement Papers P 127/1).

[21] Findlay to Nicolson, 6 January 1915 (PRO FO 95,776).

[22] Findlay to Nicolson, 14 January 1915 (PRO FO 95,776).

[23] Nicolson to Findlay, undated, late February 1915 (PRO FO 95,776).

[24] '... on 27 July Emrys Hughes MP stated categorically in the House of Commons that there had been "a special intelligence department at Scotland Yard which carefully forged diaries and letters ..." To test the veracity of such a statement it seemed wise to approach Richard Crossman who, as British Director of Political Warfare against the Enemy and Satellites or as Assistant Chief of the Psychological Warfare Division of SHAEF, might reasonably have been expected to inherit whatever machinery was used in the previous war. He elicited help from Donald McLachlan,* who had held a number of propaganda posts which came loosely under the heading "Naval Intelligence" ... it was his guidance which led to

the discovery that Hall had heard of Casement's alleged proclivities twenty-one months before the execution, and not long afterwards Hall discovered the whereabouts of the traitor's personal luggage' (Sawyer 1984, 137). *Donald McLachlan (1908–71), an Oxford-educated Scot, was head of Naval Propaganda and Commander of Naval Intelligence Division NID 17Z in WWII.

[25] Nicolson to Findlay, undated, late February 1915 (PRO FO 95,776).

[26] At the time homosexual acts were criminal acts, and therefore the defamation was criminal in nature.

Appendix I

There has been much misinformation and confusion about Christensen's role in the events of 29–31 October, and particularly about how he came to be in the legation on the 29th. His version is that he was contacted by an Englishman in the hotel, invited outside and taken in a large car to the legation, where he was asked about his master by Lindley. This version was undisputed until the Inglis biography of 1973, in which Inglis wrote that 'the Foreign Office files told a different story'. The new story was that Christensen went entirely on his own initiative with the intention of betraying Casement. Scrutiny of those Foreign Office files reveals, however, that they do not tell 'a different story' because they do not tell any story at all. Nowhere in those files is there any account of how Christensen came to be in the legation on the 29th. At no later time did Findlay account for his presence on that day. Only on 17 February does Findlay state that Christensen arrived *on 30 October* 'of his own accord'. This is true for all three visits, since he was not compelled. Therefore Findlay's comment *does not contradict* the account of first contact given by Christensen to Casement on the 29th, nor is there any documentary evidence to prove that Christensen's account is false.

The Inglis citation is simply an unsupported insinuation that was taken up by later authors. One of these is B.L. Reid, who continues: 'In his first account of these events, sent to Sir Edward Grey on 31 October 1914, Findlay wrote that Christensen had simply presented himself at the door of the British Legation at 79 Drammensvein in the *late afternoon* of the twenty-ninth'. This is wholly untrue. Findlay's letter of the 31st does not contain this apparently paraphrased written statement attributed to him by Reid. Here is the relevant extract of Findlay's letter: 'The man called at the Legation about 11 a.m. and asked to see me alone. He went over much the same ground as he had covered with Mr Lindley on Thursday evening.' In this letter there is no reference anywhere to Christensen's arrival at the legation on the afternoon of Thursday 29 October. Therefore Reid has misinformed his readers by *falsely attributing* to Findlay his own false account of Christensen's arrival on the 29th (Reid 1976, 213).

Ó Síocháin's (2008, 393–4) version is even more duplicitous:

'… Two versions of what happened survive. According to the *British legation account*, Christensen had presented himself at the door of the legation, intimating that he had information on a well-known "Englishman" involved in an "Irish-American-German conspiracy". Francis Lindley, the first Secretary, was the first official to interview Christensen. While cautious, he was willing to hear more, and *asked his visitor to return the following day* …

Casement's version painted a very different picture. According to it, *early in the afternoon of* 29 October, Christensen was approached by a stranger in the hall of the hotel and taken by car to a large house, which Casement later ascertained to be the British legation; here he was questioned about his master … Over the course of three visits, *Christensen's hosts*, Findlay and Lindley, quizzed him about his master, whose *identity legation officials were very interested* in … Christensen claimed to have driven a hard bargain and to have, ultimately, extracted a promise of £5,000 in gold for delivering Casement … Christensen, *it seems likely*, was playing *a double game*, seeing possible advantages for himself, especially financial gain, on both fronts.

During his *encounters* with Christensen, *Francis Lindley received from him information* on Casement's homosexuality: "He implied that their relations were of an unnatural nature and that consequently he had great power over this man who trusted him absolutely" … In addition to Christensen's *hints* to Lindley and Findlay, the latter subsequently acquired *corroborating information from a Norwegian* …' (emphasis added).

This is almost entirely invented. (1) There is no 'British legation account' and no evidence in the 'memo' or elsewhere that Lindley 'asked his visitor to return the following day'. (2) Christensen met both Lindley and Findlay alone, not together, as suggested above. (3) Findlay himself claims that Casement was identified at the second meeting, and therefore Christensen was not 'quizzed' about this 'over the course of three visits'. (4) Lindley had only one encounter with Christensen. (5) There is no 'information on Casement's homosexuality' in the 'memo'. (6) The quotation in the last paragraph comes from Findlay's letter of 31 October and not from the 'memo' or from Lindley. (7) There is no proof of any 'hints' made at any time. (8) The 'corroborating information' refers to the Olsen story, the falsity of which has been demonstrated.

Conspicuously missing from Ó Síocháin's duplicitous version is any reference to the 'memo'. While he mentions Christensen's sworn deposition of April 1915 he does not quote from it, preferring to quote Findlay instead. The 'double game' theory emerged only in 1973 with Inglis and in 1976 with Reid. The theory is very weak and easily disposed of by the following undisputed facts: (1) Christensen did not betray Casement when the *Oscar II* was boarded by the British Navy; (2) he did not blackmail Casement, who was in possession of a considerable sum of money; (3) he informed Casement of all his legation visits; (4) he gave Casement the 'earnest money' given to him by Findlay at the third meeting; (5) he persisted with Findlay for two months to obtain the bribe in writing; (6) he did not betray Casement when he had the written bribe; (7) *he at once gave the written bribe to Meyer in Berlin*; and (8) he later gave a newspaper interview about the Findlay Affair.

This voluntary surrender of the written bribe is of vital importance because it demonstrates that Christensen never had any intent to betray Casement. Casement's biographers are sensitive to these verified facts but they overlook that the handing over of the written bribe renders utterly untenable the theory of a double game. The undisputed facts show that there was but one game—the deception and entrapment of Findlay. Therefore, since there was only one game, the biographers' claim that the first contact was on Christensen's own initiative is not credible.

Christensen's account is very detailed and very plausible. He gave no information to Lindley and was not invited back by Lindley. He did not tell any 'story', as the 'memo' claims, nor did he show any papers to Lindley. He also guessed on the 29th that he was in the British legation. Christensen gives the numbers of the taxi-cabs used on his two visits on the 30th. He records the 100 kroner 'earnest money' as a single banknote. He gives precise times. He gives the contact name and address given by Findlay on the 30th, saying that it was written in block capitals on legation paper with the top address torn off by Findlay. The contact name and address was later confirmed to Casement as being that of an employee of the Norwegian lawyer representing the British legation. Findlay confirmed giving the contact address in his long draft of the 31st. Christensen's sworn deposition was made before the US vice-consul in Berlin in April 1915.

Appendix II

Lindley's private letters of 1914–15 reveal a rather mediocre personality but one who was fully complicit in Findlay's plotting against Casement. His private letters do not mention the events of 29 October; this silence can be explained by the fact that the 'memo' was secret and confidential. In a letter dated 21 February 1915, after Casement's open letter to Grey had been 'spread all over the place', Lindley wrote briefly about 'the Findlay Affair' without revealing his meeting with Christensen or his role in the 'memo'. There is no mention of the written bribe issued on 3 January that had provoked Casement's letter. Lindley writes: 'The truth is that Casement is a b—er … His "friend" a blackguardly young Norwegian American came up to the Legation and supplied us with a lot of very valuable information about Casements [sic] plans and accomplices. Finally after a good many visits and after we had got a lot out of him he fell out about the money, wanted a big sum down before he had supplied the goods.' Since the 'very valuable information' had proved to be false and worthless long before 21 February, Lindley seems to be out of date or misinformed, or is simply covering up the mess created by Findlay.

Appendix III

There is considerable written and circumstantial evidence indicating that Findlay was in contact with British Intelligence during this period. Given that it was wartime and that Norway was in a strategic position, it would be surprising if he were not in such contact. In his draft letter of 30 October Findlay writes: 'I am arranging to obtain news of what this man does after arrival in Germany'. The only way such news could be obtained was through agents and spies in Germany. It is reasonable to deduce from this that he also had contact with agents elsewhere. Casement records that his hotel was being watched constantly from the time of his arrival and that his taxi was followed on the evening of the 29th. From these circumstances it would not be unreasonable to conclude that Findlay had been pre-alerted to Landy/Casement's arrival in Oslo. He had been under surveillance while in the US until 14 October, when, by subterfuge, he boarded the *Oscar II* in New York, and his disappearance thereafter must have been noticed.

In his draft letter of the 30th and his short letter of the 31st to Grey, Findlay wrote: 'The alleged Casement is described as very tall ...' and 'The man alleged to be Casement is described as very tall, dark, heavy jaw ... he is now clean shaved and is said to have formerly worn a beard'. This information does not appear in the 'memo' and is not attributed to Christensen. The most probable source is British agents in the US, who would have seen a bearded Casement before his departure. Use of the passive 'is described' twice conceals the source of the information. These deductions strongly indicate that Findlay was in contact with intelligence agents in relation to Casement. This helps to explain his actions and motivation; it also partly explains his failure to publicly rebut the accusations in Casement's published letter to Grey.

Epilogue—
A brief demonstration that the 1911 Black Diary was not written by Roger Casement

Précis: the multiple contradictions on page 27 of the 1911 police typescript are the result of human error. They can be attributed to Casement only if we accept a fallacious circular argument and accept that he was delusional.

The police typescript dated 1911 is replete with internal errors, anomalies, inconsistencies and contradictions of many kinds that render it impossible to accept as a copy of a diary written by a responsible, rational British consular official. This is particularly true of the entries from 19 to 23 December, which was Casement's last week in the Amazon. On 24 December he left Pará on a ship bound for Barbados. The entries in the typescript for these days show a level of incoherence and contradiction which defies all comprehension and is impossible to reconcile with the Casement known in 1911, knighted that year and appointed by Foreign Secretary Grey to this delicate and dangerous mission.

These entries constitute page 27 of the police typescript and this Epilogue examines an apparently inexplicable cluster of contradictions. What follows is a reduced version of a longer analysis and it does not deal with all the inconsistencies on that page. The reader is advised to study page 27 of the typescript carefully (see image right).

It is a verified fact that the 1911 typescript was typed in June 1916 by Scotland Yard staff on the specific instructions of Basil Thomson and others acting in concert. It is a verified fact that the various typescripts were shown during May, June and July 1916 to a considerable number of influential persons, who were told that the typed pages were faithful copies of diaries written by Casement. It is undisputed that the motivation for these actions was to destroy Casement's reputation, thereby eliminating support for any possible reprieve. It is undisputed that those who conducted the smear campaign with the police typescripts were British officials who *before his trial* had determined that Casement must be hanged. These undisputed

Page 27.

19th Tuesday.
Steaming down the river past the hills of Framba and Sierra
Jutahy and at 5 near Gurupa entrance to the Channel. We
should arrive in Para before 6p.m. tomorrow evening I hope
but I am not sure of it as we are behind where Atahualpa was
last year. I am a bit better but not very well. and wonder
what news I may get, from Tyrell - if any. Arr. Para 5.40
anchored and fired guns but Saida and no agents.
20 th Wednesday.
Health vist 7. 10 and Customs 7,20 and got ashore just 15
hours after we arrived. To Hotel Commercio and after bath
down to Camiseria Moderne and lo there he was at door in new
pants and it down left thigh- huge and enormous and he lovely
beyond words. Went in and tried to buy necktie askinghim.
Saw him often after and met in street. Heis quite splendid.
To Tavares, Cardoso too, several times, but no Augusto! To
Pogson and letter from Tyrell saying B. A. is given to Mackie
of Congo. Alack. Alack. So I am clear done out of that.
What a shame. After b'fast to B. Campos at 11. 30 till 12.30
and also b Palace Square and saw many on seats and in trams
and lots of huge ones-perfect monsters. A lovely young police
man at Hotel, Caboclo, with big limbs, hands, softface and
huge curved one. He shook hands and we clung long. I loved
him and followed to street. Out at 6 after early dinner to
Palace and then very soon white work boy nice, followed long
but I to B. Campos when "practicanta" of "Hilda" wanted and a
small boy (lovely) with huge one. Tried but Praticanta
spoiled by intercepting. To Nazareth where huge one on seat
(biggest ever seen) and after long round to Paz Theatre, etc.
At last a darkie with a very big one. Wanted and pulled
it and gave 5$000 and home at 1. a.m. New police in Para.
Many caboclos.
21st Thursday.
See Y&dy's entry, in error made under Wednesday. I only
landed to-day at 8. 30a.m., Got a few letters by "Anslem"
to-day but none from Nina - poor old soul, and Charlie and
Miss Causten and Mrs G. and Agnes O'Farclly.
          "5,000 X   to Darkie at Paz Gardens."
22nd Friday.
In house and out at 8. 30 to Pickerell and got my luggage
only from Customs at 5p.m., near 48 hours after landing, and
with immense difficulty after 5 visits to Customs Warehouse.
To dinner on "Anselim" and after a visit to B. Campos 6 - 6-30
seeing one fine type on seat. After dinner with May &c.
an "Anselim", left at 8-40 and to B. Campos, None, and
Nazareth none and then Paz where a young moco tried - and
then the darkie who entered finally and hugely - pulling
down pants and stripping. Again later on met him again and
still more furiously, never anything like it. He asked
"Kbom"? when putting in with awful thrust - saw several
others.
23rd. Saturday.
Spent day mostly in Hotel. Kup and Coulson to lunch and then
on "Anselm" to see Mays off at 1. Then to B. Campos for an
hour but none and back to Hotel and to Pogsons but Darkie came
just near door so I crossed Paz Gardens and on to Mrs. Kup
and Ornstein's and then after dinner out to Palace Square and
B. Campos and Nazareth. At Palace Square several and one
splendid young mulatto like "Aprigio", beautiful limbs and
clothes and huge one on seat at corner - but shy and finally
home with none all night.
24th. Sunday.
Embarked on "Denis" for Barbados at 9 a.m.. Fine boat and
only 5 passengers for Galveston - so heaps of room.
25th. Monday.
Christmas Day on "Denis". Spent day reading mostly - old
books and loafing. Weather cool and fine - poor old Hya-
cinthus is not well and won't eat. Ran 258 miles from
10-50 a.m. on Sunday. Barbados 941 miles.
26th. Tuesday.
Cold morning - & sea - Ran only 301 miles leaving 640
miles to Barbados.

facts condition any interpretation of the status of the typescripts that were produced by officials of proven hostility to Casement.

Those who claim that page 27 is a true copy of an original diary recognise the confusion and are constrained to attribute this to Casement. To attribute the confusion to Casement in an original diary is, however, to assume without evidence the material existence of a diary in June 1916; it is also to rely upon the fallacy of *petitio principii*, a version of circular argument. In simple terms, the argument from confusion admits that there are contradictions and claims that, since page 27 is a faithful copy of an original diary, these contradictions were made by Casement, who was 'confused'. The attribution is untenable because the conclusion derives exclusively from the unsubstantiated assertion about an original diary. This leaves only one explanation for the contradictions, which is that they were made by the anonymous officials during the process of creating the typescripts in 1916. Moreover, the nature of the contradictions and the confusing attempts to remedy them are consistent with errors that arise from hasty *joint endeavour* rather than from one person. Along with the unsubstantiated assertion and the circular argument, we are also required to ignore the manifest hostility of the officials and to attribute to them total integrity despite the vilification campaign which they planned and conducted over several months.

On page 27 we have events recorded before they purportedly happened, events recorded which did not happen and events recorded days after they did not happen. If the work of one person, this is more than confusion—it indicates a disturbed mind.

On the hypothesis that page 27 of the typescript is a copy from an authentic Casement diary, scrutiny of that page leads to the following reconstruction of the writing sequence of the contradictory entries. The entry under Wednesday 20th is, we are told, an account of events on Thursday 21st which has by mistake been written in the blank space for Wednesday. This error is noted in the short entry dated Thursday 21st. This misplaced entry therefore records events not on Wednesday but from Thursday morning to 1am on Friday morning and was therefore written at some time after 1am on Friday. This is followed by the short Thursday entry with its remedial sentence referring to the misplaced entry above; this short Thursday entry was therefore also written after 1am on Friday.

In turn, this is followed by the Friday entry, which was written at some time after 8.40pm on Friday and possibly on Saturday. The Friday entry adds a third contradiction to those already recorded. These concern the times stated for the diarist's landing and going ashore at Pará. Logically this going ashore is an event that can happen only once, but three contradictory times are cited in the following order:

1   In the entry for Wednesday 20th: '... Customs 7.20 and got ashore just 15 hours after we arrived', hence landing soon after 7.20am on Wednesday 20th.
2   In the entry for Thursday 21st: 'I only landed today at 8.30 am', hence landing at 8.30am on Thursday 21st.
3   In the entry for Friday 22nd: '... got my luggage only from Customs at 5.p.m., near 48 hours after landing ...', hence landing around 5pm on Wednesday 20th.

In respect of the hypothesis, these three entries were written in the above sequence and all were written after 1am on Friday 22nd.

It is evident that two of these recorded landings did not happen, since arrival and going ashore can happen only once. That two did not happen does not imply that the third landing time is the true one. It is impossible to determine whether any of the three recorded times is true, but it is certain that at least two are false. Their falsity does not depend on the putative truth of the third event. Therefore the entries on page 27 of the typescript refer to three landings recorded as being real events but two of which did not happen as recorded. On this hypothesis, Casement recorded two non-existent events and remained unaware of the contradictions.

To recapitulate: on Friday 22nd at some time after 8.40pm Casement states that he landed 48 hours earlier than 5pm that day, therefore at around 5pm on Wednesday. This contradicts the earlier correction in the short Thursday entry stating that he landed at 8.30am on Thursday. Thus at some time on Friday he writes the long misplaced entry, then writes the short Thursday entry with the correction, and after 8.40pm on Friday he writes another landing time of 5pm on Wednesday which contradicts what he has written earlier that same day in the misplaced entry and its subsequent correction. It is impossible to understand how anyone could be so profoundly confused about the timing of a very recent event that happened once only. The diarist has *on the same day* recorded three conflicting times for a single event. To maintain that page 27 is a true copy of Casement diary entries made on these days requires a credible explanation for the cluster of contradictions purportedly written on Friday 22 December. Such explanation can only be that he lost touch with reality on that day and was delusional.

In science and jurisprudence an explanatory hypothesis must be both testable and potentially falsifiable for it to merit consideration. The hypothesis that Casement was delusional on Friday 22 December cannot be tested. Since no test is feasible, the hypothesis cannot be falsified. This being the case, the explanation from delusion does not qualify as a hypothesis; it is at best a necessary but groundless speculation. Thus it is demonstrated that the claim that Casement wrote the entries can only be defended by a groundless speculation that he was disturbed. As a speculation it might appear compelling, but only because no alternative has been considered. That he was delusional on Friday 22 December is not compatible with known facts about Casement before or after that date. His correspondence in the preceding days of December is lucid and coherent; it includes letters to Foreign Secretary Grey, Secretary of State Spicer, Gertrude Bannister and Travers Buxton. There are also fragmentary diary writings in December that are equally lucid. By 9 January 1912 Casement was in Washington, where he spent three days with British Ambassador Bryce and meeting US officials and US President Taft. Bryce's letter to Grey of 12 January reports his talks with Casement; there is no mention of any mental instability. Casement's report to Grey of 5 February is lucid and highly detailed.[1] The speculation of a delusional state must be dismissed because it is groundless.

This signifies that page 27 of the typescript cannot be a transcript of real events recorded in an original diary. It follows that the typescript is a document that confusedly mixes imaginary events with a minimum of verified facts. Those facts are that Casement travelled to Pará on the *Hubert* and left Pará on 24 December to travel to Barbados and then to New York.

The explanation for the contradictions on page 27 of the typescript must lie elsewhere since there are no credible grounds for attributing them to Casement. Page 27 was typed in June 1916 by anonymous Scotland Yard staff who were provided with the text by anonymous British officials. The nature of the text provided cannot be ascertained since there is no material evidence. It cannot be ascertained whether the text was a diary since there is no independent testimony that such a diary existed in June 1916. The existence today of a 1911 diary does not entail that it existed in June 1916.

The incoherence of the page 27 entries does, however, have an explanation that is compatible with verified facts and with undisputed motivations. This explanation proposes that the page 27 contradictions are a product of human error that occurred not in 1911 but in a later time-frame—indeed, at the time of the typing operation. The explanation does not accept that page 27 is a copy of anything written by Casement at any time because there was no proof then that it was a copy, nor is there any proof today.

A further contradiction indicates hasty and careless improvisation of the page 27 typescript entries in June 1916. The diarist notes after 5pm on Tuesday 19 December that arrival at Pará is anticipated before 6pm on the following evening (the 20twh). Three lines below, however, the same entry states that arrival has already happened at 5.40 on the 19th. Since this arrival entry was purportedly written on the 19th after 5.40, an entire day of travel has disappeared. If we are to believe that these contradictions were faithfully copied from a diary written by Casement, the search for an explanation would tempt us towards the irrational, towards the absurd conclusion of time travel, but no rational person will propose a science-fiction explanation for what looks like a human error, however puzzling.

Yet another verified fact determines the fate of the hypothesis that page 27 is a copy of a Casement diary. The local newspaper *Folha do Norte* in its 'Mares e Rios' column on Friday 22nd reported the arrival on 21 December of the *Hubert* from Manaos. It named five first-class passengers, including Casement, and reported that he was British consul at Rio and was staying at the Commercial Hotel. Thus on that Friday the local newspaper reported to its readers the arrival of Consul Casement on Thursday 21st. Nonetheless, that same Friday a delusional Casement wrote three conflicting arrival times in his diary, quite unaware that hundreds of Pará citizens already knew when he had arrived.

Brian Inglis, author of the most influential biography of Casement, wrote of the diaries in 1973 that '… a single mistake in any of them would have destroyed the whole ugly enterprise'. This implies that no mistake was made. Page 27 contains dozens of mistakes of every kind. Inglis added the logical conclusion: '... and if one was forged, all of them were ...' . The factual evidence above demonstrates that in order to believe that the 1911 typescript is a true copy of a Casement diary one must believe either in the fantasy of time travel or that Casement was delusional. The first is an impossibility, while the second is a desperate speculation.

Note
[1] The correspondence referred to can be found in Angus Mitchell (ed.), *Sir Roger Casement's heart of darkness: the 1911 documents* (Irish Manuscripts Commission, 2003).

Bibliography

Brendon, Piers and Whitehead, Phillip 2000 *The Windsors: a dynasty revealed*. Pimlico, London.

Curry, Charles E. (ed.) 1922 *Sir Roger Casement's diaries*. Arche Publishing, Munich.

Daly, Mary (ed.) 2005 *Roger Casement in Irish and world history*. Royal Irish Academy, Dublin.

Doerries, Reinhard R. 2000 *Prelude to the Easter Rising: Sir Roger Casement in Imperial Germany*. Routledge, London.

Gaffney, Thomas St John 1930 *Breaking the silence: England, Ireland, Wilson and the War*. Horace Liveright, New York.

Gwynn, Dennis 1930 *The life and death of Roger Casement*. Jonathan Cape, London.

Hall, Sir Reginald 2017 *A clear case of genius: Room 40's code-breaking pioneer* (with commentary by Philip Vickers). The History Press, Stroud.

Hambloch, Ernest 1938 *British consul: memories of thirty years' service in Europe and Brazil*. G.G. Harrap, London.

Horgan, John 1949 *Parnell to Pearse: some recollections and reflections*. Browne and Nolan, Dublin.

Inglis, Brian 1973 *Roger Casement*. Hodder and Stoughton, London.

Jones, Sir Thomas Artemus 1944 *Without my wig*. H. Evans and Sons, Liverpool.

MacColl, René 1956 *Roger Casement: a new judgment*. Hamish Hamilton, London.

McHugh, Roger 1960 'Casement: the Public Record Office manuscripts'. *Threshold* 4 (1), 28–57.

Mackey, Herbert 1966 *Roger Casement: the forged diaries*. C.J. Fallon, Dublin.

Maloney, William J. 1936 *The forged Casement diaries*. Talbot Press, Dublin.

Mitchell, Angus (ed.) 1997 *The Amazon Journal of Roger Casement*. Lilliput Press, Dublin.

Mitchell, Angus c1999 *Sir Roger Casement's heart of darkness: the 1911 documents*. Irish Manuscripts Commission, Dublin.

Mitchell, Angus 2001 The Casement Black Diaries debate: the story so far. *History Ireland* **9** (2), 42–5.

Mitchell, Angus 2003 *Casement*. Haus Publishing, London.

Mitchell, Angus 2012 'Phases of a dishonourable phantasy'. *Field Day Review* **8**, 84–125.

Mitchell, Angus 2013 *16 Lives: Roger Casement*. O'Brien Press, Dublin.

Mitchell, Angus 2016 (ed.) *One bold deed of open treason: the Berlin diary of Roger Casement 1914–1916*. Merrion Press, Dublin.

Monteith, Robert 1932 *Casement's last adventure*. Privately printed, Chicago. (Revised edition: M.F. Moynihan, Dublin, 1953.)

Noyes, Alfred 1957 *The accusing ghost, or, Justice for Casement*. Victor Gollancz, London.

Ó Síocháin, Séamas 2008 *Roger Casement: imperialist, rebel, revolutionary*. Lilliput Press, Dublin.

Parmiter, Geoffrey de C. 1936 *Roger Casement*. Arthur Barker, London.

Ramsay, David 2008 *'Blinker' Hall, spymaster: the man who brought America into World War I*. The History Press, Stroud.

Reid, B.L. 1976 *The lives of Roger Casement*. Yale University Press, New Haven.

Sawyer, Roger (ed.) 1984 *Casement: the flawed hero*. Routledge, London.

Sawyer, Roger 1997 *Roger Casement's diaries, 1910: the black and the white*. Pimlico, London.

Smith, F.E. [Lord Birkenhead] 1926 *Famous trials of history*. George H. Doran, New York.

Stuart, Sir Campbell 1920 *Secrets of Crewe House: the story of a famous campaign*. Hodder and Stoughton, London.

Sullivan, A.M. 1952 *The last serjeant: the memoirs of Serjeant A.M. Sullivan*. Macdonald, London.

Taylor, Rex 1970 *Michael Collins*. Hutchinson, London.

Thomson, Basil 1922 *Queer people*. Hodder and Stoughton, London.

Thomson, Basil 1939 *The scene changes*. Collins, London.

Weale, Adrian 2001 *Patriot traitors: Roger Casement, John Amery and the real meaning of treason*. Viking, London.

Wilson, Mairead 2000 *Roger Casement: a reassessment of the diaries controversies*. Athol Books, Belfast.

Wyllie, James and McKinley, Michael 2015 *Codebreakers: the secret intelligence unit that changed the course of the First World War*. Ebury Press, London.

Index